WHAT'S YOUR EVEREST?

Advance Praise for *What's Your Everest?*

'An inspirational account of the importance of never giving up on your dreams. This is a tale of self-discovery and perseverance in the face of insurmountable odds'

Anupam Kher

'*What's Your Everest?* is: when you get knocked down, you get up again. Everest is tough. [This] is a great achievement'

Peter Hillary, mountaineer and son of Sir Edmund Hillary

'A moving and insightful exploration of grit and resilience. This book will inspire you to rise above adversity and chase your dreams'

Krishnamachari Srikkanth, former captain of the Indian cricket team

'A testament to the unbreakable human spirit. This story of two climbers battling the world's tallest peak is not just about the mountain but about the strength it takes to rise every time you fall. Inspiring and unforgettable'

Mingma Tenzi Sherpa, 11-time Mt Everest summiteer

WHAT'S YOUR EVEREST?

A PATH TO PASSION AND PURPOSE

SAURAJ JHINGAN
SAMIR PATHAM

BLOOMSBURY
NEW DELHI • LONDON • OXFORD • NEW YORK • SYDNEY

BLOOMSBURY INDIA
Bloomsbury Publishing India Pvt. Ltd
Second Floor, LSC Building No. 4, DDA Complex, Pocket C – 6 & 7,
Vasant Kunj, New Delhi, 110070

BLOOMSBURY, BLOOMSBURY INDIA and the Diana logo
are trademarks of Bloomsbury Publishing Plc

First published in India 2025

Copyright © Sauraj Jhingan and Samir Patham, 2025
Illustrations copyright © Samir Patham, 2025

All photographs from the authors' personal collection,
unless mentioned otherwise

Sauraj Jhingan and Samir Patham have asserted their right under the
Indian Copyright Act to be identified as the Authors of this work

All rights reserved. No part of this publication may be: i) reproduced or transmitted in any form, electronic or mechanical, including photocopying, recording or by means of any information storage or retrieval system without prior permission in writing from the publishers; or ii) used or reproduced in any way for the training, development or operation of artificial intelligence (AI) technologies, including generative AI technologies. The rights holders expressly reserve this publication from the text and data mining exception as per Article 4(3) of the Digital Single Market Directive (EU) 2019/790

ISBN: PB: 978-93-61319-40-2; eBook: 978-93-61317-68-2
2 4 6 8 10 9 7 5 3 1

Typeset in Minion by Manipal Technologies Limited
Printed and bound in India Gopsons Papers Pvt. Ltd., Noida

To find out more about our authors and books visit www.bloomsbury.com
and sign up for our newsletters

Contents

Foreword ix
Preface xi

Prologue 1

PART 1: PASSION
1. Management or Mountaineering 5
2. The Mountains Call 17
3. From Frustration to Freedom 28
4. The Odyssey Begins 37
5. Mission Everest 2015 50
6. Everest Base Camp: Home Away from Home 60
7. Avalanche 71
8. Relief and Rescue 80

PART 2: PURPOSE
9. Resilience 91
10. Everest 2017: Back to Base Camp 103
11. To Climb or Not to Climb 118
12. The Climb up Everest 127
13. The Death Zone: In the Eye of the Storm 140
14. The Aftermath of Failure 151

PART 3: PERSEVERANCE
15. Resurrection 167
16. Summiting Possibilities and Unexpected Alliances 175
17. In the Shadow of Everest: A New Odyssey Begins 180
18. Unpredictable Paths 188
19. The Western Cwm Beckons 195

20	Entering the Death Zone	202
21	The Final Push	208
22	Triumph Written in Snow and Sky	217
23	The Return	225
24	Finding Purpose	237

Epilogue   247
Acknowledgements   251
Note   253
Index   255
About the Authors   261

Foreword

Mountains don't yield to the timid. They respond to quiet strength, unwavering resolve and the kind of courage that keeps going even when breath is short and belief is running thin.

What's Your Everest? is more than a story of two young men climbing a peak. It's a mirror held up to all of us. Because each of us, in our own way, is trying to rise – beyond limitations, beyond doubt, beyond fear. As someone who has stood on Everest's summit and looked down on the world from its highest point, I can tell you this: no two journeys are the same. But the essence is always there – grit, failure, fear and the fire that refuses to die.

There was a moment in my journey that changed everything. At Camp 3, I was buried under an avalanche. In those silent, suffocating moments beneath the snow, I faced the edge of everything I knew. And yet, I didn't give up. What could have ended my climb instead became the turning point. It made me stronger, and a week later, I reached the summit. And I realised: sometimes, the mountain within us is steeper than the one beneath our feet.

Sauraj and Samir's story isn't just about reaching the top of the world. It's about choosing purpose over comfort, heart over hesitation and resilience over retreat. Through storms, heartbreak and unimaginable challenges, they stayed true to their dream, and in doing so, they reminded us that the highest summits aren't only in the Himalayas. They're within each one of us.

We all have an Everest. Maybe it's not a mountain. Maybe it's a dream, a fear, a fight or a goal that scares you just enough to know it's worth it. Whatever it is, you have to choose it. And then climb it with everything you've got.

As you read this incredible story, I hope it inspires you the way it inspired me. May it stir something within you. And may it gently ask: What's your Everest?

Bachendri Pal,
Padma Shri, Padma Bhushan,
First Indian woman to reach the summit of Mount Everest

Preface

In the tumultuous year of 2020, when the world found itself confined within walls, when the ordinary rhythms of life ground to a halt, Sauraj Jhingan and I, Samir Patham, embarked on a different journey. While the world wrestled with a global pandemic, we found ourselves delving into the recesses of our memories, chronicling a remarkable expedition that had unfolded years earlier – the ascent of Everest in 2018. The following pages are not a work of fiction nor the creation of established authors. These are but an amateur attempt at documenting a life of adventure.

What's Your Everest isn't your conventional self-help guide offering a simple formula for success. Instead, it is an authentic, first-hand account of two individuals navigating through the extraordinary, marked by relentless determination, passion and a willingness to embrace the highs and lows of life's journey. Sauraj Jhingan and I chose to diverge from the well-trodden path of corporate careers, daring to chase our passion for mountaineering and pioneer an entrepreneurial venture in an industry still finding its footing. It was amidst the challenging backdrop of a recession that we defied conventions and set forth on a path less travelled.

Our story isn't one of overnight success but of perseverance through adversity. The creation of our adventure company marked merely the inception of an arduous journey – one that would culminate in scaling the world's highest peak, Mt Everest, but at great cost. Along the way, we encountered trials that tested our resilience: earthquakes, avalanches and snowstorms at unfathomable altitudes.

Our ascent to the summit of Everest was not without setbacks. Failure became a companion, a relentless teacher, urging us to ponder a profound question: How much are you willing to endure in pursuit of your dreams? It's a story of audacity, a narrative not confined to mountain slopes but resonating with the essence of human determination and the undying spirit to conquer the metaphorical Everest in each of our lives.

As you embark on these pages, we invite you not only into our world of extreme altitudes but also into the realm of unwavering determination, resilience and the unyielding pursuit of dreams. May our tale ignite the spark within you, urging you to ponder your own Everest and the lengths you're willing to go to make it a reality.

Prologue

Avalanche

'I can't breathe! Oh God! Why can't I breathe?'

I gasp with shock, feeling like I've just woken up from a nightmare.

'Why can't I breathe?'

I try to open my eyes, but everything is dark. I panic, afraid I've lost my sight. The nightmare hasn't ended!

It feels like a lifetime ago that Tashi Sherpa had pulled me into the dining tent, dragging me under the flimsy aluminium table. It happened so fast, right after we saw the source of our terror. A massive wave of snow, ice and rock – literally, a mountain – was crashing down on us. Avalanche!

Seconds later, it hit. The impact felt like a sledgehammer against my chest and crushed the air from my lungs. I remember suffocating not only from the force of the impact but also from the snow that stifled the air, entering my mouth and windpipe as I gasped. It felt like someone was holding my head from behind and pushing it underwater.

It takes me a few moments to realise that the avalanche has destroyed everything, crumbling the structure of our tent and table. We've been completely buried under snow and debris with the entire weight of the metal frame and the canvas of the tent on us. It's very quiet now, and I can hear my heart racing, trying to jump out of my chest while I struggle to suck air into my tortured lungs. I can hear Tashi and Ghanshyam somewhere behind me, praying loudly in fear. Earlier, through the roar of the avalanche, it had sounded like innocuous ramblings. I'm scared to move. I can't feel my right leg, and I'm sure that I must have broken it. Tashi asks, 'Samir, are you okay?' Surprisingly, I hear myself say, 'Yes, Dai!', using the Nepali word for elder brother.

We start digging, lifting the weight of the tent. As my leg is freed, I feel the blood rushing back and, with it, a sense of relief. My body is bruised and battered, but I think I'm going to be okay. Slowly, Ghanshyam and I push the debris away as we make our way to the surface. Fortunately, there isn't much snow, and in moments, we emerge into the open. The sudden brightness of the snow glare hits my eyes, leaving me dazed and shocked. There's nothing left: no landmarks or tents. There is just a trail of destruction across the glacier, resembling a scene from an air crash. I can't even feel my hands, so I must be in shock. It's only when I start shivering that I realise that I'm drenched in snow and extremely cold.

As we pull away the frame of the tent to free people, I realise that Sauraj is missing! 'Where's Sauraj? Where's Sauraj Dai?' I ask a confused Ghanshyam. I don't remember him being under the tent with us and there aren't any signs of life near our camp. As several minutes pass, I begin to search frantically, looking behind every ridge of the glacier. There is no sign of Sauraj, and with each second, my terror rises.

PART 1

PASSION

1

Management or Mountaineering

> There will come a time when you believe everyth[ing] finished. That will be the beginning.
> — Louis L'Amour, *Lonely on the Mo[untain]*

Sauraj

In July 2005, I found myself taking the very first steps into adulthood, having just turned twenty. As I walked through the gates of the Symbiosis Institute of Management Studies (SIMS), Pune, with my suitcases in hand, I stopped and looked up at the massive glass dome of the academic block, admittedly nervous about starting my two-year residential MBA programme. The admission letter in my hand read: 'Student Manager – Sauraj Jhingan, PM and HRD; Personnel Management and Human Resource Development'. I was still processing how I had got there.

The last few months had gone by in a blur with graduation, entrance exams, interviews and a series of college applications as I grappled with the harsh reality of becoming an adult. I needed to have a 'profession' or, in other words, a well-paying, reputed job. I projected – or so I hoped – an air of quiet confidence but was internally wracked with misgivings about whether the whole MBA thing was really for me.

With the advantage of my military family already being stationed in Pune, I reached the institute early on a grey, wet morning as the city was inundated with monsoon rains. My early arrival was not to be confused with enthusiasm but was driven by a desire to leverage prime communal real estate when our hostel rooms were to be allocated. I was alone when I entered the room that I had to share with two other students and quickly called dibs on the bed closest to the window, which promised a better view (and ventilation). Having stayed in a hostel before, I knew what was important in a co-sharing space. Satisfied with my smart thinking, I waited around for a bit, pretending to explore the space. In reality, I was hoping for my new roommates to turn up so that I could unmistakably establish my claim on this bed. After an awfully long wait (of ten minutes), my patience wore thin. On a large piece of cardboard, I hastily scrawled a brief note – 'My bed. Do not touch. Sauraj Jhingan' – and left it on the brand-new mattress that was still wrapped in plastic. There really wasn't anything else to do. So, with a set of room keys in hand, I left my still-packed cases behind and rode my bike back home.

It was late in the afternoon by the time I returned to the hostel. The door to my room was locked from the inside, rendering my keys useless. Suspecting the worst, I banged loudly on the door, eager to rescue my bed. I assumed that it had already been taken by one of the strangers I had to share the room with. When the door opened, I quickly rushed in and was pleasantly surprised to see my cardboard sign exactly where I had left it. I turned around to see a boy about my age looking at me quizzically while still holding the door open. He was almost as lean as me, probably a little broader, about the same height, clean-shaven and decidedly non-threatening. I took the initiative and held out my hand. 'Hi! I'm Sauraj.' The boy looked at me with an amused smile and replied, 'Yeah, I figured from the cardboard. I'm Sam.'

He seemed likeable enough, but I wasn't one to be fooled by the 'hail-fellow-well-met' sorts. I sauntered to the end of the room and was relieved to see that my possessions and property had been left undisturbed.

Since there was nothing else to do, I sat down on the coveted metal cot and tentatively initiated a conversation with my new roommate. We would be the only two sharing this room as the third student had opted out. After exchanging initial introductions to our respective lives, I was pleasantly surprised to learn that, like me, Sam was more interested in outdoor sports than an MBA. Finding him a keen listener, I told him all about the basic mountaineering course I had just completed that summer at the Nehru Institute of Mountaineering in Uttarkashi. This intense thirty-day programme is designed to train budding mountaineers to navigate terrains involving rock, snow and ice, establishing a strong foundation for climbing expeditions and outdoor survival.

The Nehru Institute of Mountaineering, an extremely prestigious academy, was established in 1965 to honour Pandit Jawaharlal Nehru's desire to create a subset of the population specially trained in mountaineering. The institution soon gained a tremendous reputation in India and around the world. Sam listened raptly to every word, asking questions about the course and what it felt like. Having grown up in New Delhi, he had spent a large part of his life training and working with a river-rafting company in Rishikesh, Uttarakhand. His obvious interest made me realise that he was an amateur adventure sports junkie himself, and I found myself feeling less like a misfit. The hours flew by as we sat up talking late into the night, the stuffy confines of the room fading away in the tales of the mountains.

The next few months flew by in a blur of academics. Our schedules were packed with brand-new subjects such as Regression and Correlation, interspersed with Balance Sheets and P&L Statements. When not in class, we were swamped with assignments and early-morning presentations. I still wasn't quite sure what I wanted to do in life. After my bachelor's degree in computer applications, pursuing an MBA had initially appeared to be the next logical milestone. However, unlike most other MBA aspirants I had interacted with, getting into the corporate world had not been my first choice.

It wasn't lost on me that this was a fairly odd way to go about a postgraduate education. To put things in perspective, when you join a B-school, you expect to meet a lot of people – the engineers with a couple of years of work experience who are hoping to leverage their MBA as a fast track to middle management, the finance whiz kids and the young hopefuls – all trying to gain a foothold in the corporate world with dreams of a lifestyle with fancy gadgets, luxury cars and weekends spent on the golf course cracking multimillion-dollar deals. I was an outlier, a kid simply waiting for the afternoon classes to end so I could skip off to the nearest hill for a quick trek before nightfall.

Surprisingly, in this entire improbable equation, Sam proved to be a willing accomplice. Over the course of the next two years as roommates and classmates, we found ourselves thrown together a lot. Despite our packed timetables and hectic study schedules, we still managed to spend more time outdoors than in the classroom. After leading our batchmates on a few local treks, in a burst of enthusiastic fervour, we formed the college's first adventure club.

During the first year of my MBA, I had heard about the Pune-based Enduro race. Reputed to be one of the toughest adventure races in Asia, Enduro3 was designed to test the physical and mental strength of its participants. The course spanned over 200 km across the Western Ghats and required teams to cover a vast geographical terrain, navigating several checkpoints while completing a series of activities such as trekking, mountain biking, kayaking, river crossing and rifle shooting.

The race and the outdoor challenge it offered immediately caught my attention. The first hurdle came up soon enough when I realised that, as per the race rules, each team of three required at least one female team member. I remained optimistic, however, primarily because of the demographics of our MBA class. In 2005, our MBA batch of 300 was almost equally represented by female and male students. Sam and I had both opted for the human resources programme. In this section, the gender diversity was skewed 11:1 in favour of women. Once I had roped Sam in for Enduro3, we began scouting for a female member from the class. We were confident that, among the fifty-five women, finding someone willing to race cross-country with no sleep and very little food for three days would not be a challenge. I was obviously very wrong.

Our attempt to identify the right talent became synonymous with a military recruitment drive. We created flyers, pooling in our limited pocket money to splurge on colour printing, and prominently posted our 'wanted' ads on the college noticeboards outside the administration office. We sent out reminders and bulletins on the school email IDs. Yet no one volunteered. We soon resorted to walking up to female batchmates, suggesting that they appeared to be in great physical shape and that they might enjoy roughing it out with us. That we didn't get beaten up was a miracle. Finally, our friend and classmate Preeti Sharma agreed to join us.

We trained hard for the race, waking up at 6 AM every day to run and cycle on the wooded back roads and by-lanes near our campus before the day's lectures started. Preeti trained hard with us, cursing constantly and threatening to abandon us after every practice session. Yet, every morning for two months, she would meet us in the pre-dawn

December chill, in front of the girls' hostel as we fell into our warm-up routines.

Enduro3 proved to be as challenging as I had anticipated, but I was pleasantly surprised to find that the weeks of training had paid off. On race day, I felt strong and confident. As per the rules of the race, we had to have our own supplies as we bicycled, hiked, sailed and kayaked across the difficult terrain while navigating the race hurdles together. We carried our food rations and bike repair kits on our backs for over two days with hardly any stops for rest or sleep, desperately focusing on completion rather than competition with the other seasoned athletes. All our efforts eventually paid off, and we won the Enduro trophy, finishing second after having completed the race in just under thirty hours.

As we turned our attention back to academics, I found some unlikely champions and influencers who have continued to be a part of my unorthodox passion. One of my earliest sources of encouragement was Advocate Shekhar Bhonagiri, our labour-law professor. On the morning of Enduro, Sam, Preeti and I were shocked to see him standing at the starting line to flag off the race. Prof. Bhonagiri, who could make one of the driest subjects in the course come alive, was something of a superstar in the classroom. I was in complete awe of him. What I didn't know at the time was that he also shared my passion for adventure sports. I later learnt that he was a close friend of the Enduro race organisers. We walked up to Prof. Bhonagiri to greet him, catching him completely by surprise. He wasn't expecting to see his MBA students participating in an endurance race. From that moment on, he began to take a personal interest in my development.

Winning Enduro3 was a huge feather in our cap. Soon, many of our batchmates actively sought us out to plan outdoor experiences as the SIMS Adventure Club finally gained momentum. In our second year, we were the seniors on campus, and as the new batch of MBA students joined the institute, Sam and I were given the tedious task of waking them up early in the morning during their orientation week and taking them for a long run. We, of course, did this with relish.

As the second year of our MBA programme continued, I was beginning to find my place in the institute. Sam and I, as part of the adventure club, became the go-to guys for student weekend adventure getaways and hiking trips. Our brief run-in with Prof. Bhonagiri during Enduro3 resulted in even the faculty taking note of me, and Prof. Bhonagiri became something of a mentor.

One of the toughest aspects of our second-year assessment was the labour-law oral examination, where students were expected to recite the Bare Act as stipulated in the legislation. Prof. Bhonagiri, a man known for his unrelenting standards, was not just an excellent teacher but also a perfectionist when it came to gauging how well students had grasped the intricate details of his subject. The long corridor outside the examination room felt like the waiting area of a courtroom, with each of my classmates emerging through the door looking thoroughly defeated. I overheard fragments of conversations: the professor was relentless, grilling each student mercilessly on the course material.

I sat on a bench, feeling my stomach churn with nerves as I waited for my turn. The walls of the corridor seemed to close in as a voice suddenly called out, 'Roll No. 46.' My heart sank. With shaky legs, I walked into the classroom, my mind racing. I sat across the table from Prof. Bhonagiri, bracing myself for the onslaught of legal questions that I was sure would follow. Instead, something unexpected happened.

As I met his gaze, the professor's expression softened, and a grin spread across his face. He recognised me from the Enduro race. Without missing a beat, he launched into questions – not about the Maharashtra Shops and Establishments Act but about my experience in Enduro. He seemed genuinely curious, asking me how I had trained for the event, sharing his stories of the outdoors and marvelling at the physical and mental demands of such an endeavour. For a moment, it felt like the walls of the classroom had faded away, replaced by the expanse of nature that had shaped my Enduro journey. Time seemed to stand still as we exchanged anecdotes, his enthusiasm for the outdoors mirroring my burgeoning passion. When I paused, waiting for him to pivot to the examination material, he casually glanced at his watch and announced that our time was up.

I walked out of the classroom in a daze, unsure of what had just transpired. Sam, waiting in the corridor for his turn, rushed up to me. 'What questions did he ask?' he demanded eagerly. I could barely speak, motioning for him to follow me outside. Once we were alone, I recounted the surreal encounter. Sam stared back at me, his expression a mix of disbelief and confusion. 'Are you serious?' he asked, shaking his head. He walked back to the corridor, muttering under his breath, while I stood there, still processing the moment.

Looking back, I realise how that seemingly inconsequential interaction became a pivotal moment in my life. It wasn't just a lucky break during an exam – it was a reflection of the invisible forces shaping my journey. My passion for the outdoors, which had been quietly growing, found validation in unexpected places, nudging me towards a path I didn't yet know I was destined to follow. Perhaps it was no coincidence that someone like Prof. Bhonagiri, with his love for nature, happened to notice and encourage that spark within me. Sometimes, life has a way of weaving seemingly random threads into a tapestry that only makes sense when viewed in hindsight.

On a separate occasion, when the professor learnt that our adventure club was leading a students' hike to the nearby Torna Fort, he offered to lend us some rope that he used for his expeditions. Despite having attended a basic mountaineering course, I had little experience of working with rope, and Sam and the others had even less. However, when your college professor suggests you use a rope during a trek, you don't say no. Early one Saturday morning, we duly found ourselves outside the professor's house, holding a long and surprisingly heavy coil of rope. As it turned out, I had reason to be grateful. During our night-long trek to Torna that monsoon, we encountered harsh weather, rain and strong winds. The rope, despite our amateur knots, ensured the safety of the entire team.

During my first term in college, I met Karan Sharma, a fellow student who would become a lifelong friend and a key enabler of my passion for adventure. Despite our different interests – Karan being more academically inclined and active in the student body – we bonded quickly. By the second year of our MBA, Karan, Sam and I were roommates. Karan, ever the diligent class representative, often marked my attendance while I pursued outdoor adventures or simply skipped dull lectures. Thanks to him, I graduated with an astonishing 120 per cent attendance rate, much to the administration's disbelief.

Karan's deeply religious nature added a unique dynamic to our shared space. Each morning, he followed an elaborate routine: bathing at dawn, praying at his self-made shrine and preparing incense as a mark of devotion. One morning, Sam's younger brother, Satyen, who was crashing in our room, stirred awake to the sight of Karan meticulously rolling incense. Mistaking the activity for something far less pious, Satyen excitedly asked, 'Dude, are you rolling? Can I get a puff?'

The scene that followed was priceless. Karan, fresh out of his spiritual zone, looked utterly baffled. When the penny dropped, he turned red with embarrassment, vehemently denying any association with illicit substances. Sam and I, unable to contain our laughter, reassured Satyen that there was nothing to 'share'. That memory remains one of my fondest, perfectly capturing Karan's sincerity and the hilarity of our college days.

During my time at SIMS in 2006, by sheer chance, I became acquainted with Malli Mastan Babu, one of the biggest influences in my life. This Indian mountaineering stalwart soon became my role model, and his story continues to inspire me to this day. In college, I rarely read any newspapers unless it was the *Economic Times* for finance assignments. As luck would have it, a stray copy of the *Times of India* found its way into our room one day, and while casually flipping through the pages, an article caught my eye. Consigned to a corner of the sports page, it briefly stated that Malli Mastan Babu from India had created a world record by becoming the fastest person to climb the Seven Summits, a feat he achieved in a mere 172 days. The Seven Summits are the seven highest peaks on each of the seven continents and include Mt Everest in Asia, the holy grail for serious mountaineers. I secretly entertained a fantasy of being able to travel across the world to each of the seven continents and climb to the highest points. Besides Mt Everest (8,848 m) in Asia, there is Mt Elbrus (5,642 m) in Europe, Mt Kilimanjaro (5,895 m) in Africa, Mt Denali (6,190 m) in North America, Mt Aconcagua (6,961 m) in South America, Mt Kosciuszko (2,228 m) in Australia and, finally, the remotest peak, Mt Vinson Massif (4,892 m) in the white continent, Antarctica.

Intrigued, I immediately began researching Malli Mastan Babu. The bare bones of the story of an exceptionally determined mountaineer began to emerge from brief internet profiles. Malli came from a humble farming background in Andhra Pradesh. He studied in Sainik School close to their small temple town where he did well academically and displayed a real aptitude for sports, especially mountaineering through school treks.

As a youth, Malli Mastan Babu went on to pursue engineering and, later, an MBA from the prestigious Indian Institute of Management Calcutta. Subsequently, he turned down lucrative placement offers to pursue his passion for mountaineering. I became obsessed with his story, and as luck would have it, at the time, my father was posted by the Indian Army as the principal of the Sainik School in Satara. I asked my father to help me with Malli Mastan Babu's contact details through the school alumni network and got in touch with him over a phone call. I was immediately touched by his warmth and humility. I learnt that, like me, he too had pursued his mountaineering course through the Nehru Institute of Mountaineering. Subconsciously, his story had begun to influence the course of my life. Malli would continue to play an integral part in my life in the years to come, representing a beacon of hope that life and a career in the mountains could still be a possibility.

At the time, I was unaware of it, but looking back now, I can trace the subtle patterns that were quietly steering my life toward discovering my true passion. What fascinates me is how this journey was shaped by both my internal drive and the profound impact of external influences. The individuals I came to admire and the friendships forged during this period became the cornerstone of my life, shaping not just my path but also the person I would become.

As my MBA programme slowly came to an end, our entire batch was gripped with placement fever. I found myself conforming to the mass hysteria, waiting anxiously for companies to shortlist my resume. By the end of day one, some of our batchmates had received their offer letters. The next day, as the placement process continued and more companies came to campus, Karan received a confirmation along with the coveted offer letter from a leading consultancy firm. I participated in multiple group discussion rounds, hoping to be shortlisted for the personal interview. I wondered dejectedly why I had not had the foresight to join the debate team instead of spending my days in the adventure club. I wished I had a more dazzling academic record or even prior work experience to impress the interviewers. My achievements in the Enduro race, the Torna hike and all the adventure activities seemed like inconsequential accomplishments.

With each passing day, the stress of not securing a job after two years of doing an MBA weighed heavily on my shoulders. However, what seemed like a lifetime of misery was short-lived, and finally on day four of placement week, Sam and I found ourselves once again sitting side by side outside a conference room, awaiting our personal interview round for the same organisation. That evening, we both celebrated our success, having received offer letters from a US-based multinational, although he would be sent to Hyderabad and I would be working in the Mumbai office. As soon as the initial jubilation was over, that very night as I lay in bed, it occurred to me with dread that all that lay in front of me now was a life of corporate drudgery.

2

The Mountains Call

> A journey of a thousand miles begins with a single step.
> Lao Tzu, *Tao Te Ching*
> (translated by D.C. Lau)

Sauraj

Within months of embarking on my career, I began to realise that the thought of slowly working my way up the corporate ladder held little to no appeal.

While in Mumbai, I was caught up in the frenzy and unrelenting busyness of my job. Initially, both Sam and I started off in middle management at the same company as HR recruiters, despite being in different locations. Invariably, we would be on the same calls or video conferences, attending meetings together and addressing each other with formal deference. It was all very strange, and after the meetings were done, we would call each other and laugh about corporate idiosyncrasies, missed deadlines or the general air of self-importance that seemed to be part of the job. I was becoming increasingly frustrated with losing myself in this world as well as the accompanying worries like paying rent and investing in tax-saving FDs. Every time I spoke to Sam, our conversations would invariably turn towards our outdoor adventures and treks. I began to fear that I would never get to experience the thrill of hiking again. I spent about a year in Mumbai before switching to Standard Chartered Bank.

The disconnect from the outdoors began to haunt me, and I knew I had to act. I had to do something about it. Maybe I could just pick up a rucksack and wander off into the great unknown. Soon, the clarion call of life outdoors became impossible to ignore. At this point, I turned to my inspiration – Malli Mastan Babu, who had climbed Everest in 2006. Malli had done the Everest Base Camp trek and, in a heartbeat, told me to seize the opportunity. He said, 'Just go for it. It will be a life-changing experience.' In retrospect, it really turned out to be one. A couple of years later, when I was deeply entrenched in the corporate world, I got the opportunity to meet Malli Mastan Babu in person in Pune. He stayed at my place for a few days, and I got to know him much better. Once again, I couldn't help but admire his passion and commitment to the sport and the mountains. Despite the accolades and his achievements, I was struck by his simplicity. He lived in relative penury despite his IIM credentials, devoid of all materialistic aspirations in pursuit of a life dedicated completely to mountaineering and preserving the planet's ecosystem.

In 2008, my life would change forever, taking a radical tangent from the course of the corporate career I was apparently predestined to follow after doing an MBA. I had been working for a year already when the opportunity to trek to Everest Base Camp presented itself. I knew nothing about the details of the trek, but after speaking to Malli, the idea just sounded fascinating. Having heard and read about Mt Everest, the prospect of seeing it in person excited me. Even though I had absolutely no idea what this trek would entail (how long, difficult or expensive it would be), I wanted to go for it.

The first challenge was to apply for leave. It wasn't a question of a few days or even a week. This incredible adventure would require a commitment of fourteen days, with the trek starting and ending in Kathmandu. Now imagine yourself as a young executive just two years into your corporate career, especially given that you have spent only four months in your new organisation. Most people I spoke to said it was an absurd idea and that there was no way I would get fourteen days off.

Summoning the courage, I walked into the office one day and approached the director with a very passionate appeal for leave. After several days and many conversations back and forth, eventually, with luck (or persistent pestering), the fourteen days of blocked leave were approved, an extremely rare phenomenon in the corporate world. I had talked so much about hiking and my upcoming trek that, eventually, I even managed to inspire my boss to attempt the trek with me. Once it was official, I immediately called up Sam to ask him if he would like to be part of this adventure. Unfortunately, Sam had just switched jobs to Infosys less than a month ago to move back to Pune from Hyderabad and wasn't allowed leave for this trip.

Since I was in Mumbai, I began travelling to Pune almost every weekend to go on treks in the Western Ghats near the city as part of the training and preparation. Sam made it a point to accompany me on all of these hikes even though he would be missing out on the actual trip to Everest Base Camp. By March, I had been on a substantial number of treks, exploring all the nearby forts around Pune, and was in excellent physical form.

In April 2008, I finally set off for Nepal to make this wild fantasy come true. From Delhi, I flew to Kathmandu to start my journey. On landing in Kathmandu, I made my way to a hotel located in an area called Thamel. I remember being extremely fascinated with Thamel on that first visit. Thamel is the tourist hotbed of Kathmandu with streets lined on both sides with shops selling high-end mountaineering gear. The air was vibrant with the sounds of live music streaming from pubs and cafés as I explored the streets with wide-eyed wonder.

Early the next morning, I joined my cohort, and we set off for the domestic airport to catch our flight to the Everest Valley. Nothing, however, had prepared me for the actual plane ride to the infamous Lukla Airport located at the start of the Everest Valley at a height of 2,843 m. The short trip from Kathmandu to Lukla takes only thirty minutes but is widely reputed to be the most dangerous flight in the world. I was soon to find out why. My first flight to Lukla is also the most vivid in my memory. We flew to Lukla in a small, twelve-seater Dornier 228 aircraft, operated only by the most experienced pilots in the world. The pilot manually controlled the small aircraft, avoiding the surrounding mountains with incredible skill and, once the plane approached Lukla, began the descent for landing at one of the smallest airstrips I had ever seen. It appeared to be completely impossible to approach. I was terrified and exhilarated in equal measure. Imagine the feeling of being on a roller-coaster, wanting to scream and laugh out loud at the same time, and then multiplying that tenfold. The view from the plane was as magnificent as it was terrifying. As the plane neared the mountain, the runway came into view – a startlingly short landing strip carved into the incline, rising steeply up the mountainside. The wheels hit the ground with a jarring thud, and the plane surged forward, racing up the slope. Gravity took over, rapidly slowing us down, but not before my eyes locked onto the sheer rock face looming at the runway's end. The brakes engaged with a jolt, and we came to a sudden, breathless stop, mere feet from the wall. Only then did I realise I had been holding my breath, my heart pounding like a drum in my chest. Around me, I could see my emotions reflected on the faces of my co-passengers. Some had goofy grins, while others sat tensed and braced. Some were even chanting prayers, their eyes squeezed tightly shut.

Our trek began from Lukla as we slowly made our way on foot through the incredible mountain vistas of the Himalayas along a meandering river. We gradually gained altitude. On day two, we made our way to the iconic Namche Bazaar, the official capital of the Khumbu district in the Everest Valley. My first glimpse of Namche Bazaar was surreal. We trekked for hours through steep and narrow mountain paths surrounded by dense pine forests, arriving at this Shangri-La for weary travellers. This small town, perched in the lap of formidable mountains, offered both hardened mountaineers and curious trekkers every creature comfort of modern life. It brought to mind childhood memories of summer vacations spent in the hill stations of India.

The narrow streets of Namche Bazaar – better described as wide footpaths, given the absence of vehicles in these mountains – are dotted with cafes, bakeries, ATMs and even bars. Yet, despite its charm and amenities, Namche remains a strikingly remote outpost. The nearest road is over 300 km away, and everything in the valley – be it food, fuel or building materials – must be carried up on the backs of men and mules or flown in by helicopter.

I stayed at a teahouse, one of the many guesthouses operated by local families. These teahouses, vital sanctuaries for mountaineers, have a fascinating history. They began as modest tea stalls serving hot drinks to the rare hiker on the Everest trail. Over time, as waves of Western climbers and trekkers arrived, these simple stops expanded into guesthouses offering a range of accommodations. Today, they cater to all kinds of travellers, from those seeking basic, no-frills rooms to those indulging in relative luxury. Despite these comforts, the logistical challenges of maintaining such facilities in such isolation are a testament to the resilience and ingenuity of the local people.

My first glimpse of the snowcapped mountain peaks in the Everest region was from a viewpoint close to Namche Bazaar. I felt a thrill go down my spine as I feasted my eyes upon the vista in front of me. No amount of research and hours spent googling images of Mt Everest had prepared me for the visual impact of seeing the tallest mountain in the world. As I stood there revelling in the grandeur of being surrounded by the highest mountain range in the world, I found myself speechless. At once, I was captivated by the icy, stark beauty of Mt Everest. At this point, it seemed nearly impossible for me of all people to even think of attempting to scale the highest peak on the planet. Yet, even as I thought how laughable it was for a guy like me to even dream about standing on the summit of Everest, I think the idea was already taking root somewhere deep in my subconscious mind.

From Namche Bazaar, our little group made its way to the famous Tengboche Monastery. The trek to the monastery was tough and really tested my endurance. At a height of 3,867 m, this Tibetan monastery is revered by locals as well as mountaineers. Most people attempting to scale Everest make it a point to come here to offer prayers for a safe return. The monastery itself is majestic and dominates the Khumbu landscape. From the monastery, we continued on our journey to the base camp.

The most anticipated day on the trail finally arrived. On day nine, we started early in the morning from Lobuche and set off for Gorakshep, the closest settlement to Khumbu Glacier, where the campsite was located. The walk to Gorakshep took us over the 5,000 m altitude mark, where even the most resilient climbers start slowing down due to the altitude. We stopped at Gorakshep to catch our breath and tried eating a meal while we waited for our porters to arrive with our bags so we could settle them into our rooms. Once everyone was well rested, we set off for the glacier, spirits soaring, towards Everest Base Camp.

From Gorakshep, we gradually climbed onto the side of the massive Khumbu Glacier through broken ground that was scattered with huge rocks and completely devoid of any vegetation. As we walked through this landscape that looked more like the surface of the moon, we would occasionally hear rockfalls and ice scraping as the glacier shifted under the grinding weight of the ice. After two hours of carefully making our way through this trail, we could see a city of tents in bright colours of yellow, red, orange and green perched precariously between the ice and the rock of the glacier. Each expedition team had a campsite. The city of tents seemed to extend for almost a kilometre on the glacier. As trekkers, we could only visit the campsites but were not allowed to spend the night. It had taken us such an effort to reach this point that I could not even begin to imagine what it was like for the climbers to live in this extreme environment for thirty to forty-five days in their quest for Everest. All I can say is that this journey alone is worth every penny and will change your life forever! Pictures and descriptions of the sense of unbounded joy I felt on reaching Everest Base Camp can never do the trek justice.

On this trek, I was travelling with a small group of five people from India, all of us from different cities. Luckily, all the team members were quite fit, each one having trained well for this trip, and we all made it to the base camp at around the same time as a group. It was the first time any of us in our small group had experienced being at an altitude of 5,380 m. After having spent only about fifteen minutes at the base camp, a few people in our group began to experience headaches and fatigue. I was to learn that these were both common symptoms that affect anyone not acclimatised to the decrease in oxygen and air pressure at this altitude. As a precaution, our group unanimously decided to head back down immediately.

However, I couldn't help but show my disappointment. After eight days of hiking, I couldn't bear to leave so soon. I wanted to explore and spend some more time there. So I decided to stay back to make the most of this opportunity and then, later, hike back at a faster pace to catch up with my group. I was hoping to meet some 'real' climbers and began walking further into Everest Base Camp. I made my way towards the Khumbu Icefall, way beyond the point where amateur hikers usually venture.

As I walked around, I was encouraged by the sight of more tents scattered across the glacial moraine, transforming this extreme habitat into an almost village-like encampment, temporary but thriving. Soon, I spotted a small group of people who appeared to be fellow Indians. I walked towards them, introduced myself and asked them if they were trekkers to the base camp like myself or climbers attempting to summit that year. As luck would have it, I found myself face to face with the first police team from India attempting to climb Everest. The team were spending an extra few days at the base camp when I met them. They explained that they had been compelled to take a forced rest since the Chinese government had cordoned off both sides of the mountain for the next four days. As it was the year of the Beijing Olympics, the Chinese climbing teams were attempting to take the Olympic torch to the summit of Everest.

I was completely awestruck by this chance encounter. I vividly recall my conversation with the expedition leader – a very senior, soft-spoken IPS officer, Atul Karwal, who would later go on to summit Everest and write a thrilling account of his experience in a book titled *Think Everest*. He enquired about my experience of the trek to the base camp. I was so impressed that I found myself feeling uncharacteristically bashful and couldn't ask all the questions I normally would have. At that moment, I felt so inspired by my interaction with the IPS team that I would have even asked him for his autograph had I not been too shy. As I trekked back down alone to the village of

Gorakshep, a new dream gripped my soul – one so gigantic that I could barely articulate it to myself.

As this aspiration began to take form, I was overtaken by a Sherpa walking at breakneck speed. I increased my pace and eventually caught up with him, only slightly out of breath. I struck up a conversation with him, and he was kind enough to slow down and walk with me for part of the way. I had so many questions about climbing Everest, and he did his best to answer them. I was even naive enough to tell him that I was fit to undertake the arduous climb to the summit and willing to extend my trip by a few days if he knew any team with a slot available for me to climb to the top. I offered to pay upfront, completely ignorant of the exorbitant expedition cost or the time required to achieve this enormous task. I was confused when the Sherpa looked at me and started laughing. He shrugged in good humour and walked on ahead.

I continued on my solitary trek down to Gorakshep. By now, I was firmly in the grip of mountain fever. I kept wondering who these people were, these professional mountaineers who alone had access to Everest. Were they celebrated in the highest strata of mountaineering professionals? Were they featured on the covers of adventure sports magazines? What were their qualifications that they alone could conquer the highest peak on the planet? And most importantly, what would it take for someone like me to even attempt an ascent to Everest without being scoffed at by the Sherpas?

As our group made its way back to the village of Lobuche, we came across two young girls from the United Kingdom and New Zealand who had also reached Everest Base Camp and were on their way back. In a casual interaction, I learnt that they were 'budget travellers' and had been travelling through Southeast Asia for the last four months as part of their adventure. Besides carrying all their belongings themselves, they had trekked to Everest Base Camp without a guide and were on a shoestring budget. Their plan was to cover the distance of two days in a single day so they could save a small buck on stay and food. I was absolutely amazed by their courage. It occurred to me that taking this kind of time to experience life is something we Indians are just not accustomed to doing. I was thrilled by their travel stories. Their sense of freedom and desire to travel and trek was contagious.

After a four-day descent and an adventurous flight back to Kathmandu, we finally returned to the hustle and bustle of the city. However, I had left a piece of my heart in the Everest Valley. For our final dinner, we headed to the famous Rumdoodle restaurant and were presented with a huge cardboard cut-out of a Yeti foot. The restaurant was particularly famous for these 'Yeti foots' where each group could write a message and leave a signature on the foot, which was then nailed to the wall of the restaurant. The restaurant had hundreds of these on the walls. It was an unofficial tradition for all Everest Base Camp trekkers and a fitting end to this incredible experience.

Though our group celebrated the success of the trek several times with lots of beer on our way down, somewhere I knew this was only the beginning. In my mind, I was left with more questions than answers about the highest mountain in the world. I was awestruck. I had an intense feeling that this was not the end of this adventure but merely the start, as if the mountain had a magnetic pull on my soul. Why was I the only one from our group to feel this way?

It wasn't just the trek to Everest Base Camp that left an indelible mark on me; it was the revelation that came with it – the understanding of what it felt like to be truly passionate about something. Up until that moment, my life had been a series of motions dictated by societal expectations: working diligently in a corporate job, climbing the corporate ladder and measuring success by material achievements. However, as I stood in the shadow of Everest, I was overwhelmed by a profound sense of belonging and purpose. The mountains stirred something deep within me – a sense of freedom and fulfilment I had never felt before.

Back in Mumbai, the contrast was stark and unrelenting. The brightly lit office, the ceaseless buzz of deadlines and the pursuit of pay cheques seemed hollow. My days revolved around reports and meetings, but my mind was back in the Himalayas, traversing trails and breathing the crisp mountain air. For the first time, I realised the difference between existing and truly living. The clarity I felt on those trails – the raw connection to nature, the simplicity of life and the fulfilment of achieving something deeply meaningful – was the antithesis of the disconnect I felt in my corporate role.

This realisation wasn't a sudden epiphany; it was a slow awakening. Each memory of the Everest trek felt like a beacon, guiding me towards a life that was no longer just about surviving but thriving. I wasn't merely yearning for the mountains. I was beginning to understand what it meant to dedicate oneself to a cause. I wanted to channel this newfound passion into something bigger, something that could inspire others to step outside their comfort zones and find their own mountains to climb. It wasn't just about reaching Everest but about redefining what success and fulfilment truly meant to me.

3

From Frustration to Freedom

> The privilege of a lifetime is to become who you truly are.
>
> Carl Jung, *Memories, Dreams, Reflections*

Sam

In the spring of 2008, I got the opportunity to shift to Infosys in Pune. I had spent more than a year in Hyderabad, and work had lost its charm. Sauraj, too, had left a few months earlier to join Standard Chartered Bank, and with him gone, the daily corporate drudgery seemed overwhelming. Though the work was comfortable, I desperately wanted something more, something better, something more meaningful.

Starting work with Infosys was incredible (at least in the beginning). I was completely in awe of the absurdly modern campus with its food court and incredible infrastructure. Their progressive ideology of process-driven and system-driven management seemed to be the stuff of corporate dreams. This was a new environment – so much to learn, so different from what I knew. I believed the organisation was one of the most recognisable brands in India at the time, a name that people respected. After all, I thought to myself, it would certainly add value to my credentials and maybe even my self-worth. The fact that I had been rejected by this company during my campus placement drive seemed to add a feeling of smug satisfaction. 'I had managed to get in.' With tremendous excitement and with the added perk of Pune as a location, I moved bag and baggage from Hyderabad. My girlfriend, Karishma (a.k.a. 'Kay'), had just gotten admission into SIMS, my alma mater, and I would now embody the very cool image of the 'corporate-employed senior' visiting campus every time I went over to meet her. It seemed like life was suddenly falling into place perfectly, like a script from a movie. Finally, I could shrug off that feeling of monotony from my previous job.

Around this time, Sauraj had started talking about planning a holiday in Nepal and the possibility of trekking up to the base camp of Mt Everest. He kept trying to tempt me to join him, but I could not even begin to contemplate asking for leave as I had just started working. Though excited for him (and incredibly jealous), I joined him and his boss on several practice treks around the city of Pune. Sauraj's enthusiasm made me all the more desolate that I would be missing an amazing adventure. As the time came for this incredible odyssey in April 2008, I followed their progress with rapt attention. Their return was celebrated with the fanfare of conquering heroes. I lived vicariously through their experience, imagining each step of the journey during its retelling.

The glamour and excitement of my new job soon faded away within the first few months. Sauraj had subconsciously ignited a spark with his Everest Base Camp adventure. Joining them for practice hikes had felt fantastic, while the drudgery of sitting at a desk felt boring. The rest of the year dragged on with days turning into weeks and, slowly, into months. The fancy campus lost its sheen, the food in the three enormous cafeterias lost its appeal and the monotony of the corporate job began to set in once more with alarming rapidity. Due to the sheer size of the organisation, I soon became aware of the harsh reality: I was just another cog in the wheel, an employee number. The frustration of not being able to meet Kay despite living in the same city due to my fourteen-hour workday and the constant deluge of emails and phone calls that kept me bound to my office desk all began to feel very familiar. This meaningless drudgery felt exactly like my previous job.

The constant feeling of apathy and lethargy and the endless cycle day after day, week after week, took its toll. I could feel something inside me wither away as I tried in vain to make peace with my chosen profession. Cigarette breaks with chai, followed by chai breaks with cigarettes, became the much-sought-after escape from the harsh, white computer screen. My fitness regime petered away, and soon my health suffered as I started putting on weight. Other than the enforced social interaction at work, I began to cut myself off from friends and family, missing important events and social engagements, explaining it away with the hectic work schedule, unavailability of time and inability to take leave. I was depressed, and I didn't even know it.

One day, as I vacantly stared at the employee portal flashing on the computer screen, going through the motions of approving forms, I received a call from Sauraj. Stepping out of the office complex, I picked up his call, hoping he was visiting Pune and wanted to meet up for a drink. Little did I realise at that moment that 'that' fateful conversation would change my life . . . forever.

'Hey, man! What's up? Are you in Pune?' I asked.

'Can you talk?' asked Sauraj, skipping the initial pleasantries in a tone that instantly put me on alert.

'Yeah! All okay?' I asked, concerned.

'You remember our pet project from college, the adventure club?' he baited me. 'What if I told you we have an investor who wants to make it happen?'

I was already hooked. It seemed like a tiny glimmer of light had suddenly emerged at the end of a very dark tunnel, and my imagination began to run wild.

'Dude! Stop messing with me. What are you talking about?' I asked, unable to contain my excitement, yet a little pissed in case this turned out to be his idea of a cruel joke. It just seemed too good to be true.

'Listen, I can't talk now, especially over the phone just yet, but there is a possibility it may happen,' he said cryptically. 'We are coming down to Pune over the weekend. Can you meet us at SIMS?'

'Yes, of course. I'm guessing you're coming down for recruitment. But who's "we"?' I asked.

'My senior colleague and I. Just be there, and I will explain everything in person,' said Sauraj. Then he hung up. In a state of shock, I turned around and stumbled back into my cubicle.

Suffice to say, the rest of the week was excruciatingly long. I was already dismissing the conversation as my overactive imagination. 'It could just be another job offer with Standard Chartered in recruitment,' I thought. I didn't want to get my hopes up only to have them dashed. On Saturday, I tentatively walked into the SIMS campus. As I entered the academic block, I looked up at the dome with reverence, a practice I had done a million times during my student years. This very structure had laid the foundation for my career, and it appeared that it may play yet another pivotal role in my life. I crossed the foyer, greeting Sauraj and his colleague with more formality than usual, as befitted the solemn dignity of the surroundings, and was quickly ushered into an adjoining classroom. As luck would have it, this was the very same classroom I had sat in for two years as a student manager preparing for the corporate world.

I sat down at one of the desks, and Sauraj nonchalantly straddled the lecturer's chair. Meanwhile, his colleague picked up a marker and began to outline 'the plan' on the whiteboard. For the next two hours, with his usual high energy, he began to outline his master plan for starting up his main money-making venture – an MBA institute. This institute would be the parent company with a subsidiary adventure company in partnership with Sauraj and me. This would all be funded by the students' fees. We would provide outdoor management training through adventure activities, and we would have complete autonomy to pursue other adventure-related activities. All we had to do was spend a year helping him set up the MBA institute, and then we were free to run the adventure wing.

I sat and listened with rapt attention, caught up in the fairy tale of it all, like a drowning man in an ocean of despair clinging to a piece of driftwood, my only hope of salvation. Of course, I asked some perfunctory questions, hoping to sound intelligent, but my desperation was written all over my face. The way I saw it, this was my opportunity to quit my job yet continue drawing the equivalent of my current salary. At the age of twenty-six, I would become the director of my very own adventure company. Details like what kind of adventure activities we would pursue were insignificant at this point and could be tackled at a later stage (or so I thought).

With big grins and much backslapping, we walked out of that classroom feeling like adventurers who had just discussed a plan of action over a treasure map and were embarking on an epic journey to El Dorado. Now all I had to do was wait for the signal for the parent company to be registered and start executing 'the plan'. Together, we would form the best MBA institute in Pune and, eventually, in India. I had already begun to imagine the institute, despite it just being a castle in the air. There were no signs of a campus, students, staff, teachers or, for that matter, any existence of this institute other than in our minds and somewhat haphazardly on an erased whiteboard in that classroom at SIMS. I didn't really care if Sauraj was in; I was good to go.

Three weeks later, as I vacantly stared once again at the employee portal flashing on the computer screen, I received a message from Sauraj. 'Registration done!' it read. 'THE MBA INSTITUTE, successfully approved. Looks like we are on.' I was grinning like an idiot. It was happening. I felt incredible, euphoric. I was taking charge of my destiny. 'What now?' I asked myself, and my frenzied mind immediately provided a surprising answer. I knew I had to serve a three-month notice period in this organisation. I was working on the employee portal anyway, so I thought, 'Why not? Carpe Diem!' I held my breath as I moved the cursor down the dashboard and, with shaking fingers, clicked on the resignation button. Though this would merely initiate a lengthy process requiring a cascade of approvals, I had cast the dice and was willing to wait it out.

I messaged back, 'Brilliant! I just resigned!', hoping to have made as dramatic a statement. Instantly, my phone rang with Sauraj's name flashing across the display. I walked out of the building to avoid eavesdroppers and, finding a secluded spot on the grass lawn, picked up his call.

'Are you serious?' he asked in shock.

'Of course! I have to serve three months, so I will still end up getting out only by April,' I said, trying to explain the simple logic of my decision.

'Yeah! That makes sense,' he said uncertainly. 'But are you sure? Don't you want to talk to someone about it? Your parents or Kay?' he asked again.

'No, dude! If you're sure about this gig, then I'm all in,' I said. 'And honestly, there's no way I can continue here. I'm really done,' I added with finality.

Sauraj laughed. 'That's brilliant, man. Well done!'

I served the next three months of my notice period with all the enthusiasm of a prisoner serving the last leg of a prison sentence. Eventually, Sauraj quit too, exiting his company within two weeks of resigning. Then began the process of forming the MBA Institute. We poured our hearts and souls into the formation of the college: from infrastructure to admissions, from curriculum design to conducting lectures. The work was immensely fulfilling. Right before our eyes, we saw our creation take shape, attracting students, imparting education and becoming a full-fledged academic institute.

However, we did not get our fairy-tale ending. From an initial prediction of 300, we had only 30 students and were compelled to work harder to gain more admissions for the following academic year. The commitment of salary at par with our last drawn corporate pay cheque proved to be a fallacy as there was no money to pay out. Our dreams of pursuing our ambition to provide adventure sports experiences were confined to a company that existed just on paper. Despite several assurances and commitments, neither were we able to pursue and promote the adventure aspect of the business nor were we made stakeholders in the MBA Institute, adding to our growing sense of frustration. We seemed further away from our endeavour of creating an adventure company than when we were still in the corporate world. Finally, with a heavy heart and a tremendous sense of betrayal, Sauraj and I took a stand and, in 2010, parted ways with the management, our very first lesson in failed aspirations.

I was done with people telling me what to do and using me. I was willing to take that chance and start our dream venture. If nothing else, the last year had taught me an important lesson: If you believe in something hard enough, it will happen. After all, we had started an MBA Institute from scratch; at this point, I had nothing else to lose. Sauraj, unfortunately, was not so lucky. He was as angry and disappointed as I was and felt encumbered by his sense of responsibility towards me. Due to house loan EMIs, however, Sauraj had no choice but to look for a corporate job. He joined a small IT startup called

Druva Software. Joining as their HR manager, he would later go on to see the company grow from 35 to 300 employees, personally recruiting their numbers and watching them open offices across India and the US.

The thought of embarking on the business aspect of the venture alone was daunting. As Sauraj and I had conceived this plan together when we were in college, I couldn't imagine him not being a part of it. So with some emotional blackmail and cajoling, we came up with a plan. Between us, we decided that I would be fully part of the 'adventure venture' and Sauraj would provide the financial security with the corporate job. In addition, he would commit himself to projects, especially on the weekends when we had events, thus working twenty-four hours a day, seven days a week. We also decided to play to our strengths and focus on mountaineering, specifically, high-altitude trekking and climbing as the domain of adventure we would specialise in.

Through a series of several discussions – and available domain searches – we finally narrowed down on a name. Adventure Pulse was born on 17 July 2010 with our first trek to Torna Fort in Maharashtra, where we led a group of sixty-five people.

Over the next four years, from 2010 to 2014, Sauraj and I embarked on an incredible journey, leading trekking expeditions to Stok Kangri (6,153 m) and the Chadar trek in Ladakh, scaling Mt Kilimanjaro (the highest peak in Africa), guiding multiple treks in Nepal and offering our flagship experience – the Everest Base Camp trek that had sparked this entire adventure.

Being in the outdoors, surrounded by nature's raw beauty and challenges, gave us a profound sense of freedom and fulfilment. Leading people on these treks, often into environments that pushed them far outside their comfort zones, was an extraordinary privilege. Each expedition wasn't just about the physical journey; it became an opportunity to build experience – not only in trekking techniques but also managing people under incredibly difficult circumstances. These were moments when emotions ran high, tempers were tested and perseverance was the only way forward.

In many ways, these experiences laid the foundation for something deeper. They subconsciously began shaping the purpose of our lives – helping others step beyond their boundaries and discover their strength while finding immense joy and meaning in the process. Each trek taught us about not just mountains but also people, resilience and the shared human spirit that thrives even in the harshest of environments.

4

The Odyssey Begins

> Obsession is the wellspring of genius and madness.
> Michel Foucault, *Madness and Civilization:*
> *A History of Insanity in the Age of Reason*

Sauraj

By 2013, as part of Adventure Pulse, Sam and I had both led multiple treks to Everest Base Camp and gained considerable mountaineering experience. Over the last five years, I would often think about my first visit to Everest Base Camp and the naive conversation with the Sherpa where I expressed my desire to extend the trek by a few days and climb Everest. Now, occasionally my trekkers would ask me a similar question, and I would smile, enjoying the humour. For me, the inception of climbing Everest had taken place when I first set eyes on the mountain. 'Could I actually reach this summit one day?' I had learnt a lot more about Everest and had developed a deeper appreciation of all the planning and preparation it would entail. Also, in this endeavour, I knew I would not be alone. Sam was as crazy about the mountains as I was.

Over the last few years, I had often spoken about this desire, even though it had felt like nothing more than a wishful fantasy. One afternoon in October 2013, Sam had come home for an informal 'work meeting', and the topic came up again. I knew I truly wanted to make it happen, and there seemed to be only one way to approach it. We would need to treat this like any other Adventure Pulse expedition – professional, structured and strategic.

Our MBA backgrounds and corporate experiences proved to be invaluable at that moment. The skills we had developed – strategic planning, leadership, crisis management and organisational insight – added tremendous value to our approach. These experiences taught us that education and life skills can create unique opportunities and equip us with a versatile toolkit for challenges, often ones we might not initially expect. They gave us a unique lens to view this dream, providing not just the technical know-how but also the confidence and strategic thinking to make Everest more than a personal goal. It could actually become a business endeavour.

Who knew? If we were disciplined and professional enough, we might just be able to make climbing Everest part of our business portfolio.

'The first thing,' I remember saying to Sam, 'is to freeze on a date to climb and then work backwards.' Sam listened patiently, with a smile. I had been doing a lot of reading and realised that the window to climb Everest is just before the onset of the monsoons in the Indian subcontinent. Getting the timing right is crucial and can make or break a climber's summit attempt. In a perverse way, nothing about climbing Everest can be anything less than perilous. Climbers must brave the challenges of high altitudes, endure extreme temperatures and face the risk of altitude sickness, all while dealing with bad weather conditions for most of the year.

Due to its sheer altitude of almost 30,000 ft above sea level, Everest and a handful of other Himalayan peaks graze the stratosphere and are subject to powerful, cold jet-stream winds pretty much all year round. There is a reason why, in most pictures of Everest, you see a dark expanse of rock juxtaposed proudly against a blue sky. The plume of cloud often seen drifting from the summit is, in reality, the jet-stream winds at 150 km/hr, 9,000 m above sea level, blowing the snow from the face of the mountain. These winds are cold and fast-moving, battering the top of Everest constantly and making it impossible for climbers to summit.

There is just one exception, a brief period just before the onset of the monsoons on the subcontinent. The 'climbing window', as it is called, opens as the monsoon winds start moving north in the Bay of Bengal. This powerful weather system collides with the jet streams above Everest, creating a high-pressure region that calms the winds and results in a brief period of perfect weather, usually in May. This window can last anywhere between two days and three weeks. During this time, wind speeds may plummet to less than 10 km/hr, providing ideal climbing conditions. From all the information I had read, spring was the season to plan an Everest expedition, just before the onset of the monsoons. However, if this weather window was reduced to just a few days, hundreds of Everest aspirants would rush to try and reach the summit, causing the notorious Everest traffic jam.

The internet and several mountaineering books became my constant sources of research. The chief concern that doomed most Everest aspirants was the funding required to finance this climb: approximately $45,000 per climber. This translated roughly to about ₹28–₹30 lakh per person. Raising the finances and working out the logistics seemed formidable, requiring effort and skills similar to those needed to run your own company. I realised that the expenses would start piling up before we even set foot in Nepal.

There were several costs that added up to this. One was just the climbing permit or royalty fee paid to the Nepal government for Everest, which was approximately ₹7 lakh for each climber. This fee was non-negotiable and non-refundable and had to be paid irrespective of the outcome of the expedition. The next big expenditure was the cost of the expedition itself, which included liaison officer fees, park fees, yaks, porters, icefall ladders and fixed ropes, waste deposit, travel, insurance, tents, food and fuel. All this added up to a whopping ₹12–₹14 lakh for one person.

I was already beginning to feel light-headed looking at these numbers when we were confronted with the fact that climbing to the top of the world in the rarefied air would require supplemental oxygen. We would each require six to eight cylinders for ourselves and the Sherpas to provision enough for the summit and a safe return. At ₹35,000 a bottle, this was to set us back by another ₹7 lakh. To survive for any duration of time in extreme weather conditions, low wind chill and the harsh terrain, we would require some very specialised equipment. Shoe shopping for Everest, too, turned out to be quite interesting. I soon discovered that, at the time, there were only two companies in the world that made shoes specifically for climbing Everest. They cost a small fortune, approximately ₹70,000 a pair. In addition, we would have to set aside another ₹2–₹3 lakh for tipping support staff and sundry expenses for training climbs before the summit push.

We began by breaking down the tasks into smaller steps. We ensured that no matter how busy we got with Adventure Pulse, we spent thirty minutes a day planning and reviewing progress on our Everest expedition. We could leave nothing to chance. From raising the funds and planning the logistics to ensuring our physical readiness, we had our work cut out for us.

Though Sam sat listening to me outline the logistics of the expedition in a calm, practical manner, I could see him freaking out about the sheer amount of money we had to collect.

'Fifty thousand dollars! And that too, per person?' he suddenly exclaimed. 'How much is that in rupees, 30 lakh? Shit!'

Just the enormity of it was staggering, making him express considerable doubts and consider abandoning this sheer madness.

In our desperation and hope for salvation, we turned to our law professor, Shekhar Bhonagiri. In the years since our college days, we had established a strong bond with him. He had an uncanny ability to cut through the bullshit, identify the core of a problem and then give us a completely different perspective that invariably left us bewildered by its simplicity. In addition, he and his family had also been among the very first clients we had taken to Everest Base Camp in 2010. If anyone could relate to our madness and understand our passion and desire to climb Everest, it was him. We were really looking for a co-conspirator.

When we met Prof. Bhonagiri, we voiced our desire to climb Everest, followed immediately by a list of all the reasons why it was close to impossible. Surprisingly, he dismissed our misgivings and said with a smile, 'It's about time. I was wondering when you boys would come around to it!' With absolute ease, he simplified the challenge in a way that should have been sheer common sense, making us feel a bit ridiculous. 'Just break down the amount into small steps,' he said. 'You mean to tell me that you don't know twenty-five people who can give you one lakh?' he asked. 'Start putting down names on the list. You can put my name first, and that's one less to go,' he said with a smile. That fateful evening set the ball rolling, giving us the courage and motivation to start.

I was keen to look at April 2014 for Everest at first, just five months away, but we later realised that this was far too ambitious. Realistically, we would need at least eighteen months to prepare. This timeline would hopefully allow us to juggle fundraising, physical preparation and the day-to-day running of Adventure Pulse at the same time. Honestly, when I look back, I don't really know how we managed to get the money. I think the most important thing we started doing was talking about wanting to climb Everest to every single person who was willing to listen. We spoke to friends and family. We spoke to ex-colleagues and batchmates. We shared it on Facebook and wrote emails. Around this time, we were introduced to the concept of crowdfunding. After much research, we shortlisted a relatively new India-based crowdfunding platform called Milaap. This became yet another effective medium for us to start promoting our Everest campaign. It possibly reached a stage where people looked at us and already knew what we were going to ask for. Then our family and friends, seeing our energy and enthusiasm, started sharing it as well.

Slowly, the money started trickling in. We received support and finance from both immediate and distant family as well as friends. Our campaign to climb Everest really did become a rallying cry, for in our attempt to climb the highest mountain in the world, we were also inadvertently spreading the message to 'follow your dreams'.

One of the most innovative attempts we made at raising money was through Druva Software, the IT company where I was working. They commissioned us to write a series of twelve blogs for every month leading up to the expedition. They agreed to give us a substantial amount per blog, which became a huge part of our fundraising campaign. In the months leading up to the expedition, we put our heads together, working meticulously to cover as much information as possible and do justice to the agreement. Inadvertently, this also helped us by increasing our knowledge of the subtle nuances that go into the logistics of setting up such an expedition.

For Sam, one of the most touching moments was when he received a contribution from his ninth-grade biology teacher with the simple message: 'I believe in you.' We were moved by the incredible support we received from colleagues and classmates living around the world who reached out and declared their support and monetary contribution to our Everest campaign. Slowly but surely, the finances crept in, and before we knew it, by February 2015, we were within a few lakhs of our target. To make up for the shortfall, as a measure of their appreciation for my dedication to the company, Druva Software stepped in again by pledging to match the amount contributed by any of its employees towards the expedition campaign, a gesture for which I will always be deeply grateful.

I was always a lot more confident about the finances, overriding Sam's scepticism. For me, a more realistic worry was the physical and technical readiness required. On 18 April 2014, Everest witnessed a massive tragedy. A huge serac (a vertical column of ice) collapsed off the western face of Everest onto the Khumbu Icefall, killing sixteen Sherpas while they were climbing up from Everest Base Camp to the higher camps. The scale of the tragedy and the damage to the route effectively put a stop to the climbing season. This was a gruesome reminder of the raw danger we had signed up for.

To be prepared physically and to hone our skills as mountaineers, beginning sometime in July 2014, we set ourselves a very ambitious target. We would spend the next three months in the mountains, taking on some of the most demanding peaks in the world. In order to do this, I had to leave my job as the HR manager at Druva Software, my last link to a stable corporate career, and join Sam in the full-time operations of Adventure Pulse. This step was driven more by necessity for I was aware that to have a real shot at summiting, we would need to be in the best shape of our lives, physically, mentally and emotionally. There could be no half-measures.

The first challenge we were to take on was Mt Nun (one of the toughest summits in the world), standing at an impressive 7,135 m above sea level in the Kargil district. We would then drive from Kargil to Leh via NH-1A, where we would lead a team to climb Stok Kangri (6,153 m), the highest mountain in the Stok Range in the Ladakh region. These climbs would pave the way for our thirty-day Advanced Mountaineering Course at the Nehru Mountaineering Institute. Finally, in October, we would conclude the season by leading a trek to Everest Base Camp with a team of twenty-two schoolchildren. We were hoping that this would be sufficient experience. In theory, it looked foolproof. I am a cautious climber. I have to be since I am responsible not only for myself but also, very often, for the lives of other people. Yet, I learnt during our eighteen-month Everest preparation that sometimes the best-laid plans go awry and that the mountains are wilful and unpredictable, much like life itself.

Before the Nun expedition, I was in excellent physical shape and in high spirits. We reached Srinagar, the capital of Jammu and Kashmir, from where we were to drive to Kargil and then onwards to Nun Base Camp. On the morning of our departure, as I was shifting some heavy equipment, I suddenly felt my back spasm. I released the bag I was holding and was in excruciating pain. I couldn't move. Since I was in the room and out of earshot, I realised that crying for help would be of no use. Painfully, I tried to move and half-crawled to the bed where I collapsed, unable to move.

Sam found me there an hour later when he came upstairs to tell me that everyone was ready to leave for Kargil. He stepped inside the room and immediately realised that I was in no position to move, let alone ascend a mountain. I knew I was holding everyone up but was completely helpless and in excruciating pain. I insisted that he should not miss out and should leave after asking the hotel staff to find medical assistance. However, Srinagar was perhaps not the best place to have a medical emergency, and although it is the largest city in the Kashmir Valley, we were not familiar with it. Worried, Sam informed the rest of the group and decided to stay with me long enough for me to consult a local doctor or book a flight to Delhi to get my back fixed. After a few hours, although still in terrible pain, I was able to move enough to visit the government hospital. Unfortunately, the doctor was not of much help. Sam stayed on with me for another two days until I felt strong enough to fly out from Srinagar to Delhi. My father met me at the airport and immediately rushed me to orthopaedic specialists who diagnosed the injury as a compressed disc needing intensive treatment. Then began a slow, month-long journey of recovery and physiotherapy. During this time, I found myself growing increasingly frustrated and annoyed. I could not believe that after months of preparation, I was laid up, out of action due to an incorrectly lifted bucket that could not have weighed as much as my backpack for the Nun climb, which was upwards of 25 kg.

Although I was glad that Sam could have a go at climbing Nun, I could not help but feel sorry for myself as I spent most of my time in bed or in physiotherapy. The recovery was slow, but I was determined to get back on track as per schedule for our Stok climb. What I did not know at the time was that Nun turned out to be the archnemesis of the entire team. Despite staying on with me at the Srinagar guesthouse for an additional two days, Sam managed to catch up with the group at base camp. The tide thereafter turned for the group of climbers, who found themselves stuck in a terrible snowstorm close to the summit. With provisions for only a few days and extreme conditions, they came perilously close to not making it back. Finally, when the weather cleared for a day, they were able to descend the mountain and retreat to safety.

Against all odds, after a month of complete bed rest, I somehow recovered in time to make it back to Srinagar and then on to Ladakh to attempt Stok Kangri. As per plan, Samir met me in Leh but looked visibly shaken from his ordeal on Nun. We discussed his experience at length and concluded that he should go back home for some rest. Despite the failures and setbacks, we believed that by the end of the year, after completing the advanced course and the Everest Base Camp trek, we would still be adequately prepared. My back having recovered so recently, I was also grappling with my own demons. Stok Kangri would be the acid test for me to determine whether I was truly ready to take on Everest in the next six months. Thankfully, our expedition went well, and I was able to summit not just once but twice on consecutive days without incident, my body adapting and responding well to the challenges of the climb. These were important life lessons that would time and time again remind us to keep moving forward and not dwell on past failures. More importantly, each of these experiences was further forging bonds of trust in our friendship.

In September, Sam and I continued our adventures with the Advanced Mountaineering Course at the Nehru Institute of Mountaineering in the Garhwal Himalayas of Uttarakhand. I felt strong and confident, especially after the recent success of Stok Kangri. The advanced course was not easy, but I sailed through it, finally feeling perfectly prepared for Everest. However, during the course, we once again had cause for anxiety when Sam fell some 12 ft off a mountain face during the final ice-climbing assessment. Other than a knee injury, which did not trouble him much at the time, he appeared to be all right. We both completed the course with an A grade and received our certification.

After the advanced course, we returned home to Pune for a short respite before setting off once again to Nepal. This time, we were accompanied by twenty-two students from the Bishop's School, Pune, for a guided Adventure Pulse trek to Everest Base Camp. The school had just completed its 150th anniversary, and as part of the celebrations, these students would attempt to reach Everest Base Camp in Nepal and raise the school flag. The trek with twenty-two teenagers was challenging, to say the least, but all the children reached the base camp and back safely, a fantastic achievement for us. Things were finally falling into place. Yet, time was running out, and once back in Pune, sometime in mid-November 2014, we could no longer ignore the daunting challenge of raising the ₹70 lakh needed to finance this mammoth project.

It was touch-and-go with lots of frantic scrambling, but in the nick of time, we managed to bring in the financial wherewithal. An important lesson for me was that a bid to reach the top of the world takes not just determination, physical grit and mental toughness but also uncanny resourcefulness in mobilising such huge funds. I developed more 'business acumen' in the six months before our summit attempt than in all my years of an MBA, a corporate career and running our own business put together.

While running around for finances from pillar to post between November 2014 and March 2015, we also had to focus on our physical conditioning. The preparation for Everest needed two crucial aspects: the overall mountaineering experience built over time and the immediate physical conditioning that starts at least eight to ten months prior to the expedition. Having successfully completed three of the four mountaineering challenges we had set for ourselves, we felt reasonably prepared. Yet, we still had to focus on our constant physical readiness.

To help, I roped in Mangesh Ravlekar, a trainer I had met at the local gym in Pune that I used to visit. Over time, I realised that he was as passionate about physical fitness and training as we were about climbing. His determination to get us into physical shape for the climb became as obsessive as our desire to succeed. Without him, we would never have been Everest-ready.

As much as we would have liked to take a break, we didn't have the luxury of time. In November 2014, we drew up our training schedules, including early morning 10K runs at 5 AM, followed by gym sessions for muscular strength-building. Just as we were getting into the rhythm of training, we faced a major setback. In the second week of our morning runs, Sam's knee injury from the advanced course, despite him having completed both the course and a trek to Everest Base Camp, began to flare up. During a run, he suddenly cried out in pain and stumbled, forcing us to rest. The intense pain effectively put a stop to the morning runs.

I was still convinced that there was nothing that some rest could not fix. However, when the discomfort did not subside, Sam finally consulted a sports injury specialist. The prognosis left us both shocked. He had a major meniscus injury, and surgery seemed to be the only option. The downside was that the surgery would require him to rest for at least a month without putting any weight on his leg. This was a complete disaster. The atmosphere in our office was sombre when we sat down to discuss the way forward. I was beginning to get very anxious, but I didn't want to let it show since I could see how disappointed he already was. We were already in mid-November, and from what the doctor had said, it would be mid-January before he could begin to bear weight on his leg, let alone recover enough to resume training. I was worried that Sam would have to drop out.

We had been in this together from the start, overcoming all the challenges the last year had thrown at us. I didn't want Sam to have to pull out so close to the finish line. I even tried to dissuade him from the surgery, but after assessing the damage, he realised that without it, he would never be able to climb Everest. It was the only option that would give him a fighting chance to make it to the top of Everest. Towards the end of November, after weeks of pain and discomfort, Sam finally had the surgery.

I continued with my training schedule with Mangesh, but the fear of Sam being unable to make it constantly nagged at me. The first two weeks after surgery, he was completely bedridden. From then on, he was only allowed to walk a few metres with support within the house. With just three months to go before we flew out to Nepal, in mid-December 2014, Sam broached the subject, confirming all my worst fears. In a deliberately calm voice, he said to me, 'Dude, there is a high probability that I may not be ready for the climb if the recovery takes longer than expected.' I could see the effort it took him to remain calm and hide his distress. I found myself unable to stay as composed. 'Are you doing your physio regularly?' I challenged him. 'Because if you are,' I continued, 'you will recover. The surgeon clearly knew you needed to start running again soon, so let's just wait and see how it goes.'

With constant encouragement and several anxious weeks, Sam diligently powered through his physiotherapy with ruthless determination. By Christmas 2014, less than a month after his surgery, he was back on his feet and walking around – a true testament to his determination and commitment to our cause. As they say, there is a very fine line between determination and obsession.

By mid-January 2015, he had resumed workouts at almost his regular intensity and, by the end of January, even ended up leading the Frozen River–Chadar trek in Ladakh, considered one of the coldest treks in the world with night-time temperatures dropping to −30°C. Though his recovery was fantastic, we were both still under considerable stress. There was the pressure of his full recovery within the timelines, especially as he had to be careful not to overstrain his knee before it healed completely. After all, you aren't supposed to climb the highest mountain in the world less than four months after major knee surgery.

There's always that storybook idea: when you commit to a noble cause, the universe aligns, the stars shine and the journey becomes a smooth, effortless voyage. Reality, however, has a way of writing its own narrative. The past year felt less like a serene sail and more like an unrelenting struggle against the tide, with the odds stacked high and each wave testing our resolve.

5

Mission Everest 2015

> Why do we climb?
> Because it's there!
>
> George Mallory

Sauraj

By February 2015, despite all the ups and downs, things had miraculously fallen into place. We were physically fit (Sam somewhat less so) and adequately financed. Our Everest dream was closer than ever. I was as ready as a rocket about to take off, and I could see that my enthusiasm was infectious, helping Sam overcome his apprehensions about his physical fitness. Despite all the setbacks, we were ready, but more importantly, we were mentally focused on the goal ahead. This time, we hoped we wouldn't just stop at Everest Base Camp but go all the way to the summit of Mt Everest, literally to the 'top of the world'.

Most climbers (experienced or amateur alike) go about their expedition by signing up with a company that helps with organising the logistics. This help includes the entire gamut of logistical support, right from securing the climbing permits to bringing together a team of experienced Sherpas to enable the climbers and the support team to carry and set up tents and food supplies at base camp and higher up. Essentially, these teams cater to all the needs of the climbers for the two months it takes to summit Everest, allowing the mountaineers to focus on the actual climb.

We, instead, opted to self-organise our expedition. By now, having led multiple base camp treks, we were both confident in operations in Nepal and decided we could make it happen. It was, nonetheless, an extremely ambitious undertaking. It meant that in addition to focusing on our physical fitness and ensuring proper acclimatisation and practice hikes, we would also have to be actively involved in the entire expedition management. This required us to plan each step of the expedition and ensure all the moving parts came together. By January, we had interviewed some highly experienced Sherpas, applied to the government of Nepal for a climbing permit and assembled a team of twelve staff members, which included a base camp manager, cooks, Sherpas' helper boys, the kitchen boy and so on.

We soon realised that there was only so much we could do while sitting in Pune. So we made a four-day trip to Kathmandu in the third week of January 2015. We personally took stock of all the climbing equipment and food stores, purchased new regulators with masks and identified suppliers of oxygen cylinders. We met our dear friend Ghanshyam Sharma, who would be our base camp manager, and finalised our Sherpas for the expedition. It was particularly important to meet the Sherpas in person, as during the expedition, our lives would depend as much on their experience of the mountain as on our skills and physical fitness. We were introduced to Tashi Sherpa from Rolwaling who would be our climbing sirdar (the head Sherpa). A seven-time Everest summiteer, Tashi Sherpa was a very reassuring presence and had excellent climbing credentials. His maturity and experience would soon prove to be the difference between life and death for the entire team. With Tashi Sherpa and Ghanshyam, our base camp manager, we got down to the brass tacks of ensuring that everything on our list – amounting to over 1 tonne of equipment and supplies – was procured and properly packed to fly with us to the Everest Valley by March.

During this time, as we approached the end of January 2015, I once again reached out to Malli Mastan Babu via email a couple of months before leaving for Nepal. I immediately received a response from him, a brief note wishing our team the very best and stating that he himself was soon leaving for South America where he would be climbing fifty peaks in the region. He promised a longer correspondence once he was back. His endorsement and wishes, despite his remote location, were a tremendous source of reassurance for me.

Back in Pune after our visit to Kathmandu, we were satisfied with our preparation, and Samir was recovering well. Our trainer in Pune, Mangesh, continued to help ensure our fitness was on track. Soon it was March 2015, and Sam and I were once again on our way to Nepal with a group of trekkers who had signed up with us for an Everest Base Camp trek.

A large part of our funding had been raised through promoting these base camp treks. The thrill of not just trekking up to the Everest glacier but also being part of an Everest expedition team built tremendous excitement for our trekkers and, in a way, included them in this aspiration to reach the summit. We planned to lead them to the Everest Base Camp, after which our guides would take them back down to Lukla while we stayed on at base camp in readiness for our summit attempt. Finally, I would no longer be just one of the base camp trekking guides watching Everest climbers enviously from the sidelines. I was now going to be a part of that small and very exclusive club.

Before our Everest Base Camp trekking group reached Kathmandu, Samir and I arrived a week earlier to make sure that all our supplies for Everest were in place. Within a few days of being in Kathmandu, I was thrilled to receive a call from the office of the prestigious Himalayan Database. This nonprofit organisation maintains an extensive database of all climbing expeditions to Everest and other peaks of the Nepalese Himalayas higher than 8,000 m. The Himalayan Database continues to be the most credible record of mountaineering and Everest summit attempts. Developed by Elizabeth Hawley, an American journalist, it has records of climbs since 1903. The publication contains the most painstakingly researched data available on successful Everest summits and is the most recognised authority that verifies and lends credibility to mountaineers' claims of success. Receiving a call from the office of the Himalayan Database made me realise just how close we were to achieving my lifelong dream.

On our last day in Kathmandu, we caught up with our friend Pem Dorjee Sherpa at dinner. He and his wife, Moni Mulepati, hold the unique distinction of being the first (and only) couple to have married at the top of Mt Everest, an incredible feat never attempted again. He had a lot of advice and tips to offer about climbing this mountain, things that I had never even considered. We listened intently amid the bustle of the Kathmandu restaurant, grateful for his insights and excited about the beginning of our adventure.

The next morning, on 20 March 2015, we once again boarded a flight from Kathmandu to Lukla, only this time in a chartered aircraft and accompanied by 1,000 kg of equipment and rations, which made up only a part of the supplies we had to transport to the Everest glacier. Our friends from the trekking group joined us a day later from Kathmandu, giving us sufficient time to send these supplies up by yak caravans. Despite having made the trek from Lukla to Everest Base Camp many times before, this trip felt very different. We discovered that as intrepid mountaineers with a bona fide intent to summit Everest, we had to take part in several customs. For me, one of the most significant moments was seeking the blessings of Lama Geishi, the head lama at the upper Pangboche Monastery on the way to Everest Base Camp. The Sherpas of the Khumbu Valley hold Lama Geishi in extremely high regard, and receiving his blessings before an Everest expedition is a rare privilege.

Our climbing sirdar, Tashi, being an established mountaineer and a senior member of the community, was able to organise an exclusive prayer ceremony with Lama Geishi. This rare privilege lasted for thirty minutes featuring an elaborate pooja ceremony personally performed by Lama Geishi. The ceremony engulfed me in a sea of calm, and I found myself enjoying the serenity of this deeply spiritual moment. After the frenzy of the last few months of logistics and coordination, I was finally able to experience a sense of peace and truly live in the moment. As I looked at the rest of my team, I saw the same sense of calm reflected on each of their faces. The blessings of Lama Geishi had deeply touched each of us, and we were all brimming with confidence and determination. This exclusive time spent with one of the most revered Buddhist monks in the shadow of Everest marked an incredibly auspicious beginning.

After the pooja ceremony, we rejoined our trekking group to move ahead towards base camp as planned. We continued our journey and arrived at Everest Base Camp on 28 March 2015, to the spectacular views of Everest and much excitement among our trekking group. However, we realised that it was still early in the season, and we were among the first few groups to arrive at base camp. As we discussed our plans over the phone with Ghanshyam, who was in Kathmandu, we realised it would be some time before we could set up camp, as there was a forecast of heavy snowfall in a few days. We concluded that it made more practical sense to walk back down halfway from base camp to Deboche with our trekking group, wait out the bad weather and enjoy the hospitality of our favourite teahouse, the

Rivendell Lodge. After all, once we were at base camp, we would be sleeping on a glacier for the next two months. Our trekking group was also pleased to learn that we would be joining them for the next two days on their return journey. Sam was especially happy as his wife, Karishma, had also accompanied us up to that point as part of the trekking group. They had been given some unexpected bonus time together.

Two days later, as we bid our friends goodbye at Deboche, the reality of the project began to sink in. We turned in early that night to get a good night's rest and woke up the next morning to find the place transformed by a couple of inches of snow. True to the forecast, it had snowed all night and continued through the rest of the day. The weather remained grim with overcast skies over the next couple of days, punctuated by periods of very heavy snowfall. Our spirits began to sink, and the isolation of the teahouse in this remote part of the Himalayas weighed heavily on us. Ghanshyam called us at the Rivendell Lodge, informing us that much of our equipment and supplies were stuck en route due to bad weather and would take longer to reach base camp than originally planned.

However, one of the most disturbing updates reached me completely unexpectedly. I received news that Malli Mastan Babu had perished while climbing solo after a successful summit attempt of Tres Cruces Sur in the Central Andes located on the border of Argentina and Chile. I was shocked and deeply saddened by his untimely demise. He had been an inspiration, a mentor and, more importantly, a friend. Despite my grief, my resolve to summit Mt Everest only grew stronger. Given the disturbing news and frustrated by the delay, on 3 April, Sam and I decided to trek further down to the comfort of Namche Bazaar.

Over the span of our annual Nepal treks, I had come to think of Namche as my second home in the Khumbu Valley. Being the largest village in the valley and a popular haunt for trekkers and mountaineers, Namche had far more recreational avenues for us to pass the time. We even went to relax at some of the popular bars despite not having had any alcohol for months and it would be another two months before we would allow ourselves celebratory mugs of beer after successfully summiting Everest.

At Namche Bazaar, we ran into many other prospective summiteers who, like us, had decided to rest here before heading up to base camp. Our conversations with them made us realise that we were still at least a week ahead of schedule before the start of the climbing season. As always, we were staying at the Khumbu Resort teahouse in Namche. There, I met Melanie, and we got talking. She appeared to be in her late forties, and I assumed she must be one of the trekkers on the Everest Base Camp circuit. As we talked, I realised she was there to climb Mt Everest. A seasoned mountaineer, she had already successfully summited Lhotse, which is adjacent to Mt Everest and is the fourth-highest peak in the world. Summiting Everest would make her one of the oldest British women to accomplish this incredible feat. Over the next few days, we spent a lot of time in her company, benefitting from her experience and wisdom. By the time we were ready to leave Namche, we felt well acclimatised to the altitude of 11,000 ft. Everest Base Camp, which was to be our home for the next two months, was much higher, at an altitude of 18,000 ft.

We waited in Namche Bazaar until 7 April for Ghanshyam to catch up with us along with our supplies for base camp. Together, we started making our way up the Khumbu Valley once again, a relatively more sober ascent without the chatter and excitement of the trekking group. The trek to Everest Base Camp passes through many iconic landmarks, but few are as sobering as the Thukla Pass, also known as the Everest Memorial. Nestled at an altitude of approximately 4,830 m, this high mountain pass is a natural amphitheatre for emotion.

As we approached, the landscape shifted dramatically – steep, rugged trails gave way to an expanse of windswept ridges dotted with rows of stone chortens and plaques. The pass is a place of quiet reverence, a reminder of the immense risks and sacrifices that the mountains demand.

Each memorial stone here tells a story. Among the most notable is the plaque for Scott Fischer, the celebrated American mountaineer who tragically lost his life in the infamous 1996 Everest disaster. Fischer, known for his charisma and deep connection to the mountains, was a pioneer of guided climbs in the Himalayas. His memorial stands as a poignant tribute to a climber who dared greatly but paid the ultimate price.

Another striking memorial belongs to Babu Chiri Sherpa, a legend in his own right and a national hero of Nepal. Babu Chiri holds multiple records on Everest, including spending an astonishing twenty-one hours on the summit without supplemental oxygen – a feat few can fathom. His contributions to mountaineering and the Sherpa community are celebrated worldwide, and his loss is a sombre reminder that even the most experienced climbers are not immune to the mountain's unpredictability.

Walking through the pass, we stopped often to read the inscriptions, each etched with names, dates and heartfelt messages left by loved ones. The chill of the wind seemed to carry whispers of their stories – dreams pursued, triumphs achieved and lives cut short in the pursuit of something extraordinary. It's impossible not to feel the weight of their legacy. Thukla Pass isn't merely a waypoint on the trek; it is a solemn threshold where every climber pauses, reflecting on the fragility of life and the indomitable spirit that drives humanity to reach for the heavens.

I was filled with a sense of remorse as I sat and looked out at the sheer number of memorials dotting the landscape of this windswept mountain pass. Instinctively, I reached into my rucksack and pulled out the *katha* (a silk Tibetan blessing scarf) I had received at the monastery. I climbed to the highest point on the pass and tied the *katha* to the colourful prayer flags fixed to the rocks. Bowing my head, I said a silent prayer for my friend and mentor, Malli Mastan Babu. He had lived life to the fullest, inspiring me and teaching me so much about the mountains. I fondly remembered our conversations and the way I had confided in him many years ago about my dream of building an adventure company to make the mountains more accessible to people. Although appreciative of my enthusiasm, he had advised me to always ensure the sanctity and preservation of the mountains. To this day, his words continue to carry tremendous weight, and I remain acutely aware of my responsibility to conserve this delicate ecosystem in order to offset the commercial aspect of our organisation.

We continued our journey onwards. Since one of the basic tenets of mountaineering is to climb high and sleep low, we decided to add another pit stop on our way to Everest Base Camp, an attempt to summit Lobuche East. By gaining higher altitude above the point where we planned to rest, we were allowing our bodies to better adapt physiologically to the thinner atmosphere. At an altitude of 6,119 m, it would serve us well not only for acclimatisation but also as good practice for the days to come. Located very close to Everest, Lobuche most closely simulates the conditions we expected on Everest, in terms of geography, terrain and atmosphere. Having climbed this mountain a few years ago, we were excited to test our physical fitness before attempting the dreaded Khumbu Icefall. As we made our preparations to climb Lobuche, Ghanshyam, along with the yak caravan, pressed on to occupy Everest Base Camp.

On 10 April, we started our Lobuche climb in the early hours of the morning, gaining 1,100 m in 7 hours to reach the summit at 7 AM despite the sub-zero temperatures and harsh snow conditions. My weariness vanished as I looked ahead at the gigantic Everest Massif towering over us. Even though I had combed through numerous images of Everest, having spent the better part of the last two years with a single-minded focus on reaching its summit, nothing had prepared me for the commanding presence and sheer grandeur of it right before my eyes. From the summit, Tashi Sherpa pointed out Everest Base Camp to us and suggested we test our walkie-talkies while we were here. Excitedly, I radioed Ghanshyam at base camp, half expecting him to be asleep. But within minutes, over the crackle of the radio, we heard Ghanshyam answer smartly, 'Ghanshyam here from base camp, Dai. Congratulations on your Lobuche summit [6,119 m]. I can hear you loud and clear.' I replied promptly, 'Great to hear your voice, Ghanshyam. The radios are working fine. Please have a good dinner ready. We are finally coming home to base camp.'

6

Everest Base Camp: Home Away from Home

> It's hard to be away from home, but I'm glad I am home now!
> Miriam Makeba, *Makeba: My Story*
> (co-written by James Hall)

Sauraj

Brimming with enthusiasm, we made a swift descent back to Lobuche High Camp, packed our belongings and headed towards Everest Base Camp, arriving sometime in the late evening. I passed by the last point at base camp accessible to trekkers, reminiscing about the day I had stood at this very spot for the first time six years ago, dreaming of climbing Everest. Words couldn't come close to describing my excitement as I marched on towards our very own camp. It was located near the end of the glacier towards the mouth of the infamous Khumbu Icefall. We received a warm welcome to the camp from Ghanshyam and the entire team with lots of congratulations on our successful summit of Lobuche. The highlight was sitting down in a warm dining tent with a hot cup of coffee and indulging in some pakoras and samosas prepared by Bhim Dai, our head cook.

After spending time with the team in the dining tent, we were given a quick orientation of our expedition base camp by Ghanshyam. The kitchen tent had been placed strategically, 20 m from the dining tent, to facilitate easy access to food and hot water. Our store tent stood behind the kitchen tent, placed protectively between two huge boulders. Beyond this lay the Khumbu Icefall. Though uncomfortably close to this volatile feature of the glacier, it provided us with an uninhibited approach during our climbs as well as easy access to flowing water. Our two toilet tents were placed discreetly at either end of the camp. This consisted of a simple setup: a big blue drum lined with plastic, placed below a stone ledge, with a small tent positioned over it to ensure privacy. Once the drums were full, the Nepalese governing body, the Sagarmatha Pollution Control Centre (SPCC), mandated that they be sealed and carried all the way down the valley for proper sanitation and processing.

Each climbing member was assigned a dedicated sleeping tent, arranged in a neat row diagonally behind the kitchen tent, facing down the valley, away from the wind. After the orientation, we made our way to our individual tents. My tiny 6×5 ft tent was to be home for the next forty-five to sixty days. Despite having spent innumerable nights in tents during our other climbs, this was different. This was the longest duration I would be staying in a tent, and for another, this was on the Everest glacier, the dream of a lifetime.

I decided to get organised to make it a functional space for myself for the coming weeks. So I divided the tent into an inside space of 6×4 ft and started by laying out my sleep mat before allocating space for other activities. Then I realised that this was it. That was all the private space I had for myself for the next fifty days or so. I was keenly aware, too, that having a personal tent was a luxury. As we moved to higher camps, we would be sharing tents. At Camp 3 and Camp 4, very often, there would even be three people in one tent.

That first night in my tent on the Khumbu Glacier was not particularly comfortable. I didn't sleep too well due to the combined effects of the excitement of sleeping at Everest Base Camp and the extreme cold. At Everest Base Camp, you are effectively sleeping on a slab of ice, thinly protected from direct contact by a layer of tent fabric and the sleeping mattress. During the night, the cold and damp from the glacier seeped in, and more than once, I woke up in a clammy sleeping bag in −30°C temperatures.

The next morning, we decided to explore the other campsites and get to know our neighbours. We started by going around the base camp, identifying the important camps and landmarks. We first walked over to familiarise ourselves with the Himalayan Rescue Association (HRA) tents, which housed a team of three doctors specialised in high-altitude medicine. These doctors volunteer to stay at Everest Base Camp for two months every year, taking care of the medical needs of all climbers. Every climber must go to the HRA tent and register with the camp doctors so that they are aware of the demographics and number of teams at Everest Base Camp at any given time.

For me, the most interesting camp was that of the Indian Army contingent, who, like us, were hoping to make a successful summit bid. Having grown up surrounded by the military, I was very excited to meet them and, especially, the expedition leader, Major Jamwal, whom I had first met through my father when he was in the Indian Army. As an experienced climber, he had already summited Mt Everest twice and was a source of inspiration for me. He had been instrumental in guiding me during my pre-Everest preparation, and the fact that he was physically here was extremely fortuitous. That morning, he graciously welcomed us to the Indian Army dining camp, and over cups of hot tea, he once again shared advice and safety tips with us. As a veteran Everest climber, he made us feel at home and took us under his wing, making us feel like part of the Indian Army family at the base camp. He told us to approach him for anything we needed, however small, and they would be glad to help. This was especially reassuring as our two-member climbing team was probably the smallest contingent on Everest that year.

Since Sam and I shared a deep fascination for Everest, we were already fairly aware of many of the base camp traditions. For instance, we knew of the deep reverence that the Sherpas held for the ceremonial pooja tradition at Everest Base Camp. They believe that Sagarmatha, the mother goddess of Earth, would protect them and their loved ones. Offering prayers and seeking the blessings of the mother goddess before stepping onto the Khumbu Icefall is the most important of these Everest rituals. This tradition dates back to the first British Everest expedition of 1953, and all Sherpas, young and old, religiously follow it. I was very moved by this reverential practice, viewing it as a significant moment while embarking on this journey of a lifetime. So, when our climbing sirdar, Tashi Sherpa, announced that the pooja had been organised for 16 April, I was as excited as the rest of the Nepali team. Bhim Dai (our cook) spent the entire day preparing a variety of snacks that would serve as offerings for the pooja, and Tashi Dai asked us to bring out all our technical equipment to be blessed by the lama. Ghanshyam brought out the other equipment, including ropes, oxygen cylinders and even the satellite phone, to receive his blessings. As luck would have it, it started snowing again that afternoon, and I began to worry whether the auspicious ceremony, which is always conducted outdoors, would continue as planned. I was once again reassured by the quiet confidence of Tashi Sherpa. 'Don't worry, Dai,' he said. 'It will stop snowing tomorrow. It never snows on pooja day.'

His optimism, in this case, was misplaced. The next morning, when I woke up, it was still snowing, and the weather gods seemed to be conspiring against us. On the day of the pooja, a Buddhist lama from the Tengboche Monastery arrived in person to conduct the ceremony. The lama had already arrived at camp, and we were to begin the pooja within the next hour. I began to worry about the impact on the morale of our small team in case the pooja didn't go as planned. With the calm stoicism that I was now getting accustomed to, Tashi Dai once again reassured me, 'Don't worry, Dai. We will do it indoors.'

We shifted the pooja inside the dining tent, and the entire staff chipped in to make arrangements indoors. We cleared the tables, prepared the space with customary pooja decorations and laid out the *prasad* (food offerings to the gods) that Bhim Dai had painstakingly prepared. As we laid out the food offerings, I was surprised to notice that along with small portions of Bhim Dai's freshly prepared snacks and some rice, the prasad tray also comprised chocolates, a soft drink and even beer and whiskey! I learnt that the pooja offering to God must include whatever one has at home or in the camp, as our base camp was our home. The Sherpas believe that the pooja is the only way to appease the gods and ensure a safe passage on the mountain. Our Buddhist lama had travelled to Everest Base Camp from Tengboche Monastery and had conducted dozens of pooja ceremonies there. He performed the pooja, which took about an hour, and I found myself enthralled by the mysticism of this high-altitude ceremony, even though outside the sanctuary of our tent, it continued to snow.

Once the pooja ceremony concluded, the entire façade of the camp was transformed with colourful prayer flags strung across the entire camp, their ends all tied together to a makeshift altar of stones. Luckily for us, by the time the pooja ceremony ended, the snowfall had let up a little, and we all trooped outdoors joyously to set up the central console and raise the auspicious prayer flags. The central console is considered extremely holy, serving as the place where the team would offer prasad and light incense sticks every day throughout the expedition to seek God's blessings.

On this central console, we also hoisted the Nepali and Indian national flags side by side, signifying the nationalities of our team members and support staff. Looking at the Indian flag at our camp, I felt a surge of patriotic pride. The pooja was also particularly symbolic as it signified that our Everest climb had now officially begun. Tashi Dai and Ghanshyam were extremely pleased with the ceremony, and Tashi pronounced, 'Dai, very good pooja. Tomorrow, we go into the icefall to Camp 1 and come back.'

Listening to Tashi Dai, I was gripped by both excitement and fear in equal measure. The Khumbu Icefall is a fearsome feature that poses a unique challenge for Everest mountaineers approaching the summit from the Nepal side on the south face route.

The Khumbu Icefall, one of the highest glaciers in the world, is an immense, ever-shifting river of ice that defies imagination. Stretching nearly 4 km (2.5 miles) in length and rising from an altitude of 5,486 m (17,999 ft) to over 5,800 m (19,000 ft), it is a colossal frozen cascade wedged between the towering Nuptse on the right and the western shoulder of Everest on the left. The icefall resembles a giant frozen waterfall, its surface fractured into massive blocks of ice, some as small as a car and others as large as multi-storey houses. These blocks, known as seracs, teeter precariously, constantly on the verge of collapse due to the immense gravitational forces acting on the glacier.

The Khumbu Icefall is in a perpetual state of flux, its ice shifting and grinding under its own weight, creating a cacophony of groaning and cracking sounds. This movement gives rise to deep, treacherous crevasses – gaping cracks in the ice, some spanning several metres wide and plunging to unknown depths. At times, entire towers of ice collapse without warning, sending thunderous avalanches of ice shards cascading down the slope. The sheer scale and volatility of the icefall make it one of the most dangerous sections of the Everest climb, where every step demands focus, precision and a deep respect for the mountain's raw power.

Given the precariousness of the feature and the fact that all climbers must cross it multiple times during their rotations to acclimate, it is necessary to ensure that no one spends more time here than absolutely necessary. Since the 20th century, every climbing season, the Nepal government has deployed a team called the 'icefall doctors'. The icefall doctors are a specialised group of climbers (usually Sherpas) on Mt Everest responsible for creating and maintaining the safest routes through the Khumbu Icefall, one of the most treacherous and technical sections of the Everest route. They play a critical role in ensuring that other climbers can safely navigate this perilous glacier region as they ascend or descend the mountain. Just like a doctor ensures a patient's health by diagnosing and solving challenges, the icefall doctors diagnose hazardous areas in the ice and ensure climbers' safety by establishing and maintaining routes through the icefall. For the services provided by the icefall doctors, the Nepal government charges each climbing team a maintenance fee.

Although full of trepidation, I was very curious to finally come face to face with the dreaded Khumbu Icefall. We had read much about the deadly Khumbu Icefall, known for claiming the highest number of lives on the mountain and we were also aware of the dread and reverence with which even the Sherpas spoke about it. These are men who spend a significant part of the climbing season each year navigating through the icefall multiple times. Yet, even with this level of familiarity, they can never afford to take it for granted. Only the year before our expedition, in 2014, the Khumbu Icefall had claimed the lives of over sixteen climbers, most of them Sherpas, in a deadly avalanche. The group, consisting of about fifty people, including icefall doctors, had been setting up the ropes for climbers to use later in the season when they were struck by boulders of ice and debris. Many fell to their deaths in the crevasses after being hit by the avalanche.

I reasoned that I was as ready as I would ever be to take on this challenge. That evening, Tashi Dai briefed us on how to prepare and kit up for the next morning. 'We will leave at 4 AM. We will climb through the Khumbu Icefall, reach Camp 1 and descend back to base camp by afternoon,' he reminded us.

Early the next morning, after a hurried breakfast and a quick prayer at the central prayer flag altar, we set off towards the Khumbu Icefall while it was still dark. As we took our first steps away from the camp, I was reminded of my first base camp hike in 2008, when I had seen the Khumbu Icefall from afar, trying to get as close as possible for a good photo-op. At the time, it had seemed inconceivable that one day I would be making my way through it, and yet, here I was, almost exactly seven years later about to do just that. It had been a long, circuitous journey, but in retrospect, it seemed inevitable that I would end up here.

We walked for about forty-five minutes over large blocks of ice, before Tashi Dai instructed us to put on our crampons as the incline increased. I halted and pulled out the crampons from my pack to fix them to the bottom of my climbing shoes. Once fixed, the crampons looked like the cleats footballers wear but with longer and sharper teeth designed to bite through the slick top layer of ice and provide a firmer grip on the treacherous glacier. We used our ice axes to cut through the ice and create handholds to climb over some of the almost vertical boulders of ice we encountered. It was around 5 AM, and as dawn broke, I could see the gigantic cathedral of cold, hard, blue ice of the Khumbu Icefall in sharp relief around us. As the sun rose over the horizon, the landscape gleamed with a dangerous, otherworldly beauty. Once we reached the ropes, I clipped on with my safety carabiner and then attached my *jumar*, a mechanical device that allows you to ascend a rope without risking a fall. 'This is so cool,' I called out to Sam, who was a few paces behind me. Hearing my voice, Tashi whispered urgently, 'Dai, in the icefall, no stopping and no talking loudly, please. We can't disturb nature and the ice. At any time, an avalanche can happen.' The icefall was so volatile that even talking loudly could disturb the delicate balance, dislodging the ice and triggering a chain reaction of falling slabs.

We continued climbing steadily through large columns of ice for another hour and then came across a 10-ft-long crevasse. To cross it, there was a fragile-looking aluminium ladder laid across the gaping crack in the ice. On closer inspection, I realised that two ladders were tied together end to end and fixed across both shelves of the crevasse. I flashed a worried look at Tashi, who only said in a deadpan tone, 'Don't worry, Dai. This is only a small crevasse. Just be careful, and don't fall.' Before getting on the ladder, I made the rookie mistake of asking Tashi how deep the crevasse was. 'Bottomless, Dai,' came the eerily cheerful response. 'Very deep,' he continued. 'Once you fall, no possibility of rescue.' Scared beyond belief, I turned to Sam and asked him to support me by holding on tightly to the rope securing the ladder to make it steadier. I took a deep breath and took my first step on the ladder. I had to make sure I planted each foot carefully with the spikes on my crampon aligned with each rung. Often, in trying to lift a foot to place it on the next ladder rung, my crampons snagged on the metal. Any sudden movement could have resulted in losing my balance, so I had to focus on gently pushing my foot outwards just enough to dislodge the stuck crampon. Although that first ladder crossing probably took me only a minute, in my terror, it felt like an eternity.

Later that morning, we finally arrived at Camp 1, located just above the Khumbu Icefall at an altitude of about 6,065 m (19,900 ft). Camp 1 is a small, exposed outpost perched on a mix of ice and rock, serving as a vital staging point for climbers as they prepare for their ascent towards higher camps. It offered a brief respite from the harsh conditions of the icefall but constantly reminded us of the thin air and constant exposure at these altitudes. Before we could catch our breath, we turned back. The objective of this rotation had been completed, and we were ready to get back to Everest Base Camp. To return, once again, we had to face the perils of the icefall, and I realised that while the fear I felt with every ladder crossing did not abate with time, I now knew what to expect and could carry out the process more calmly.

We made it back from Camp 1 in good time, reaching our base camp by 1 PM that afternoon. We were exhausted and dehydrated but excited to be back and were warmly welcomed by Ghanshyam with hot orange Tang and biscuits. We felt like victorious conquerors back from our first battle. The date was 22 April 2015, and before we retired to our tents, Tashi announced, 'Dai, we rest for three days, and on 26 April, we go up again, this time to stay one night at Camp 1 and then push to Camp 2.' I went back to my tent, feeling satisfied with the events of the day and very content.

We spent the next day resting and hydrating ourselves. I was very happy with the progress we were making and our recovery after the excursion to Camp 1. Seeing that both Sam and I were well rested after our Camp 1 excursion, on 24 April we hiked up to the Pumori High Camp, located at an altitude of 5,800 m. Pumori is a magnificent peak with an altitude of over 7,000 m, situated towards one end of Everest Base Camp and a preferred trek for Everest mountaineers acclimatising to the conditions for the summit push. Tashi approved of the plan and re-emphasised the importance of continuing to move about and exercise at Everest Base Camp. So on the morning of 24 April we embarked on a five-hour hike to Pumori High Camp and were back at Everest Base Camp in time for lunch. My plan for the next day, 25 April, was to spend the entire day resting at camp, perhaps watching a few movies to relax, in readiness for our Camp 2 rotation on 26 April.

7

Avalanche

> You only live twice: Once when you are born and once when you look death in the face.
>
> Ian Fleming, *You Only Live Twice*

Sam

That day, 25 April 2015, started like any ordinary day at Everest Base Camp. We had enjoyed bright sunlight over the last three days and were extremely disappointed to wake up to an overcast sky and light snowfall. Sauraj was brimming with confidence from the first rotation, but I could still feel the residual fatigue. The temperature started dropping, and it looked like it was going to be another cold day on the Khumbu Glacier. As per our climbing schedule, the next day we would attempt to move our team to Camp 2, located at 22,000 ft, and occupy it for three to four days. We had just trekked up to Pumori High Camp the previous day, so the thought of spending a day resting in our tents sounded extremely appealing. This day also marked Karishma's birthday, an occasion that I had inadvertently missed for the last two years on account of being in Nepal, climbing during the peak season. Having been reminded teasingly by several members of my team, especially Sauraj, the early part of the morning was spent speaking to her remotely and wishing her all my love and a lifetime of happiness. As the entire team was together for a change, rather than ferrying loads to the higher camps, we decided to watch a movie in the dining tent on Sauraj's laptop. Incidentally, it was a documentary called *Sherpa*, which highlighted the natural disaster of the 2014 avalanche on the Khumbu Icefall. There was general fun as Bhim Dai, our cook, had made some popcorn, and each of our boys pointed and laughed as they recognised friends featured in the documentary, expressing amusement at the shy and embarrassed Sherpas being showcased in the film.

Suddenly, at 11:55 AM, there was a disturbance, and we felt the ground begin to shake. My very first thought was that the glacier was shifting below us, but then one of the Nepali boys shouted, '*Bhūkampa*!' This was a word I instantly recognised as it is the same in Hindi – earthquake! Immediately, everyone charged out of the tent to scan the glacier, watching for possible cracks and movements that could open beneath us. We struggled to maintain our balance as the ground continued to heave under our feet, the entire experience nauseatingly unsettling as the very laws of nature seemed to be uprooted. The poor visibility of the morning just about allowed us to make out the ghostly shadow of the Khumbu Icefall, the most volatile section of Everest. As the tremors began to ease, the sound of the earthquake was suddenly replaced by a huge explosion, a roar of snow and ice crashing down the mountains all around us. We squinted up at the Khumbu Icefall through the poor visibility, unable to discern the exact direction of the sound. However, as the roar increased to deafening proportions, we realised we were looking in the wrong direction and turned around to see a gigantic wall, a literal tsunami of snow and ice, racing towards us from Pumori, the mountain face at the opposite end of the glacier, giving us just moments to react. In the seconds that followed, we realised beyond a shadow of a doubt that we were going to be hit hard by a huge avalanche.

'I can't breathe! Oh God! Why can't I breathe?' I gasped in shock, feeling like I'd just woken up from a nightmare. 'Why can't I breathe?'

I tried to open my eyes, but everything was still dark. I panicked, afraid I'd lost my sight. The nightmare hadn't ended! It had happened so fast, right after we saw the source of our terror. A massive wave of snow, ice and rock – literally a mountain – was crashing down on us. Avalanche!

Seconds later, it hit, destroying everything and crushing the structure of our tent and table. The impact felt like a sledgehammer against my chest, forcing the air from my lungs. I remember suffocating, not just from the force of the impact but also because of the snow that stifled the air, entering my mouth and windpipe as I gasped. It felt like someone was holding my head from behind and pushing it underwater.

We started digging, lifting the weight of the tent. As my leg was freed, I felt the blood rushing back and, with it, a sense of relief. My body was bruised and battered, but I thought I was going to be okay. Fortunately, there wasn't much snow, and within moments, we emerged into the open. The sudden brightness of the snow glare hit my eyes, leaving me dazed and shocked. There was nothing left, no landmarks or tents, just a trail of destruction strewn across the glacier, resembling a scene from an air crash.

As we pulled away the frame of the tent to free people, I realised Sauraj was missing. 'Where's Sauraj? Where's Sauraj, Dai?' I asked a confused Ghanshyam. I didn't remember him being in the tent with us, and there were no signs of life near our camp. As several minutes passed, I began to search frantically, looking behind every ridge of the glacier. There was no sign of Sauraj, and with each passing second, my terror rose.

Suddenly, I saw movement in the wreckage of the kitchen tent, and three figures stumbled out, covered in snow from head to foot. As I ran towards them, one pulled off his Sherpa cap and shouted, 'Sam! What the hell happened?' Through the mask of snow sticking to his face, I recognised Sauraj, red-eyed, with an expression of shock. Relief flooded my senses to see him alive. I later learnt that he had been pulled into the kitchen by Kami Sherpa and had faced the full force of the avalanche entering the tent, saved only by the pile of stones in the centre used to support the cooking stove. The rest of the team stumbled out from under the debris of the camp, shaken, scared, battered and bruised but safe.

At first, an uncanny silence hung over the glacier. But then, the silence was shattered by screams and cries for help. The reality began to sink in. We had just survived one of the deadliest avalanches in the history of mountaineering, but many had not.

The avalanche that swept across Everest Base Camp on 25 April 2015 was triggered by an earthquake measuring 7.8 on the Richter scale. The epicentre was in Gorkha district, Nepal, near the village of Barpak, approximately 77 km northwest of Kathmandu, the capital of Nepal. The quake's effects were felt over a wide area, reaching regions across Nepal, with tremors reported as far as India, Bangladesh and Tibet. At Everest, the earthquake caused a huge block of ice to crack and break off from the ice cliff situated between Mt Pumori and Lingtren, directly opposite Everest, with the Khumbu Glacier and Everest Base Camp located between these two massive formations. Approximately 100,000 tonnes of ice and rock fell down a vertical height of 2,500 ft, gathering strength as it crashed down towards the Khumbu Glacier, building up tremendous momentum and kinetic energy, forming a huge avalanche and an accompanying air blast that completely levelled over 85 per cent of the expedition camps.

The avalanche hit the southern end of Everest Base Camp and rolled upwards against the gradient of the glacier, picking up rocks and ice in its path along with tents, creating a massive wave that stretched upwards, forming a crest over 100 ft high. As the avalanche rushed onwards through the glacier unchecked, entire expedition campsites simply disappeared, leaving nothing but a trail of destruction and devastation in its wake.

It was impossible to differentiate the landmarks in the glacier we had so often walked past. Our campsite had been completely destroyed. The only discernible feature was the Indian flag flapping in the wind on a tall pole above the Indian Army expedition camp. Our personal tents had been picked up by the force of the avalanche and tossed into a heap against a small hill outcrop that marked the extreme perimeter of our campsite. Fortunately, I had zipped up my tent, but Sauraj, assuming he would be returning to his, had left it open. We found it lying in a heap with half his clothes and bags embedded in snow and ice. We were still so disoriented, not really knowing where to start. The fear, adrenaline and confusion of the entire situation seemed to have mixed into one big ball of emotions, leaving my nerves completely raw.

Tashi Sherpa came to our rescue, quite literally taking charge of the situation. He immediately got us moving, probably knowing that if we sat down or began to think, we would simply be overwhelmed by the horror of it all. We went to our respective tents to try and salvage as many of our personal effects as possible. Tashi insisted that everyone wear as many warm and dry clothes as possible, especially gloves, as the weather had begun to deteriorate further with the temperature dipping and snow falling. I was sent to the kitchen along with the climbing Sherpas, Pasang and Lambu Lakpa, to help salvage the stores and try to get a tarpaulin over the frame of the destroyed kitchen tent, while Bhim Dai began to get the stove running for hot water. Sauraj's tent had sustained the most damage with almost all his personal effects completely buried in snow. When Sauraj came out of his tent half an hour later, having restored some order to it, I noticed him shivering. His hands had turned blue from all the digging in the snow, and we feared the possibility of him suffering from frostbite. Once again, responding swiftly, Tashi sent us into the kitchen to get a hot cup of tea, which helped warm his freezing fingers and did wonders for his morale. Even as I surveyed the carnage around us, I was struck by how, only the day before, we had been at Pumori High Camp, right at the epicentre of the avalanche. Had we delayed our hike by one day, we would almost certainly have perished, buried deep under the avalanche.

In the meantime, Tashi Dai and Ghanshyam began a frantic search for our communication equipment. Since all the cell phones and walkie-talkies had been kept in the dining tent for charging, they had been scattered across the glacier when the avalanche ripped through it. Fortunately, Tashi remembered using the satellite phone in his tent the previous evening and soon emerged with it in his hand. It had now been over two hours since the avalanche had struck with time slipping away in the frenzy. Phone lines appeared to be jammed, or maybe it was just the weather, but connecting to anyone in Kathmandu seemed impossible. We would later learn that the entire country had been hit by the same earthquake, leaving tremendous devastation in its wake. I then tried calling home, and the only number I remembered was Kay's. I tried twice and, both times, got a call-waiting tone. Frustrated, I tried a third time. On the fourth attempt, I finally connected. 'Hello,' came her tentative answer, not recognising the strange number from the sat phone displayed on her screen. Concerned

Avalanche

that we would get disconnected, I yelled into the phone a monologue I had rehearsed in my head.

'Kay! This is Sam,' I shouted. 'We are okay. All of us. There's been an avalanche here, but we are fine. Please tell everyone.'

'Yes, I know. There's been a huge earthquake in Nepal,' said Kay.

'Yes, it hit us here at Everest Base Camp, and that's why I'm telling you,' I said with some irritation. 'And why aren't you picking up my calls?'

'Sam!' she said. 'There's been a huge earthquake in Nepal, and it has hit the entire country! I have been getting calls non-stop to check if you're alive.'

Only then did I begin to fathom the magnitude and scale of this disaster. 'I'm so sorry, sweetheart. We are okay, and everything's fine. Our stuff got a little wet, but everything is okay. Please just let both Sauraj's and my parents know. The network is really bad, and I can't seem to get through.'

In the hours that followed, every expedition team at Everest Base Camp struggled to salvage as much equipment, food rations and personal effects as possible, which had been scattered across the glacier over hundreds of meters by the avalanche. Simultaneously, rescue efforts continued for the injured and missing, while the weather progressively deteriorated. The Everest Emergency Rescue (ER) team, run by the HRA, worked exhaustively to provide first aid and assistance to the casualties, despite having lost part of their medical tent and half of their supplies. Supported by doctors from other expeditions, they worked through the entire night, ensuring that all the injured in critical condition were ready to be evacuated by helicopter when the weather cleared. Meanwhile, over seventy climbers who had ascended the previous day were at Camp 1 and Camp 2, presumed missing or worse. Despair on account of the destruction and devastation permeated the entire glacier.

A few hours later, when radio contact was re-established, we received reports, with incredible relief, that all climbers at the higher camps were fine and that there were no casualties. The most damage had been experienced at Everest Base Camp.

We sat in the makeshift kitchen tent, huddled around the kerosene stove, trying to piece together snippets of information we had gathered. Ghanshyam and Tashi, having been able to get through to their families in Kathmandu, along with the little information I had gathered from my conversation with Kay, established that this was definitely not a localised event and was possibly a disaster of epic proportions. Sauraj was keen to go over to the Indian Army expedition team, having been acquainted with Major Jamwal for some years, but Tashi put a complete stop to the idea. 'Dai, sorry, but we must stay together. Please! Entire team staying in camp, please. Not safe, glacier. Big danger.' As he said this, we heard the distant rumbling of falling rock, and the ground began to shudder once again, fortunately subsiding in seconds. This aftershock was the first of several we would experience over the next few days – a harsh reminder that we still stood on precarious ground, extremely unstable and volatile.

As evening began to set in, Tashi sent us to our tents to put on our down suits, climbing boots, gloves and snow caps. He insisted that we keep our torches accessible in case we were hit by another avalanche, for the freezing temperatures of the night would cause instant hypothermia. The air outside was cold and brittle, carrying a strange and unsettling stillness – a silence that felt heavy with unspoken fears and the lingering echoes of the morning's chaos.

Sitting in my tent, lacing up my climbing boots, I just could not believe that this was all really happening. The mood was one of foreboding – a sharp, gnawing unease that lingered in the pit of my stomach. It was hard to shake the sense of imminent danger, as though the mountains themselves were watching, waiting. The uncertainty felt paralysing: Would we face another avalanche? Could we endure another night in these conditions?

Emerging from my tent, fully kitted out with all my gear, I walked across to Ghanshyam's tent to talk to him and saw him lying face down, motionless, his body tense. He got up the moment he saw me, indulging my nonsensical conversation. There was a quiet strength in his demeanour, but it was undercut by the sharp lines of exhaustion and pain etched into his face. Later, we would learn that during the avalanche, he had sustained a back injury when one of the tent poles collapsed on him. He was in excruciating pain.

He had bravely held out for the first twenty-four hours, enduring each moment with quiet stoicism, before the unbearable pain finally forced him to seek serious medical attention. His resilience in the face of such suffering was a stark reminder of the perils of the mountains but also of the indomitable human spirit. Still, as I stood there in the fading light, all I could feel was the cold, the fear and the uncertainty – waiting for darkness to once again consume the mountains.

8

Relief and Rescue

> How do we change the world?
> One random act of kindness at a time.
>
> Morgan Freeman

Sam

Night descended prematurely as it often does in the Himalayas on account of the weather, adding to our dread. The first night was tough. None of us had the courage to leave the makeshift kitchen tent. We kept the stove running through the night, and all eight of us sat huddled together in our down suits and climbing boots, talking softly, afraid to speak above a whisper. The usual stillness of the night was punctuated by the distant rumblings of snow slides, a constant reminder of the danger we were still in. Though physically and mentally exhausted from the strain of the entire day, sleep seemed to be the very last thing on our minds. Suddenly, we were startled as the entrance flap of the kitchen tent was pushed aside. A disembodied head appeared from the darkness of the night, squinting against the glare from our torchlight, looking around in search of a familiar face.

'Are there any Indians here?' came the question.

Sauraj recognised the face of the army expedition team's doctor.

'We are two here, Sir. How can we help?'

The doctor had been given the mandate to take stock of the Indian nationals at Everest Base Camp and identify any injuries to provide medical assistance. After reassuring him of our condition, Sauraj directed him to the other Indian contingents we were aware of. He politely refused our invitation for tea, insisting on trying to reach as many camps as possible despite the late hour and offering medical assistance wherever he could. The instant he left, Sauraj and I began to feel the necessity of considering our ability to offer assistance in our small capacity rather than worrying about the next avalanche or the glacier opening beneath our feet. This brief encounter changed our entire perspective and inspired us. Suddenly, the atmosphere in the kitchen seemed to shift to one of hope. We were eager to step out at once to see if we could help or do anything to bring an end to the long, anxious night we had to endure. Fortunately, Tashi Dai's better sense prevailed as he cautioned us once again about the unstable nature of the glacier and the mountains around us, insisting on the collective safety of our team.

'Dai, tomorrow morning, you go help, no problem. Now going, no good. Very dangerous, Dai. No experience you have, Dai. Please!'

Out of a lack of things to do, we discussed ways in which we could assist. Our first instinct was to run around camp with our tiny medical kit, but Ghanshyam reminded us of the futility of making a difference with just a few tablets of Crocin. Bhim Dai pointed out that we still had 70 per cent of our supplies, which, fortunately, had been stored behind the oxygen cylinders and had escaped the wrath of the avalanche. Simple things like organising tea and food, assessing extra clothes we might have, pitching our extra tents and basically providing the essentials of food, clothing and shelter to people who had lost everything could possibly make a difference. A large part of Everest Base Camp was made up of support teams, Nepali staff and Sherpas, who had lost everything in the avalanche. While insurance covered Western climbers to be evacuated by helicopter, Nepali staff who were not in critical condition on account of injuries had to endure the freezing temperatures of the glacier with nothing. These were the people who needed help. As we huddled together, all of us in the kitchen tent, the darkness seemed to be kept at bay in those moments of shared camaraderie. The long vigil of that night is something I will never forget, sitting in our down suits, on a cold slab of rock, with Tashi on one side and Sauraj on the other, hoping to see the sunrise the next day.

Needless to say, we survived the first night. After breakfast, we gathered up some of the Indian Army equipment that had been scattered around our camp by the avalanche and walked over to their camp, some 600 m south of us. For the first time, we witnessed the full devastation of the avalanche as we passed huge metal frames and LPG cylinders crushed like empty beer cans mixed in with the debris of clothes and tent fabric. The men at the army camp were in full cleanup mode as we moved through their campsite asking for directions to Major Jamwal. Seeing us, he smiled, not so much from relief but from a sense of reaffirmation.

'Captain Ritesh Goel told me that he stopped by your camp last night and said you were okay. Good to see you moving around. When are you going down?'

In complete shock, Sauraj and I looked at him.

'This will get sorted, right, Sir? We will be able to climb in a week or so, right?' asked Sauraj.

'Sorry, yaar, but *iss saal* expedition season *khatam hai* [the expedition this year is finished].'

I don't think the possibility of our expedition being over had sunk in until that moment. We had worked so hard in the last year, spent so much money and trained so hard. I had undergone a damn knee surgery and survived an avalanche.

For what? Suffice it to say, I was gutted. I knew that if I was feeling like this, Sauraj was feeling worse. Jamwal went on to describe how that was probably the worst disaster he had seen and survived in all his years of climbing and that we should seriously start thinking of packing it in and going home.

'What are you guys planning to do?' asked Sauraj.

'*Hum to fauj hai, Bhai* [We are the Indian Army]. We will stay and assist with the rescue and relief work.'

As we walked back to our camp, processing the conversation with Major Jamwal, our hearts could not come to terms with the inevitable finality with which he had articulated the end of our Everest dream. Probably as an attempt to delay the discussion with our team, on impulse, we decided to stop at the Snowy Horizon expedition camp. We knew Kuntal Joisher, a Mumbai climber who had attempted to climb Everest in 2014 and had had to turn back when the season was called off on account of an avalanche in the Khumbu Icefall that had claimed the lives of sixteen Sherpas. Climbing with him was Kishore Dankude, whom we knew was from Pune. He had climbed Everest in 2014 from the north side and was attempting to be the first Indian to climb Everest from both sides in two consecutive years. For Kuntal, this was a repeat of his experience the previous year, and he didn't give us much hope. Though their team had not decided on the next course of action, early the next morning, they left Everest Base Camp and trekked down the valley to be evacuated from Lukla in an Mi-17 helicopter to Kathmandu.

On 27 April, the weather cleared, allowing helicopter evacuations to take place on the Everest glacier after two whole days. The earthquake and subsequent avalanches had destroyed the route between Everest Base Camp and Camp 1 through the treacherous icefall, making it impossible for teams to descend, leaving them stranded for two days. Though safe for the moment, these climbers had limited resources and were stranded in an incredibly unstable environment that could escalate into a more volatile situation at any time. In a dramatic display of courage and skill, helicopter pilots flew to a height of 20,000 ft above sea level in one of the most treacherous mountain terrains in the world, evacuating two climbers at a time and thus preventing any further loss of life. On 28 April 2015, the Nepal Mountaineering Association (NMA) officially reported twenty-four deaths and sixty-two critically injured, confirming this as the largest and deadliest natural disaster in the history of mountaineering.

In the days that followed, though the wounded and critically injured had been successfully evacuated, a tremendous amount of work remained. With our limited capacity, we attempted to distribute extra equipment such as sleeping bags and tents to people whose camps had been completely levelled. We ensured that hot water, beverages and food were constantly available to any climbers or camps in need while continuing to assist in any way we could. The Indian Army organised a cleanup drive to gather as much debris as possible, which was scattered across the glacier in the wake of the avalanche.

'Descend now!' The panic and fear permeating the various expedition teams at Everest Base Camp in the days that followed were nauseating. Though Sherpas and climbers are mentally prepared for the risks associated with mountain climbing, a very large population at the base camp is made up of support staff such as cooks, kitchen boys, assistants and porters, people who have never had to face such dangers and risks. Historically, the base camp has been the closest place to the mountain that is safe to be in. This time, however, it seemed like the most dangerous place in the world. Random and unsubstantiated rumours of an impending bigger earthquake, constant smaller avalanches and the fear of the glacier opening up below our tents added fuel to the existing fire, creating an exodus of support staff, thus crippling even teams that had not sustained any damage.

At Everest Base Camp, the absence of government-appointed liaison officers tasked with monitoring expedition teams on the glacier appeared to contribute to the challenges of managing an already complex situation. We stayed on at Everest Base Camp for a week after the avalanche until 2 May 2015, hoping for some clarity from the Nepal government about the state of affairs regarding the rest of the climbing season as well as working to assist in any way we could.

Sauraj sat in his tent, the only one still standing among a campsite of packed gear, ready and waiting for the yak caravan to come and haul it down to Namche Bazaar. He sat in a state of stubborn denial about the harsh reality facing us: this expedition was finally over, and we would not be climbing Everest this year. Looking at him sitting in that tent alone in the middle of the glacier, I knew beyond a shadow of a doubt that life would never be the same for us. I walked up to his tent and sat down at the entrance.

'Let's go, Bhai!'

'No, yaar! Don't you think we need to stay here longer and at least wait to get confirmation that there won't be any attempts?' he said. 'Even if there is a 1 per cent possibility, I'm willing to wait.'

I couldn't argue with his logic. Arguing about the impossibility of climbing Everest in the current scenario would not be productive for anyone, and he had a point. Who was I to deny that there was a 1 per cent possibility of climbing? Chinese mountaineer Wang Jing would later prove this by flying her Sherpa team and supplies over the unstable Khumbu Icefall up to Camp 2 and summiting Everest from the Nepal side late on Friday, 23 May 2015, in one of the most controversial Everest summits to date.

Giving credence to his argument, I decided to take a different approach.

'Listen, we've been at Everest Base Camp for seven days. You have been walking up and down to other teams every day to get more information, and no one seems to have a clue about what's happening. Even Major Jamwal has no update. Let's just go down to the Namche Bazaar office and meet the SPCC officials. If nothing else, we will be in a better place to communicate with the outside world and take stock of the situation. If we see any positive development, it will take us two to three days at most to come back here. It's better than just sitting and doing nothing.'

This line of reasoning seemed to sink in but only on the condition that we promised to come back to Everest Base Camp as soon as we received confirmation that climbing would resume. As we left the glacier and climbed the wall of the moraine, we all stopped to catch our breath and take one last look at Everest. This look would end up being our final glimpse of the mountain in the entire year of 2015. As much as I hoped we would be back in a few days to resume the expedition, I knew in my heart of hearts that this was it, the last time I would be looking at the glacier for the season and maybe for the year. I was hurt, angry, upset and disillusioned by the sheer waste of all the effort and energy that had gone into this cursed expedition. I had begged, borrowed and quite literally gone hat in hand to family and friends, trying to raise the funds. I had spent months training, sustained injuries, undergone knee surgery, spent months away from home and missed birthdays and anniversaries. If I was feeling like this, I could only empathise with Sauraj for we had run out of words to say to each other in the last seven days. Each step away from Everest Base Camp made the realisation all the more painful as we walked away with aching hearts and shattered morale.

As we descended through the Khumbu Valley, we witnessed first-hand the devastation caused by the earthquake and the subsequent aftershocks. We distributed all our remaining food and rations, almost a month's supply, instead of taking it back to Kathmandu. Along the way, we stopped at a few remote villages such as Thame and Khunde located off the main Everest Base Camp trail to help in any way we could. We made good time reaching Gorakshep, stopping briefly to speak to our friend Pasang, the owner of the Himalayan Hotel. The settlement was quiet, devoid of the usual bustle of trekking groups, the only outward sign that something was amiss. There was no visible damage. Reassured that the impact of the earthquake had not left its mark, we hopefully set off down the valley. Two hours later, upon entering Lobuche, we were shocked to see half the buildings in ruins. Mother Earth, a teahouse we had stayed in on several occasions, had an entire side destroyed and resembled a giant smashed sandcastle. The sight of this brought home the horror of what the rest of the country must have experienced. We met Mingma Dai at the Peak XV Lodge and offered to leave behind the extra LPG cylinders as well as some kitchen stores, which would certainly be of better use in this remote place. We pressed on down the valley and, after three hours, arrived in Pheriche, a beautiful open valley with stone huts and stone-walled paddocks meant for yak domestication and breeding. The entire village was in ruins with collapsed buildings everywhere. Some of the villagers informed us that there wasn't a single building structurally sound enough to stay in and that those who had remained were living in makeshift tents, fearing the stability of the buildings and the possibility of additional tremors and aftershocks. We began to feel like survivors of an apocalypse as we slowly made our way down, hoping to reach some form of civilisation. The sun set behind the mountain range, and night fell suddenly, as is common in the Himalayas, forcing us to press on in complete darkness. As we turned the corner of the trail and came in sight of Pangboche village at 8 PM, we were relieved to see lights and movement through the silhouette of the trees. We made our way to Sherpa Highland, owned and run by Ang Temba Sherpa, a close friend, and found sanctuary in our home away from home.

In the face of such overwhelming adversity, it became glaringly evident that no individual, regardless of physical strength or mental resilience, could have weathered this storm alone. The aftermath of the avalanche had left us physically battered and emotionally raw, but it was the strength of the team – the unyielding support of those around us – that ensured our survival. Each member brought something indispensable to the table: a word of encouragement when morale was low, a gesture of compassion when fear threatened to take over or a calm, steady presence in the chaos.

However, the support extended beyond the immediate group. The unwavering concern of our families and friends back home, though miles away, was a constant source of strength. Their messages of love and prayers, though intangible, gave us a reason to persevere. It's often said that the mountains test your limits, but they also reveal the unseen ties that bind us – the relationships we sometimes take for granted. In those harrowing days, it became clear that survival wasn't just about individual willpower; it was a collective effort, a testament to the human spirit's capacity to endure when bolstered by the unshakeable foundation of solidarity and care.

It took us over a month after returning to Pune, returning home, leaving behind Nepal, the earthquake, the avalanche and the friends who perished in its wake. When I look back at what we faced and how close we came to injury and death, I am grateful for this second life. In the face of such a natural disaster, I'm glad Sauraj insisted that we stay to help and lend assistance in any way we could. In the process, we met some incredible people and made a few extremely close friends. By staying on, we played a small part in healing Nepal, while the people of Nepal helped us come to terms with the disappointment of our unsuccessful expedition and not feel like failures. In the face of such adversity, their resilience and generosity were valuable lessons, reminding us that the mountain still stood, mighty and proud, waiting for us to come back one day and resume our quest for Everest.

PART 2
PURPOSE

9

Resilience

> It is not the strongest of the species that survive, nor the most intelligent, but the one most responsive to change.
> Charles Darwin, *The Origin of Species*

Sauraj

Having spent about a week in the mountains in the aftermath of the earthquake on 25 April 2015, we started our descent back to Kathmandu. Both of us were distraught, and while Sam seemed to have reached a semblance of grim acceptance, I was still coming to terms with it. Lukla Airport, which was usually buzzing with activity, lay empty as most of the climbing teams had already left. It was a lonely and quiet journey back without our team or even the 1 tonne of supplies we had flown into Lukla just a few weeks earlier. Now we travelled empty-handed, having distributed everything in the villages on our way down from Everest Base Camp to help with the rehabilitation effort.

As we drove from the airport to our hotel in Kathmandu, we began to realise the impact of the earthquake. For the first time, we were confronted with the destruction of life and property that the massive earthquake had caused across Nepal. At the time, the death toll of the 2015 Nepal earthquake was estimated to be between 7,000 and 9,000. Inadvertently, Sam and I found ourselves in the midst of the 'biggest calamity' in the history of climbing and mountaineering.

The day after arriving in Kathmandu, we met Mel again at our favourite Thamel coffee shop. Despite her dashed hopes of a record-breaking summit, she remained upbeat and encouraging. Noting our dejection, she said, 'What's done is done. We need to look to the future.' Mel shared that some mountaineers were planning to petition the Nepal government to extend climbing permit validity for 2016 and 2017. This would save each climber ₹7 lakh, a significant incentive to return. While this could benefit us, I remained sceptical about the likelihood of the government waiving the fee, given its impact on revenue. After all, the Nepal government had extended permits only once before, following the 2014 Khumbu Icefall avalanche. Despite this, Mel was optimistic and planned to return in 2016. Her decision sparked a realisation – I knew I wanted to return and summit, and I suspected Sam did too. The only question was when.

From Kathmandu, we arrived in Delhi, where both my dad and granddad were at the airport to receive me. My grandfather was seventy-eight years old at the time and hardly ventured far outside the house. Seeing him there at the airport, I realised just how anxious my family had been after hearing the news reports from Nepal. I was deeply moved, and although, in typical Indian fashion, no one in my family ever spoke about it, I knew how relieved they were to have me home safe. I had come perilously close to losing my life in one of the greatest natural calamities, and they had spent many anxious hours not knowing whether I would make it back home. On the way home, my granddad, who is usually a man of few words, said, 'Don't worry. You are home safe, and that's what matters. You can always go back again and try.' I was deeply touched. Without my having explicitly mentioned it, my family knew that I was grappling with my inner demons.

As I sat in the car, the events of the past few weeks rushed to me. I couldn't shake off the images of the widespread devastation and death I had witnessed. Added to that, despite logically understanding that we had done the best we could under the circumstances, I was coming to terms with the weight of failure, of having been unable to realise my greatest dream of standing on the summit of Mt Everest. Back in my family home in Delhi, my mother put on a brave face as she met us at the door and hugged me. I knew how afraid and upset she must have been, and I admired her strength and courage as she went about making me comfortable and trying to make things appear normal. I spent some time in Delhi, relishing home-cooked palak paneer and rajma chawal, which I had missed at Everest Base Camp. After a few more days with them in Delhi, I headed back to Pune.

It was mid-May, and for the first time in many years, Sam and I were in Pune during the hottest season of the year. Usually at this time, we would invariably be up in the mountains, either leading treks or going on our hikes in the Himalayas. I longed to be back in the mountains and was beginning to feel listless and demotivated. Soon after we got home, our friends, even those with whom we hadn't been in touch for a while, began calling us, enquiring about our experience and how we were coping. Many of them made plans to meet up, and I was amazed and grateful for their support and solidarity. Although I initially found recounting my experiences painful, I soon realised how invested they had been in our journey. They cared for us and had prayed for our safe return. They were especially moved by the fact that we had stayed under the constant threat of earthquakes and further avalanches, enduring difficult conditions with limited resources to help as many people as we could. Although we hadn't given this any thought at the time, we later realised that, in doing so, we had inspired and touched the hearts of many. As word of our return spread, we were also contacted by *Headline Today* and the *Times of India* among several news agencies who wanted to cover our story in print and on TV.

Although being appreciated in such forums had never occurred to us, I felt immense gratitude. I found my resolve to go back to Everest strengthening due to all the support and kindness we received – not just from family and friends but even from complete strangers. In the aftermath of the disaster, standing at ground zero at the time, it seemed a no-brainer to assist in any way we could. Since we were better off than many others at Everest Base Camp, with some supplies and no serious injuries, we had to help people who hadn't been as lucky. Our families back home hadn't seen it that way and understandably so. In the midst of the relief work, we did our best to reassure them over the phone whenever the line connected, though it wasn't entirely true. Our intent to stay until the end of the relief work had understandably scared them. They thought it was incomprehensible that we would continue to stay on this unstable glacier with the constant dangers of avalanches and earthquake aftershocks. They worried about whether we had enough food and how badly we were injured, especially as they were constantly bombarded with distressing news reported by TV channels and newspapers across the world. Our friend Karan had been extremely vocal in his disapproval. Somehow, despite connectivity issues, he had managed to call us almost every day, imploring us to come back. In hindsight, we would always be grateful for their love and trust in our decision to stay on and help in spite of their deepest fears.

In Pune, we quickly became completely absorbed in running Adventure Pulse, putting all our energies into getting organised at work. Over the past year, as we prepared for our Everest quest, we had had to put off several business priorities due to the time, effort and, of course, money needed for the expedition. Now it was time to make up for all that. We moved our office into a bigger space and hired more people to manage operations. Soon, a month had passed since our return, and despite working side by side, Sam and I had been unable to bring up the topic of the avalanche and our plan to return to Everest. We both knew that no matter how occupied our work kept us, the question of when to return was always on our minds.

One evening, I invited Sam for a beer, knowing he likely anticipated what was coming. After finishing my first beer, I said directly, 'We should go back and climb in 2016. We can't give up now.' Sam agreed but voiced concerns about the cost. 'We need to recover the money we lost. Raising funds for another expedition might be tough. Can we really afford it so soon?' I was disappointed but understood his point. My worry was that if the Nepal government didn't extend the climbing permit validity beyond 2016, it would add to the costs. Also, if we waited two more years, we might lose motivation. Despite these concerns, I was relieved we both wanted to return. We decided to revisit the issue in a couple of weeks.

When we spoke again two weeks later, it was clear that though we were in agreement to return to Everest, we lacked the funds. We could only wait and hope for the permit extension. As months passed, I accepted that our next attempt would be in 2017, reassuring myself that 'the mountain isn't going anywhere'. Work at Adventure Pulse was thriving, and we were excited to return to SIMS to share our experience of surviving the deadliest mountaineering disaster in history. Soon after, word spread, and through our alumni network, we were invited to share our story as an example of resilience in several multinational corporations.

These sessions and other Adventure Pulse engagements kept us completely occupied for most of the remaining year, leaving us with very little time to dwell on not being able to go back to Everest. Despite our work schedule, both of us remained acutely aware of the timelines for starting our preparations for the 2017 climbing season. Towards the end of 2015, we once again started allocating time during our workday for Everest planning meetings. The biggest hurdle was once again raising the finances. While we had some experience, it was a lot trickier this time around to find new sources of funding. We were not keen on approaching friends and family, all of whom had contributed extensively towards our funds for the 2015 expedition. Instead, we decided to focus on seeking sponsorship from corporates and started working on proposals to send to some of the ones we had worked with in the past.

While brainstorming a sponsorship proposal and fundraising ideas, we were surprised by a call from Vikas Dimri, a long-time trekking client. He expressed interest in joining our 2017 Everest expedition, inspired by our experience during the 2015 avalanche. Sam and I were initially shocked and worried. Taking responsibility for our own safety was one thing, but looking out for someone else was another challenge. We knew about Vikas's demanding banking career and doubted whether he could commit fully to the extensive training and climbing experience required for Everest.

As the first step, we shared a detailed training plan with him. The foremost thing we asked him to do was to complete the basic mountaineering course at one of India's premium mountaineering institutes. We were pleasantly surprised when he took a month off from work and completed the course in the summer of 2016. Feeling inspired by his commitment and very optimistic, we decided to go to Mumbai to meet him. In Mumbai, we found that Vikas was at the peak of his fitness as per the plan we had shared and was brimming with ideas on how we could raise funds. Feeling inspired by his dedication, Sam and I realised that we now had another team member joining in on the madness. On our drive back from Mumbai, Sam and I started discussing the logistics and preparation required for organising the expedition for three members instead of two. Bolstered by

Vikas's faith in us, we were now also confident in our ability to lead him to the summit. From then on, we began conducting routine planning calls to discuss expedition logistics.

In March 2016, almost a year after the avalanche, the Nepal government formally announced that they would honour the climbing permits of 2015 for another two years up to 2017. This came as a welcome relief to us. With this announcement, the financial burden for Sam and me would now come down to approximately ₹50 lakh, which, without the reprieve on the permit, would have been around ₹65 lakh. While still steep, this was a lucky break. Meanwhile, we continued to struggle with finding sponsors, which was turning out to be a very uphill task indeed.

In May 2016, I was back in Nepal, leading a group of twenty trekkers to Everest Base Camp for what was perhaps the fifteenth time. Being back in the Khumbu Valley and knowing that I would not be climbing was especially difficult for me to come to terms with. A number of our climber friends from the previous year were back on Everest to complete unfinished business. Mel was there, of course, as was Kuntal, who had been our neighbour at the camp. Even Colonel Jamwal, who had been promoted since we last met him, was back once more, leading another Indian Army contingent. On the third day of the trek, I met Mel at Namche and assumed she must be resting before heading to Everest Base Camp. I was dismayed to learn that she had been very unwell and had been in Namche for over a week. The next day, I decided to walk with her for two hours from Namche Bazaar to the village of Khunde, which had one of the better clinics in the Khumbu region. She was diagnosed with pneumonia and advised by the doctor to rest completely for at least two weeks. This was a hard blow, I was sure, since Mel had been coming back two years in a row and not getting enough rest could derail her plans for a successful ascent to the summit. Later, I was overjoyed to learn that Mel had recovered and headed up to Everest Base Camp sooner than expected, finally summiting successfully in the third week of May. Kuntal and Colonel Jamwal also summited successfully that year, making it a triumphant season after two disappointing years for climbers on Everest.

Back home in Pune, while proud and happy for our friends, Sam and I dealt with the frustration of not being able to take advantage of the ideal climbing conditions that year. To add to our woes, we had not been able to make any significant headway in our fundraising and were feeling lost. We went back to the drawing board and started setting aside some profits from the company as well as a significant portion of our salaries towards our Everest fund. We kept our spirits up and decided not to be disheartened. After all, we still had ten months to go.

As our survival story gained attention, new opportunities emerged. Vikas spread the word about his Everest attempt and raised funds, while our friends and family, including many ex-servicemen, generously supported our crowdfunding campaign. We learned about the centenary celebration at Queen Mary's Technical Institute for Differently Abled Soldiers (QMTI), which aids disabled veterans. Having previously volunteered there during our MBA training, we decided to run a fundraising campaign for QMTI's 100th anniversary. We donated 50 per cent of the funds to the institute and planned to carry their flag on our 2017 expedition. Our fundraising initiatives truly tested the business acumen we had gained during our MBA days, forcing us to be resourceful and leverage every opportunity to finance the expedition – from crowdfunding to offering discount vouchers on treks.

Amid balancing work and fundraising, we needed to stay on top of our training. To build climbing experience for the 2017 expedition, we planned a trip to Mt Elbrus in Russia, one of the Seven Summits, known for its extreme cold. Climbing all Seven Summits is a prestigious goal in mountaineering and an opportunity to pay tribute to Malli Mastan Babu's legacy. We decided to turn this into a commercial Adventure Pulse expedition. Some of our close friends from India joined us, along with Abel and Greg from France, whom we had met in Nepal in 2013. This was our chance to climb outside the Himalayas and experience a new challenge.

Climbing Mt Elbrus, the highest peak in Europe at 5,642 m (18,510 ft), is both a physical and mental challenge – an awe-inspiring adventure. Imagine standing on a vast, snow-covered dome in the remote Caucasus Mountains of Russia, with breathtaking views stretching out in every direction. To someone who is not a mountaineer, the experience can be described as stepping into another world – a stark, pristine landscape of ice and rock where the air gets thinner with every step. The climb doesn't require advanced technical skills but demands determination, preparation and respect for the mountain. You will likely face biting cold winds, long hours of trudging through snow and the persistent tug of gravity as you ascend.

The journey begins at the base, often with acclimatisation hikes to help your body adjust to the altitude. You move through stages: from green valleys to rocky slopes, then onto endless fields of snow and ice. As you climb higher, the effort feels monumental – each step a battle against exhaustion and the thin, oxygen-poor air.

Summit day is the most demanding, beginning in the dead of night. Clad in layers of insulated gear, you navigate icy slopes by the light of your headlamp. The journey is gruelling, with steep ascents and a biting wind that tests your resolve. However, reaching the summit is an indescribable reward. At the top, you stand above the clouds, surrounded by silence and the incredible beauty of the Caucasus range. It's a profound moment – a mix of pride, humility and awe. Climbing Elbrus is not just about physical endurance; it's a mental test of perseverance and grit. It's the kind of adventure that leaves you changed, with a deeper appreciation for nature's grandeur and your inner strength.

At Elbrus base camp, we had acclimatised well, and at 1 AM on a particularly windy morning, we decided to push for the summit. The weather wasn't ideal, but with a very limited window, we chose to make the attempt. As we climbed, the winds picked up to 45 km/hr and the temperature dropped to −30°C. The freezing cold winds from the Caucasus range lashed across the mountain face, pummelling our faces. We hadn't really anticipated this, and about 300 m from the summit, we huddled together to make a decision. We were all cold, very cold, but nodded in unison to press on. Finally, by 7 AM, battling against freezing winds, we reached the top. At the summit, I had a brief bout of panic. My face was numb with cold, and my jacket had frozen after four hours of exposure to the relentless wind. I turned to Sam and asked him if my nose was still intact since I could no longer feel it. Without lingering at the summit, we quickly began our descent to base camp, hoping to pack up and get off the mountain that very evening using the ski lift. By 6 PM, we were back in our cosy hotel rooms, toasting with the famous 'Elbrus' beer and cracking up over the mystery of my missing nose. It had turned out to be a great trip and a huge boost to our confidence, having successfully climbed in such tough conditions. We parted ways with Greg and Abel, who wished us luck for Everest, and headed back to India.

The second half of 2016 remained a struggle to raise funds, but we kept at it. Giving up was not an option. Even as we faced difficulties, support continued to come from the most unlikely sources. One day, we were introduced to one of my father's friends, the highly respected international cricketer Kris Srikanth. When he heard about our Everest story and the work we had done during the rescue effort, he decided to make a generous contribution towards our Everest 2017 expedition. The monetary contribution was one aspect, but the faith displayed in us by the ex-captain of the Indian cricket team was a great boost to our morale, especially for a die-hard cricket fan who had grown up watching him.

In October 2016, Sam, Vikas and I took a quick climbing trip to Stok Kangri (6,153 m) in Ladakh to hone our skills and acclimatise to the high altitude. Back home, we intensified our fundraising and fitness efforts. Our trainer, Mangesh, kept us on our toes with creative outdoor training routines. One morning, he had us meet him at the base of a nearby hill. When Sam and I arrived in our Toyota Qualis, Mangesh sat in the car, shifted it into neutral and instructed us to push it uphill. Though initially taken aback, we pushed the car up the steep slope for 1.5 hours, covering 3 km. Exhausted but exhilarated, we collapsed at the top. It was an intense but unexpectedly enjoyable workout that tested our endurance.

Soon it was time for us to leave for Nepal once more. A few days before our departure, Sam's parents invited us to their home for dinner. Sam's father, a certified deep-sea diver with the Indian Navy and over thirty years of experience, was well acquainted with the risks involved in adventure sports. He knew that as this was our second attempt, our desire for the summit was even greater than before. He sat us down and told us to be cautious and to always put safety above everything else.

Two years had flown by in a whirlwind of Everest preparations, and, as in 2015, we were flanked by a vibrant group of trekkers making the journey with us to base camp. The presence of so many people rallying around us infused the atmosphere with an electrifying energy, helping to channel our nervous excitement. Once again, we stood at the foot of the great mountain, but this time, our sights were set on the summit. We were back at Everest Base Camp – determined, resolute and ready to conquer the peak that had eluded us before.

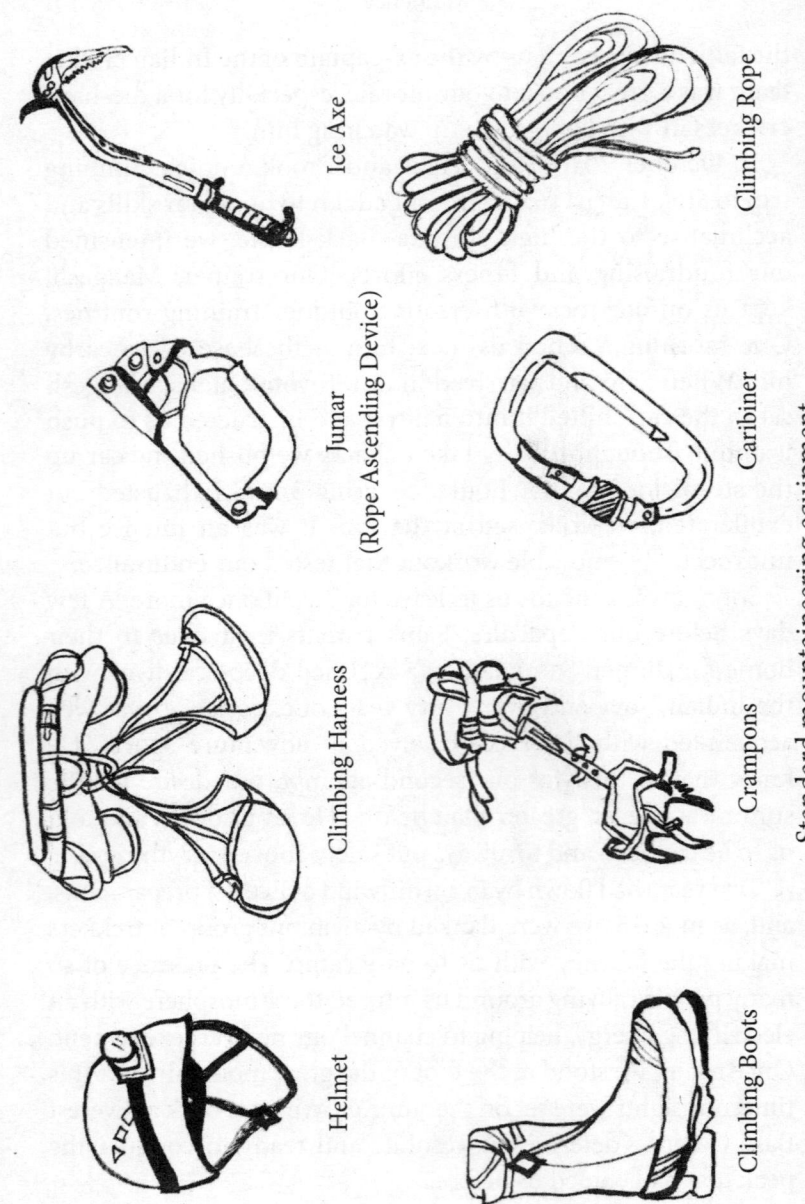

Standard mountaineering equipment

10

Everest 2017: Back to Base Camp

> We remember, we rebuild, we come back stronger.
> Barack Obama, *The Audacity of Hope*

Sam

On 25 April 2017, exactly two years after the Nepal earthquake, five of us sat in the dining tent at Everest Base Camp, sipping a cup of morning tea. I sat brooding, reliving the horror of our experience as Sauraj and Ghanshyam narrated their account of being caught up in the Everest avalanche to Vikas and Jangbu Sherpa. Being there made it all feel as if it had happened yesterday. There had been a palpable sense of tension in our camp, building up over the last few days. Our pooja ceremony this time was once again marred by bad weather, a haunting déjà vu of our last Everest expedition. As an added precaution, despite having already completed our pooja ceremony almost a week ago, the entire base camp held a special prayer ceremony on the morning of 25 April to appease the mountain gods and invoke their blessings. As for me, I was missing Karishma's birthday yet again.

Listening to Sauraj's enthusiasm about being back at Everest, I realised we had so much to be grateful for. I decided to make a distinct effort to shrug off my melancholy and focus on the fact that, despite all odds, we were back at Everest Base

Camp. As I looked around at the familiar faces – Ghanshyam, once again reprising his role as base camp manager – our cook Bhim Dai and Viru (again our kitchen assistant) walked in with big smiles on their faces, carrying breakfast. There was a certain sense of comfort derived from the familiarity of having this same team with us once more on Everest. Despite having had to pause our quest for Everest for the last two years, we were back on track with this expedition, ready to pick up from where we had left off.

Watching over us with a benign smile as we sat together was our climbing sirdar, Jangbu Sherpa, who had climbed Everest ten times. Our previous expedition sirdar, Tashi Sherpa, had immigrated to the USA a year after the avalanche and, despite our best efforts, had decided against coming back to Everest. Unlike the small, wiry frame we had come to expect of most Sherpa climbers, Jangbu was a big man with a face that distinctly resembled the image of the Laughing Buddha commonly sold in souvenir shops on the streets of Thamel. However, his real claim to fame was the record for being topless on Everest for over four minutes, a feat that had earned him the title of 'Naked Jangbu'. Having climbed with the likes of Dan Mazur (a renowned Western expedition leader), he was extremely well known throughout the Khumbu Valley. Along with him were the other climbing Sherpas: Pasang (his youngest brother), Samden (his brother-in-law) and Dawa Sherpa (a distant nephew). Between the four of them, they had a collective experience of over twenty successful Everest expeditions.

The walk up to Everest Base Camp had been hectic. We had been completely occupied by our eighteen-member Everest Base Camp trekking group, daily challenges and interesting experiences. This trek, in itself, had been a full-time commitment, helping divert our attention from the anxiety of the expedition. It also went a long way in helping us finance this climb. My cousin Alan was a part of the group. He had joined us not just as a trekker but as a videographer as well, helping us document some parts of the expedition. Growing up, I had idolised my older cousin, emulating his style of dressing and mannerisms. The fact that I could share at least a part of this experience with him was extremely rewarding for me. During the months leading up to Nepal, he had patiently captured footage of our physical training, following our eccentric workout schedules irrespective of the time of day. During the trek, his footage would also be used by a major pharma company we had tied up with to capture the experiences of smokers versus non-smokers on the Everest Base Camp trek. This concept was later remade into a TV documentary show hosted by Milind Soman to promote their nicotine gum.

After reaching base camp, we had then returned down the valley with the group as far as Pangboche. Sauraj and I bid them adieu and made our way once more to the residence of Lama Geishi in Upper Pangboche to attend his special blessing ceremony. We had even timed our itinerary such that, after the Everest Base Camp trek, we could rendezvous here with our climbing team – Jangbu Sherpa, Vikas, Ghanshyam and the Sherpas – to attend this ceremony together. Although I had interacted with Vikas several times in Mumbai, seeing him in the Khumbu Valley made the expedition feel real. The big grin and the excitement on his face revealed that the feeling was definitely mutual. At the monastery, Vikas introduced us to another Indian climber aspiring for Everest, who had coincidentally trekked up with him on the same days – Ravi Kumar from Madhya Pradesh. He, too, would be attending the blessing ceremony with us. Ravi's natural love for the mountains and exuberance were contagious. In the days to follow, we would often find him around the base camp, either at our tent or visiting other Indian teams, sharing updates on the latest news pertaining to our small climbing community at Everest Base Camp.

In the august presence of Lama Geishi wrapped in his heavy maroon robe, I took a moment to reflect on the goal we had set our hearts on. The pale yellow glow from yak butter lamps cast a soft light across a table of offerings placed before pictures of the Dalai Lama. Tendrils of smoke rose from the burning juniper incense in the corner of the room, weaving through the air like ghostly wisps, their earthy aroma deepening the sense of mystery and quiet reverence that hung in the space. The deep resonance of Buddhist mantras being chanted by Lama Geishi reverberated through the room, filling me with a sense of peace and calm. This was truly an auspicious beginning for a journey that would take us to the top of the world. After receiving Lama Geishi's benediction in the form of a protective amulet, a knotted loop of red string, we made our way out of the dark confines of his residence and stood in the sunlight.

With our team finally together and officially blessed, we were ready to begin our expedition. We moved on to the village of Chukhung to take on our first test, a training climb up Imja Tse, more popularly called Island Peak, standing at an impressive height of 6,189 m. Since this was the first time we were all working together, this climb would be critically important in assessing the team's dynamics. Three days later, we stood on the summit of Island Peak. We had fantastic weather, good team dynamics and overall a brilliant climb. On 14 April, a few days later, we charged up the valley into Everest Base Camp, feeling strong, fit and confident, ready to take on the main part of the expedition – Everest.

The first couple of days at Everest Base Camp were fantastic despite some snowfall, temperamental weather and extremely cold nights. Our spirit and morale were high as we walked around the camp getting to know our neighbours. In the next camp was Kishore Dankude once again, this time with the Satori team led by Mingma Tenzi Sherpa. Kishore, having climbed Everest from the north side in 2014, had been caught in the same avalanche with us in 2015. He was back this year, attempting to complete his record of being the first Indian to climb Everest from both sides in the shortest duration. Behind us, near the Everest ER camp, was the Giripremi Pune team. The Giripremi team, from Pune like us, is one of the oldest adventure clubs in India, more than three decades old. We struck up a friendship with Bhagwan Chawale, who would often come over to our camp for a hot cup of masala chai. This year, in addition to all the international climbers, there were some large contingents from India, such as the Indian Navy and a team from the Oil and Natural Gas Corporation (ONGC). The spring of 2017 was shaping up to be yet another busy season on Everest, a fact critical in the planning of our movement up the mountain.

The purpose of our meeting as we sat together in the dining tent was to discuss 'the plan of assault' or, in other words, our acclimatisation strategy to climb up the mountain. Having been at base camp without any adverse effects due to the altitude and considering the volume of climbers, we had to start moving further up the mountain.

The traditional approach to climbing Everest was a three-stage rotation plan. The first rotation involved a climb to Camp 1 at 6,100 m through the Khumbu Icefall and spending a night there. Coming back down to base camp from this height required a few days of recovery to allow the body to recuperate. The second rotation started after a rest period of four or five days. Climbers would climb back to Camp 1 and, after spending a night, push on to Camp 2 at 6,450 m. After two nights at this altitude, they would come back down to base camp to rest and recover. For the third rotation, climbers would try to go higher, at least to touch Camp 3 at 7,200 m.

Spending a night at this height, though theoretically good for acclimatisation, is extremely exhausting and often necessitates the use of bottled oxygen, which aids sleep and conserves energy at such a high altitude.

After returning to Everest Base Camp from this rotation, climbers rest and recover from the exhaustion of climbing in an oxygen-rare atmosphere. Some climbers even descend further below the base camp to wait out the days until the weather window opens. In this way, the careful exposure to different altitudes facilitates a physiological change that allows the body to adapt to an environment with less ambient oxygen.

During the final push for the summit, climbers, having acclimatised to heights above 7,000 m and rested well at lower altitudes, usually feel stronger. Climbing faster through the Khumbu Icefall, they move past Camp 1, spending a night directly at Camp 2 and then at Camp 3. From this point on, climbers, with the aid of supplementary oxygen, move up the Lhotse wall, entering the 'Death Zone'.

The Death Zone is a term used by mountain climbers to loosely define the high altitude at which there is not enough oxygen for humans to breathe, let alone acclimatise. This is usually at altitudes higher than 8,000 m above sea level. Mountaineers entering this region cannot survive without supplementary oxygen and may experience lethargy, hypoxia and even death without it. Most deaths on Everest have occurred in the Death Zone. This is where the final resting station, called Camp 4, is established at the South Col, located at 8,000 m, on the ridge between Mt Everest and Lhotse. After reaching here around 3 PM and resting, climbers leave the same evening at 9 PM, hoping to reach the summit the next day in the early morning after a gruelling fourteen–sixteen-hour ascent.

Though this was the classic approach, we had a better plan. During our discussion, Sauraj came up with a brilliant alternative, which even had Jangbu's approval. As we had climbed Island Peak, which was higher than Camp 1, we had technically already acclimatised to 6,100 m. If we could ensure that our resources were in place, in a single rotation, we could occupy Camp 1 the first night and then push up to Camp 2. After staying there for two to three days, depending on how we were feeling, we could even attempt to reach Camp 3 before returning to Everest Base Camp. In this way, we could not only optimise our resource utilisation but also maximise our acclimatisation and minimise the risks of climbing through the Khumbu Icefall repeatedly. With everyone in agreement, all we had to do was watch the weather and pick the right time to avoid 'traffic' on the way.

My breath strained through burning lungs as I tried to keep pace with Jangbu. On 28 April at 3 AM, it was pitch dark as we left Everest Base Camp, making our way through the lower region of the glacier. We patiently walked behind him around ice pinnacles, following the circles of light thrown out by our headlamps until we reached a point on the glacier where the gradient was too steep to climb without crampons. We paused our ascent and took time to fix our crampons onto our climbing boots, drink some water and readjust our harness. This point in the glacier was popularly referred to as Crampon Point. We clipped our safety line to the fixed rope and began the technical section of the climb.

My heart slowly settled into a steady rhythm as our bodies warmed up from the climb, dissipating the cold from our extremities. With each step, I could hear the ice crunching under our crampons and the trickle of water somewhere deep below the glacier. After forty minutes, the gradient suddenly became very steep. Fixed to the ground was a nylon rope running up the ice face, set up to provide an anchor and a guide for climbers through this incredible maze. We had just reached the most dangerous section of our climb, one that would require all our skill and concentration, the Khumbu Icefall.

The Khumbu Icefall was as daunting as I remembered from last time. Our aim was to cross the icefall during the early hours of the morning when it was partially frozen from the night before. As the sunlight warmed the region, it increased the danger of crevasses opening or blocks of snow and ice falling. The most dangerous time to cross the Khumbu Icefall was generally mid-to-late afternoon, which explained Jangbu's blistering pace. Our aim was to reach Camp 1, located at 6,100 m, slightly beyond the top of the Khumbu Icefall, by 11 AM.

Even with all the weight of the climbing equipment and the extra supplies we were carrying in our rucksacks, Sauraj, Vikas and I were keeping up with Jangbu and making good time. Our remaining Sherpas had been busy carrying oxygen cylinders up to Camp 2 over the last couple of days and were resting back at Everest Base Camp. As we clipped our safety line from one fixed rope to the next, I couldn't help but marvel at the bizarre shapes of ice all around us. We were truly in a beautiful, frightening, alien world, where a single misplaced step could be the last.

The icefall doctors, the SPCC team of Sherpas responsible for setting up and maintaining this route, had done a brilliant job. Despite the intricacy of the route – having to climb up ice towers, rappel down walls and cross huge crevasses with aluminium ladders – these guys had done an incredible job. I remembered that two years ago, my first foray into the icefall had been terrifying. At the time, being in a constant state of agitation had left me exhausted for days after our first rotation. This time, whether it was the familiarity of the terrain or just the adrenaline, my initial anxiety had given way to excitement. I was enjoying the thrill of the challenge. After all, we had worked so hard to be back here.

As we finished crossing a ladder over the last crevasse, a climber suddenly caught up with us, literally jogging through the icefall. Unlike the bulky gear we were wearing, he seemed to be wearing thermal tights and running shoes with spikes strapped onto them. He caught up with us in a matter of minutes, crossed the ladder and whizzed past us in the blink of an eye, making our ladder crossing look clumsy by comparison. I was still staring in a state of shock when Jangbu began muttering, 'Oori, Oori!' I didn't understand what he was saying at the time, but later I learnt that he was referring to the climber who had just raced past us. We had witnessed the incredible skill of one of the most famous climbers in the history of mountaineering – Swiss mountaineer and speed climber Ueli Steck. He was the first to climb Annapurna solo via the south face, considered one of the toughest mountains to climb in the world. He won two Piolets d'Or awards, in 2009 and 2014, the highest honour in mountaineering. We knew he was on the mountain this year, attempting one of the most difficult routes, the Hornbein route on the West Ridge, to reach the summit of Everest without supplemental oxygen. What would ordinarily be an exhausting seven-hour climb through the Khumbu Icefall for most people was a two-hour warm-up sprint for him. To see this legend in person was truly a big fan moment. We were hoping to see a lot more of Ueli Steck in the days to come.

We climbed over the last snow ridge and finally reached the top of the Khumbu Icefall. Below us, in the distance, one could see the tents of Everest Base Camp as a large collection of bright spots of colour, scattered amongst the black rocks of the glacial moraine. As we emerged from the broken ice, we were greeted by one of the most spectacular sights in the world. The upper region of the icefall had given way to a large, sweeping expanse of snow stretching for 4 km called the Western Cwm, enclosed on three sides by a wall of mountains that towered a kilometre into the sky. On the right stood Nuptse, just under 8,000 m. In the centre was Lhotse, the fourth-highest mountain in the world, and on the left stood the Everest Massif, with its distinct snow plume blowing off the summit. In that moment, I felt humbled, dwarfed by the sheer size of nature's splendour. We were truly tiny mortals entering a gigantic colosseum built by the gods.

Within a few hundred metres from the top of the Khumbu Icefall, at the very beginning of the Western Cwm, was Camp 1. The sight of the small cluster of tents indicated that we had finally arrived at Camp 1. We had made great time getting there, crossing the icefall in six hours and now had the entire day to walk around and take pictures. The better part of the day, however, was spent 'making' water, that is, melting snow to keep ourselves hydrated. As the sun slowly set behind the mountain range, the temperatures dropped, with cold winds blowing through the Western Cwm. We spent a fitful night listening to the constant rumbling of several avalanches rolling down the Nuptse face behind us, a very normal phenomenon considering the volatility of the terrain we were crossing. It sounded frightfully close, bringing back nightmares of our past ordeals.

The next day, we had planned a more comfortable start as Camp 2 was located a mere four hours away at the end of the Western Cwm. We packed up our gear, folded the tents and slowly made our way up the valley. Within half an hour of climbing, I could make out the distant, coloured tents of Camp 2 located at the base of the Lhotse wall. However, what appeared tantalisingly close ended up becoming one of the toughest climbs for me, as the more we walked, the further away it appeared to be. Despite appearances, the Western Cwm has a perceptible gradient, which is not to be underestimated. Being enclosed on all sides by mountains, the heat of the sun is reflected off the snow-covered walls and base of the Western Cwm during the day, creating an effect synonymous with being in a giant solar cooker. Temperatures quickly climbed, touching 40°C in zero-wind conditions, comparable to an Indian summer afternoon. The walk from Camp 1 across the Western Cwm to Camp 2 was hot, tiring and exhausting.

Vikas and I stumbled into Camp 2 at 1 PM, almost forty minutes behind Sauraj and Jangbu. Under the weight of our gear and heavy clothing, we were exhausted. I walked into our camp and collapsed in front of our kitchen. If the climb to reach 6,450 m had been so gruelling, the rest of the expedition was beginning to feel impossible. To make matters worse, I had a splitting headache. In the midst of my despair, I tried to maintain a brave façade to reassure Vikas. I must have failed terribly because Sauraj came out and, taking one look at our faces, burst into laughter. With his gentle ribbing, our fatigue began to fade away as we sipped on cups of concentrated orange juice and began to appreciate our surroundings. After three weeks (and, in a way, three years), we had finally made it to Camp 2, our advance base camp.

Not as lavish a setup as Everest Base Camp but not as spartan as Camp 1, this camp was designed to provide the basic necessities required to launch our expedition further up the mountain. We had a fully functional kitchen, sleeping tents and a store tent to house supplies such as oxygen cylinders and isobutane cooking canisters. This would act as our advance base camp, not just to facilitate our acclimatisation but also to provide a relay point for the Sherpas to start provisioning the campsites higher up the mountain. Our Camp 2 was even manned by one staff member, also named Pasang Sherpa, who would stay here for the next three weeks, looking after the supplies and acting as the high camp cook, feeding the team as they stayed here for extended periods during the setup of Camp 3 and Camp 4.

That night, in spite of the cold, I slept the sleep of the dead. Due to space constraints and to mitigate the cold, we were sleeping two to a tent. Sauraj and I paired in one, while Jangbu and Vikas shared the other. As the next day involved resting at Camp 2 with no specific agenda, we slept in late, enjoying the warmth of our sleeping bags.

I was rudely woken up by the sound of footsteps and the metallic clang of equipment being flung against the side of our tent. Intending to give the person a piece of my mind, I stuck my head out and looked around for the target of my irritation. In a small Mountain Hardwear tent, just 5 ft away, was Ueli Steck, sitting nonchalantly in his thermal tights and scraping ice from his crampons, having made a speed ascent all the way from Everest Base Camp that same day, a distance that had taken us the better part of two days. Apparently, after our first sighting of him, he had gone back down and then climbed up again. Really at a loss for words, we smiled at each other before I ducked my head back into the tent out of embarrassment. I spent the next half hour composing myself with some witty conversational starters before I had the courage to step out and introduce myself. However, unaware of my intentions, Ueli had gone into his tent and was soon fast asleep. Having now missed two opportunities to say hello, Sauraj and I were determined to at least visit him at Everest Base Camp and get a picture with him.

The rest of the day at Camp 2 dragged on in gloomy stillness as temperatures began to soar within the tent in the absence of any wind. The difference in altitude was quite perceptible, requiring all movement to be slow and gradual. Fortunately, the headache from the previous day had dissipated. The prevailing silence in that great cauldron was stifling, a precursor to the brooding storm. The weather forecast for the next couple of days was ominous, with predictions of strong winds and low temperatures. As we sat looking up at the Lhotse wall towering above us, we could make out a few bright-coloured tents against the sheer white face of the mountain, marking the position of Camp 3. At 7,100 m, it looked extremely high and very far away. The comforts of Everest Base Camp seemed a distant dream as we sat in the shadow of the mountain, its summit looming over us miles above.

The winds picked up in the evening sooner than predicted and howled through the entire night. With the tents constantly flapping, we had little sleep, once again wishing for the security and comfort of Everest Base Camp. Early the next morning, as we were getting ready, Jangbu popped his head into our tent and insisted we wear our down suits. Seeing it more as an experience to understand what it felt like to climb in down suits, we eagerly got ready, not realising the necessity of this added precaution against the cold. The winds were unrelenting as we left Camp 2, making our way at a steady pace up the bergschrund to the base of the Lhotse wall. A bergschrund is a distinct feature on a snow-covered mountain, marked by a crevasse at the junction of a glacier or snowfield with a steep upper slope.

As we tried to scramble across the crevasse and climb the first ice ridge, the winds seemed to increase in intensity, rolling down the face of Lhotse, creating spindrift and dumping large amounts of snow on us. We unwearyingly made several attempts to push past the wind up the Lhotse wall but were repeatedly hurled back. Our hands and feet slowly began to freeze in these extreme weather conditions. The numbness in our fingers and toes made the remote threat of frostbite a distinct possibility. If not for the down suits, we would have suffered even more. Finally, after ninety minutes of unsuccessfully attempting to scramble over the ice ridge, Jangbu made the call to abandon the climb and turned the team around.

Chilled to the bone and with the wind behind us, we made our way back to Camp 2, forlorn and defeated. We had not reached our objective of 7,100 m. 'How's this going to affect us?' I asked Sauraj as I kept thinking about the repercussions of this on our bid for the summit. He looked at me without comment. As we huddled together out of the wind, sitting on rocks inside the kitchen tent and sipping hot cups of tea, we discussed the possibility of trying again the next day. However, we had got our first taste of how menacing the weather could be on Everest, and it was frightening. Who knew this would only be a small precursor of things to come and that our lives would hang in the balance?

The next morning, with no respite from the weather, we made a hasty retreat down the mountain. As we began our descent, the winds, too, began to abate, and the prospect of reaching Everest Base Camp that afternoon helped alleviate our mood. We made excellent time and were already halfway through the Khumbu Icefall by midday. Every step we took filled us with renewed energy as it brought us closer to our home away from home. Slowly, we began to shrug off the fatigue of the past few days and the prevailing sense of foreboding we had experienced at Camp 2.

Everest Base Camp stood basking in bright sunlight, untouched by the weather we had faced higher up the mountain. It gave us a real appreciation for the height we had climbed to, more than a vertical kilometre above the base camp. That evening, our harrowing experience with the winds at Camp 2 became a tale of adventure with several additions in the retelling as we sat with Ravi Kumar, sipping tea in the warmth of the heated dining tent. Lulled by the sense of security in being back and drowsy from the exhaustion of the last few days, I went to sleep early, oblivious to the ever-lurking danger this extremely hostile terrain could conjure up at a moment's notice. The next day was to be a harsh reminder of this fact as Everest 2017 witnessed the first casualty of the season and a devastating loss to the mountaineering fraternity.

On 30 April, Ueli Steck set out in the early hours of the morning from Camp 2, attempting to climb Nuptse as part of his practice run. This climb was not part of his scheduled plan as his climbing partner, Tenji Sherpa, had descended lower down the mountain to recover from frostbite. Ueli was reported to have continued with his preparation and acclimatisation schedule, changing plans at the last minute to explore the route up Nuptse, one of the highest 7,000 m peaks accessible from Camp 2. A few hundred metres short of the summit, he fell an estimated 1,000 m. To date, mystery and speculation surround the reason behind his fall. His body was discovered in the Western Cwm at an altitude of 6,300 m, roughly 300 m off the main route, by Vinayak Jaya Malla, a Nepalese guide making his way up from Camp 1.

We stared up at the mountain in a state of shock. As the news spread across Everest Base Camp, people looked at each other with disbelief at the enormity of this tragedy. We watched as a helicopter was soon dispatched to Camp 2 to recover the body. It returned shortly from the Western Cwm through the breach between Nuptse and the Western Shoulder, just above the icefall, circling around Everest Base Camp and landing at the helipad next to Everest ER. We looked on, hoping for any sign that would discredit this as nothing but unsubstantiated rumours, a horrible lie. Unfortunately, the doctors at the helipad confirmed the news, and shortly after, the helicopter rose once more, setting off towards Kathmandu carrying Ueli Steck away from Everest for the last time.

11

To Climb or Not to Climb

> It is in your moments of indecision that your dreams are destroyed.
>
> Dr Marc Dussault, *Get the Best Out of Yourself and Others*

Sauraj

It was 1 May 2017, and we had already spent a month in the Everest Valley. The previous week had not only been physically exhausting but also mentally and emotionally draining. Ueli Steck's death had weighed heavily on the psychology of our entire team. To me, Ueli was one of the greatest mountain athletes in modern times; I had lost count of the number of times I had watched his speed record ascent of the Eiger in 2015. His death was a stark reminder of the dangers we had signed up for, the respect that nature commands and the mercilessness of Everest.

With our rotations done and the weather forecast looking temperamental with snow and heavy wind predictions for the next few days, the three of us had decided to descend the valley for some much-needed rest. Sam kept referring to the book *The Climb*, in which Anatoli Boukreev advocates going below the tree line to facilitate oxygenation of the system. He coined the phrase, 'Touch grass before the summit.' Boukreev was one of the most respected mountaineers and the hero of the Everest 1996 tragedy. He also features in the more popular retellings of the tragedy – the movie *Everest* and the book on which it is based, Jon Krakauer's *Into Thin Air*. Vikas and I readily agreed to make the long walk down the valley, though a considerable distance, to the beautiful Tibetan teahouse of Rivendell, tucked away in the picturesque rhododendron forest of Deboche.

Four days of rest, which entailed sleeping on a soft mattress under heated blankets, sunning ourselves on green grass and eating good food, did wonders for our morale. After having climbed to 6,800 m, the oxygen-rich environment below the tree line felt as easy as breathing at sea level. The beauty of the surrounding forest in all its colours of spring felt like heaven compared to the stark white and brown landscape of Everest Base Camp. For me, the greatest pleasure was being able to use a bathroom with indoor plumbing. The simple comforts of having a hot shower and using a Western-style toilet every day, as opposed to squatting over a blue barrel at Everest Base Camp, were bliss. We formed a routine during this period, scheduling extremely competitive bouts of Uno in the day and Monopoly Deal with our evening tea. From our table in the dining room, we had an uninterrupted panoramic view of the summit, a sight that would often make me smile. I could just picture us in two weeks, standing right there on the top of Everest.

Meanwhile, back on the mountain, the news was not good. The winds had been fierce for the past week, stopping all efforts to get the ropes to the summit on either side. At Everest Base Camp, a flu-like infection was sweeping through all the camps, with many patients complaining of high-altitude cough and other upper respiratory tract infections. We also received word from Ghanshyam regarding the second death of the season. Min Bahadur Sherchan, eighty-six, who was attempting to reinstate his record as the oldest Everest summiteer, died of unknown causes at Everest Base Camp.

On 11 May 2017, the fixed ropes and the route to the summit were opened from Tibet in the north with no foreseeable opportunities presenting themselves from our side of the mountain. Despite being the same mountain, completely different weather patterns were seen on the Nepal side. As a consequence, the corresponding delay in setting up the ropes to the summit would mean a very small summit window and a very real possibility of massive congestion caused by climbers desperate to reach the top at the same time.

After our brief respite at Deboche from the mental and physical strains of the expedition, it was time to climb the mountain again. Energised by our time spent at the tree line, we raced back up the valley, dashing past weary trekkers gasping for air as they attempted to reach Everest Base Camp. At noon, on 10 May, we picked up the trail just after the sandy plains of Gorakshep that led to the lateral moraine wall alongside the Khumbu Glacier. In just over an hour, we navigated carefully through the rugged, lunar-like landscape, stepping from rock to rock, mindful of every footfall to avoid a twisted ankle. As we turned the final corner, Everest Base Camp came into view once again. After our little vacation down the valley, it felt like we were coming home. The effects of strong winds and bad weather were visible even at this altitude with heavy snow and torn tents in different camps. Also evident was the drastic reduction in the number of people with an estimated 25–30 per cent attrition on account of the flu that had swept across Everest Base Camp a few days ago.

That night, we gathered outside to witness a bright full moon above the Khumbu Icefall, which marked Buddha Poornima (Buddha's birthday), an auspicious event that we hoped would bring an end to all the turmoil and herald the beginning of a favourable season.

However, this was not to be. Constant updates of successful summits from the north side did little to reassure us as the weather on the south side of the mountain continued to be turbulent, plunging each expedition team into a state of anxiety. Though the route through the Khumbu Icefall was maintained by the icefall doctors, Jangbu explained that the route from Camp 2 all the way to the summit was set up through a collaborative effort between the teams on Everest. The bigger teams, the likes of HIMEX (Himalayan Expeditions), Asian Trekking, IMG (International Mountain Guides) and Adventure Consultants, contributed manpower, logistics and ropes, while the smaller teams provided monetary compensation. Despite their best efforts, the rope-fixing team had opened the route only up to a feature called the Balcony located at 8,350 m, just above South Col. Subsequently, gale-force winds blowing at over 200 km/hr had prevented further progress, driving the Sherpas to retreat to Everest Base Camp. At this time, there was only speculation of a possible weather opening between 17 and 20 May. With a narrowing window, each expedition team became extremely guarded about their team's targeted date for a summit push to avoid congestion of climbers, especially higher up the mountain where the trail could be very precarious. The entire base camp was shrouded in an atmosphere of secrecy and apprehension.

At our camp, we, too, were all plagued by anxiety and confusion. Jangbu kept insisting that 17 May would be our summit day and that we should have already left for the higher camps. His source of information was a hunch and a phone call from his wife, who had consulted a Buddhist lama in Kathmandu. Our logistics partner back in Kathmandu was being just as unhelpful. In spite of his previous assurances to purchase the necessary Swiss weather reports, he had not been able to provide us with any credible information. I finally took it upon myself and reached out via email to Chris Tomer, a meteorologist in Denver, Colorado. This year, he was providing the most reliable daily weather forecasts for Everest through his company, Tomer Weather Solutions, for the princely sum of US$500. Though his reports were extremely detailed, the winds on the south side of the mountain had been so unpredictable that Chris had been forced to add a footnote disclaimer saying that 'the patterns are subject to change within the next twelve hours', which did not do much for our confidence.

Restless from having to wait each passing day, I tried getting some clarity. After spending a frustrating day making discreet inquiries at different camps, Ghanshyam suggested we meet a good friend of his, Tendi Sherpa, who ran a company by the name of TAG Nepal. With nothing to lose, Ghanshyam and I crossed over the broken ground of the glacier and, after a twenty-minute walk, arrived at their base camp. I was extremely impressed with their logistics setup and immediately recognised them as a high-end expedition service provider. Tendi Sherpa was very impressive with an amazing grasp of English. Besides his tremendous climbing experience on several mountains around the world, I learnt that he was also an IFMGA-certified guide. The International Federation of Mountain Guides Associations (IFMGA) was founded in 1965 by a group of representatives from Swiss, Italian, Austrian and French mountain guide associations and has created a set of parameters that qualify a guide to reach the highest standards of mountaineering and guiding skills.

Unlike other teams, Tendi proved to be extremely helpful, empathising with our frustration and assuring me of his cooperation. He had a client who was attempting to be the first woman from Kosovo to reach the summit of Everest, so her success was of paramount importance. While leaving his camp, we ran into a petite, short-haired blonde girl who looked like a teenager. Tendi introduced me to Uta Ibrahimi, his Kosovo client who was attempting to set the record. Apparently, there was one more Kosovo woman climber as part of another expedition at the base camp, and the competition was very close. He was full of praise for her fitness and speed, commenting that he often had difficulty keeping up with her.

The next day, we sat at the dining table, grappling with the dilemma of what our next course of action should be. This Everest season was turning out to be a unique challenge, where even the most experienced climbers at the base camp were compelled to play a guessing game. It was evident now that the weather might offer us a tiny window of opportunity to reach the summit, if at all. We wanted to be one of the earliest teams to try for the top to avoid being caught up in the crowds, but the rope-fixing teams had not yet opened the route to the summit. Did it make sense to wait at Everest Base Camp and conserve our energy or wait higher up the mountain? This crucial 'go/no-go decision' would be instrumental in deciding our success or failure. If we got stuck in a crowd of a hundred other climbers on the way to the summit, we would risk standing in a queue on the same fixed line for hours. Frustration and fatigue, running out of oxygen and certain frostbite were all certainties we would have to deal with. The price of failure could possibly even be our lives, which was just not acceptable.

As we sat together weighing the pros and cons, we heard a light tap on the outside of our dining tent. I stepped out to see Tendi Dai from TAG Nepal talking to Ghanshyam, discussing the weather forecast for the coming week. True to his word, he had decided to move up the mountain the next day and wait at Camp 2 to take up a better position when the opportunity presented itself. That evening, when we received Chris Tomer's email with the weather forecast, Sam was extremely excited. The wind patterns seemed to indicate a possible opening in the weather scheduled for 18 May. This, coupled with my conversation with Tendi, indicated that the moment we had been waiting for had finally arrived.

That evening, before dinner was served, I called the entire team to the dining tent for a meeting. Sam, Vikas and Dawa Sherpa sat with the laptop, reviewing the weather reports, while Ghanshyam continued an animated discussion with Samden and Pasang regarding the number of oxygen cylinders available for the team higher up the mountain. When Jangbu walked into the dining tent, we kicked off the meeting.

We finally had our date of departure – 15 May, two days hence. The plan was to make our way from Everest Base Camp early in the morning and push directly to Camp 2. After a night there, we would move upwards to Camp 3 and spend the night sleeping on supplemental oxygen. On 17 May, in the early hours of the morning, we would climb to Camp 4 and, after a few hours of rest, that evening itself push for the summit. All things going well, we aimed to reach the summit by the morning of 18 May 2017. Unlike the previous rotations, this time, the entire team of Sherpas and climbers would be together, which was especially reassuring to me. As an added measure of safety, every day at 6 AM and 6 PM, we would make a radio call to Ghanshyam at Everest Base Camp to give him an update on our position and situation. He, in turn, would keep us updated on the weather forecast. All we had to do now was spend the next twenty-four hours resting, repacking and mentally preparing ourselves for the climb ahead.

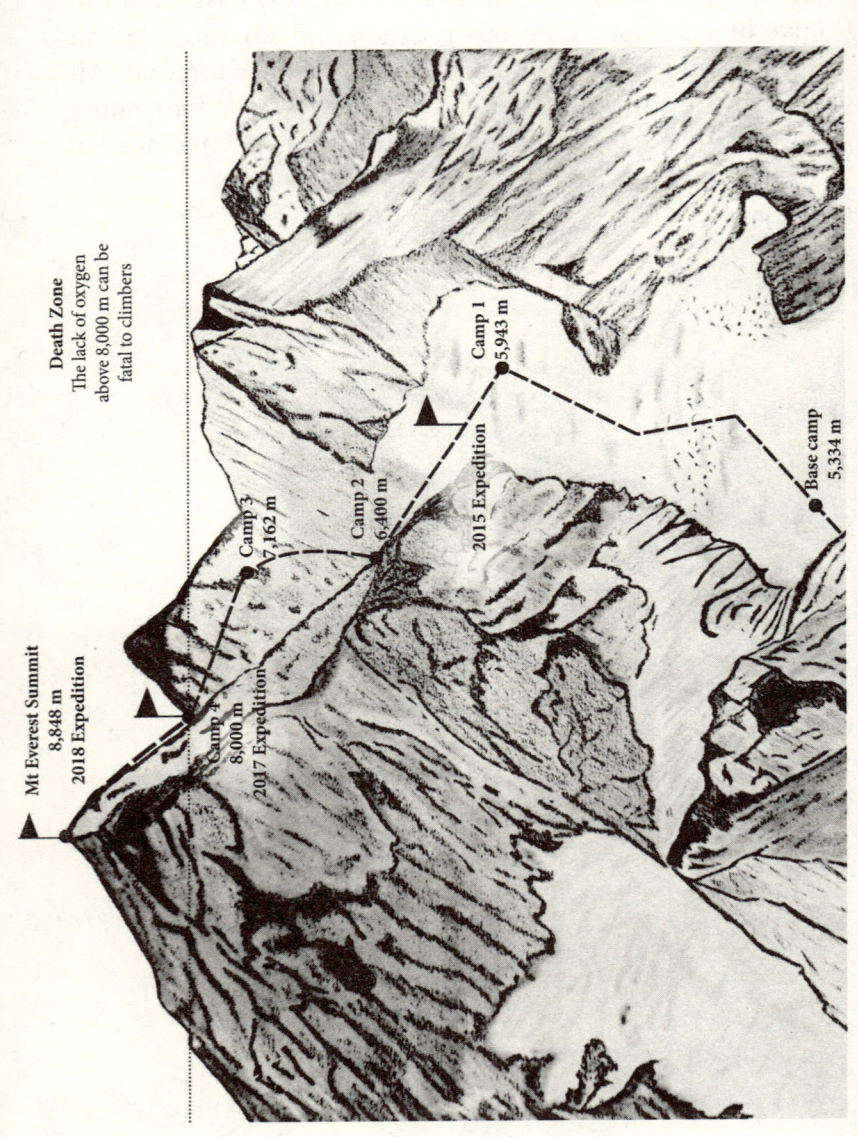

Route map of Mt Everest expedition

12

The Climb up Everest

> What lies behind us and what lies before us are tiny matters compared to what lies within us.
> Ralph Waldo Emerson, *Essays: First Series*

Sauraj

Two days later, in the early hours of the morning of 15 May, Sam woke me up to make our final preparations to leave. I was caught up in the excitement of the moment, a day I had been waiting for so long. My restlessness had kept me up until late, causing me to sleep fitfully in my eagerness to start the final push, while I spent half the night listening to Sam snoring in the neighbouring tent. If all went well, we would be standing on the summit in three days. At 3 AM, the entire camp staff had gathered to bid us a safe journey. After a brief prayer ceremony around the altar that stood at the centre of our camp, we started for the Khumbu Icefall. I was surprised to see only Jangbu with us. When I asked him, he told me that the other Sherpas were carrying the additional weight of the last batch of oxygen cylinders, which couldn't be ferried earlier on account of the weather. As we would be moving more slowly through the icefall, they would leave later and catch up with us at Camp 1. Though puzzled, I accepted the explanation without much thought, confident in our ability to navigate through the icefall as we had done before.

The Khumbu Icefall proved to be as scary as it had always been, but for us, it was a familiar adversary. With Jangbu Sherpa leading, followed by me, then Vikas and Sam bringing up the rear, we moved well through the ice, crossing ladders and navigating the vertical sections in tight formation. The clouds had descended, and there was a haze that reduced visibility to a few hundred metres. At 7 AM, Jangbu turned to me with a big smile, pointing out the faint outline of a dome-shaped structure in the distance. As I squinted at the shape in confusion, I suddenly realised I was staring at a row of bright yellow tents. We had reached Camp 1 in record time. We took our first break and sipped some hot tea from our thermos, prepared by Bhim Dai early in the morning. I had really been touched by not only this gesture but also the care and concern we had received from the entire staff. As the sun came out, the haze dissipated, replaced by a steady gust of wind blowing down the Western Cwm. Anticipating a deterioration in the weather, Jangbu urged us to get moving towards Camp 2, forcing us to leave even though our Sherpa team had not yet caught up with us. The walk across the Western Cwm was very different with the winds and lower temperatures expediting our crossing, as opposed to the usual stifling heat we had experienced the last time. Whether facilitated by the weather or having achieved better acclimatisation, we once again made excellent time, arriving at Camp 2 before noon. Exhausted from the massive height gain of more than 1,200 m, we crawled into our tents and slept.

I awoke and, for a minute, was completely disoriented. When I heard Sam's rhythmic breathing in deep sleep next to me, I suddenly remembered where we were. I crawled out of the tent, pulled on my climbing boots and stumbled towards the kitchen to get a cup of tea and some food. As I ducked into the confines of the tent, I was greeted by the rest of the Sherpa team who had arrived in Camp 2 a few hours earlier. They looked in good form despite having done the same climb with the additional weight of oxygen cylinders totalling at least 16 kg. I spent some time chatting with them, ensuring that they, too, were in good spirits. Though concerned about the weather, they seemed in good cheer, reassuring me that we were all very strong and that we would have a good summit.

Being the only one awake, I went for a walk up the path leading to the top of Camp 2 and stumbled upon Uta and Tendi Sherpa sitting in front of their camp, looking up at the mountain. Even up here at Camp 2, they had a fantastic setup with a dedicated dining tent, which seemed like an unnecessary luxury to me. I was surprised to see them still at Camp 2 despite having left a day before us. As I chatted with them, Tendi Dai explained that they had been waiting for the weather to open up and were looking at targeting the summit either on 18 May or 19 May depending on their latest forecast, which gave me tremendous confidence in the decision we had taken. I thanked him once again for being so open with his information and quickly made my way back for our scheduled call with the base camp.

When I arrived back at camp, Sam was already on the radio talking to Ghanshyam. As per the latest weather forecast, the window had shifted again and would now open on 19 May instead of 18 May. The other bit of good news was that the route had finally been opened to the summit from the south a few hours back. A team of Sherpas and climbers from British Gurkhas, frustrated with the delays, had taken it upon themselves to open the route. After braving fierce weather and opening the route from the Balcony, they reached the summit of Everest around 2 PM. We also received word that there were a few teams at South Col hoping to get to the summit on 16 May.

Taking this update into consideration and keeping in mind Tendi Dai's advice, I conferred with the team, recommending that we wait an additional day at Camp 2 and move to Camp 3 on 17 May instead. Though disappointed and eager to get the summit done, it was critical to be patient. Later in our tent,

Sam confided, 'That's a relief, man. I was just not looking forward to one more day of slogging up the Lhotse Face. This will give us a chance to rest and recover.' Sam was right. That day had been a long one and a hard climb, coupled with a sleepless night at the base camp. I, too, could do with a good night's sleep. Who knew what the mountain would bring as we entered the Death Zone?

On 17 May, after an incredible day spent recovering at Camp 2 and an unusual breakfast of steamed dal and rice (which I highly recommend), we departed at 6:30 AM from Camp 2, wearing our down suits with our gear and climbed towards the bergschrund at the base of the Lhotse wall. As in the past, the four of us left earlier, with the Sherpa team planning to follow shortly. This was extremely disconcerting as we were now embarking into unfamiliar territory, and I would have ideally liked the team to stay together. I voiced my concern to Jangbu, who placated me by expressing his confidence in our ability to handle this section of the climb. From Camp 3 onwards, he assured me that we would all be together. Accepting his rationale as well as understanding the burden of the additional weight the Sherpas were carrying, I let the matter drop.

With clear visibility and gentle winds, we could see all the way up to Camp 3 even at this early hour in the morning. Within a few hours, we crossed a large crevasse and reached the same ice ridge at the bottom of the Lhotse wall where we had got stuck during our rotation. This time, with the weather in our favour, we moved easily up this section, clipping onto the fixed ropes and pulling ourselves up the steep ice wall. We climbed upwards in the same formation, with me following immediately behind Jangbu, Vikas behind me and Sam bringing up the rear, moving slowly and carefully up the hard surface. This section of the Lhotse wall was made up of hard ice without a layer of snow, forcing us to be extremely careful to place our crampons into the steps already cut into the ice.

The Climb up Everest

A single misstep would cause a climber to slip and slide all the way down hundreds of metres to the bottom of the wall. I learnt this the hard way when I accidentally dropped a climbing mitten while shifting my safety line across the fixed ropes on an anchor. I watched helplessly as my mitten slid past Vikas despite my warning shout. I had already begun to picture frostbitten fingers as a result of trying to climb further up without a protective mitten. Fortunately, Sam, who was 60 m below us, heard my warning and reached out to catch the mitten as it slipped down the ice. A small lapse like that could be extremely dangerous at this altitude and temperature.

The climb up the Lhotse wall was long and tedious. The gradient of the slope reduced marginally as we climbed higher but still required us to stop frequently to catch our breath. As I looked up, the climb looked endless with Camp 3 hidden behind the contours of the slope. Halfway up the wall, I saw a distinct band of yellow rock, which marked one of the prominent features we would have to tackle tomorrow. The top of Lhotse, right above us, was clearly visible, and it looked very, very far away. Towards the left and even higher than the top of Lhotse was the summit of Everest, impossibly high and distinct even in the glare of the sun. Behind me, I could see the entire expanse of the Western Cwm, with Camp 2 below us and even Camp 1 visible at the bottom of the gorge.

I looked down to check if Vikas and Sam were doing well, giving them the thumbs-up signal. Vikas was moving well, just 10 m below me, but Sam seemed to have dropped back further. A little surprised, for a moment I thought I'd stop and check on him, but Jangbu kept pushing the pace. Since Sam was moving steadily up the mountain, I figured he would catch up with us soon. We had now been climbing on the wall for almost three hours when I caught up with Jangbu as he took a break for a sip of water. I asked if we should wait for the guys since the gap had opened up quite a bit between me and Vikas. Fortunately, Sam had caught up with Vikas, and they were climbing together. Jangbu smiled and, once again, pointed up the mountain. Just over the ridge, along the line of the fixed rope we were climbing, I could make out bright-coloured pieces of fabric fluttering in the wind. I recognised them as prayer flags and realised that they were tied to someone's tent. With Camp 3 just beyond the next ridge, a mere thirty minutes away, I realised that we had finally arrived at our destination for the day.

My first impression of Camp 3 was an absolute shock. I had read several books over the years that described every aspect of an Everest expedition, but nothing could have prepared me for this moment. The entire campsite was located precariously at an angle. While most campsites are fairly level, located on relatively flat areas, Camp 3 has tents perched on narrow ledges cut by climbers into steep slopes of 40–50 degrees' incline of the Lhotse Face at 7,350 m above sea level. Two or three tents were pitched together in a row on a natural ice shelf levelled and cut from the oblique ice, slightly wider than the width of the tent itself. The rows of tents were tiered one above the other on either side of the main fixed line, with subsidiary ropes running in between. These subsidiary lines were crucial not only to secure the tents but also to allow climbers to clip their safety lines onto the rope and move between tents, preventing them from falling one vertical kilometre down the Lhotse Face. This was even essential when answering nature's call. Here too, a single misstep would involve a long, slippery slide to the bottom of the wall. The history of Everest has several instances when, at night, a climber going for a pee did not clip on and fell hundreds of metres below.

Jangbu and I made our way to our tent, which was located on the uppermost section of the slope. Though frustrating, especially after a long climb, I kept in mind that every single step higher was one less we would have to take the next day. Due to limited space, we had only one tent pitched on a ledge next to another team's tent. Since it was unoccupied, Jangbu said it was okay if we borrowed it, apparently a practice common at these higher camps when resources were scarce. For the Sherpas, the only space available was on a ledge 10 m below, which we reserved by leaving our rucksacks there. The climb had been exhausting, and the effects of the thin air were evident. Twenty minutes later, when the guys climbed into camp, Sam collapsed next to me, breathing heavily. 'Damn! I really felt that. Man, you guys were on fire. You just took off.' I laughed. 'I was just trying to keep up with Jangbu.'

The rest of the afternoon was spent resting and trying to acclimatise to the altitude. There were some other recognisable faces among the climbers at Camp 3. Uta and Tendi Dai had arrived earlier, and I could see Kishore along with the entire Satori team on a camping ledge below us. Our Sherpa team arrived a few hours after us along with an extra tent, which was to be pitched on the ledge we had held for them. This also became our makeshift kitchen with basic tea and coffee along with noodle soup out of steel mugs prepared by Samden using the small portable iso-butane cooking cans. Sam decided to forgo this meal completely due to his aversion to instant noodles ever since his experience on Nun in 2014. Being stranded by a storm in a tent for three days at the summit camp of Nun with only raw instant noodles to eat had left him with a permanent loathing for this staple mountain diet. Fortunately, having learnt from this experience and prepared for this eventuality, Sam had carried a lot of extra food such as dry fruits, chocolates and biscuits at the expense of a heavier rucksack.

It had been an excellent day as the entire team had reached Camp 3 safely without any adverse reactions to the altitude. The weather looked calm, and we were treated to an unforgettable sunset above the Himalayas, viewed from a height of 7,350 m with the skies filled with shades of orange and pink. Tonight would be the first night we would sleep on supplementary oxygen. While awake, we were functioning well and could actively breathe more deeply if required, but while sleeping, the body reverted to its subconscious pattern of breathing. To mitigate any adverse effects, we slept with our face masks on and the regulator turned to a very slow (0.5 l/min) flow rate of oxygen. This was part of our oxygen utilisation plan, and we used the cylinders stashed at Camp 3, which had been ferried up by the Sherpas a few days earlier. Though it was only 7 PM, we would be making an early start the next day, and the climb to Camp 4 was going to be much tougher than what we had experienced that day. As I watched Sam connect his cylinder, he immediately gave me a thumbs-up. 'Wow! I can feel the difference,' he said, his voice muffled by the oxygen mask covering his face. 'That's weird!' I said. 'I can't feel any change.' When Jangbu came to check on us, he realised that my cylinder was absolutely empty. Shocked at this discovery, Jangbu calmly reassured me that we had enough backup cylinders. 'Dai! What to do? In mountain, this happens,' he said. With the mask on, I laid my head down, positioned myself in our sloping tent and tried to fall asleep.

I sat awake, staring at the roof of my tent. Sam's deep breathing while he slept was beginning to really irritate me. He had always had this incredible knack for just switching off, irrespective of the situation, even before exams in our college days. The mask had felt uncomfortable on my face within the first hour. Drops of water kept forming on the inside of the mask due to condensation from my breath. Every time I tried to sleep, these droplets would fall on my nose and eyes, forcing me awake. As the night progressed, I began to feel anxious, thinking about the climb ahead and the fact that I had never been to this altitude before. I tried my level best to stay calm. At some point, having drifted off to sleep, I suddenly awoke with a start, convinced that it was early morning. However, it was still only 11 PM by my watch, and I had a long six hours to go. It was going to be an extremely long night, and I just couldn't wait to start moving.

The next day, 18 May, marked our one-day countdown to reaching the summit. I was woken up by Sam with a gentle shake. 'Time to get ready. It's summit day,' he said with a smile. The night had been long and painful, and I was glad it was over. Sam got ready first and was already out of the tent, giving me enough space to manoeuvre. However, unlike the early-morning silence at our previous camps, I could hear the loud commotion of climbers outside, interspersed with the sound of blowing wind. As I continued to get ready, Jangbu began shaking the tent, asking me to hurry and have breakfast, eager to get our team onto the fixed ropes before we got stuck behind the crowds. I stumbled out of our tent, struggling with my crampons, when I noticed Vikas was also in the same state of disarray as me. It was extremely windy and frightfully cold, making it difficult to put together the equipment with freezing fingers. Only Sam stood ready to go. Jangbu placed a full cylinder of oxygen in my rucksack, adjusted the rate of flow to 1.5 l/min, and draped the mask and connecting hose over my shoulder in readiness to go on oxygen as we departed camp. At this rate of flow, according to Jangbu, the cylinder would last us the five to six hours it would take to reach Camp 4. With Jangbu leading and Sam already on the fixed line, I got behind him with Dawa Sherpa, while Vikas clipped on behind me, followed by Pasang and Samden. In Jangbu's agitation to leave, we completely forgot our 6 AM radio call with the base camp for a weather update.

We set off at a blistering pace, trying to overtake some of the slower climbing teams that had already started crowding the fixed ropes. Within an hour, I could feel myself gasping for air. It felt like trying to run uphill while breathing through a straw. Though tired, I pushed hard to keep up with the pace of the team. At some point, I noticed that our Sherpa team was no longer with us. Unable to speak clearly through the mask and trying to conserve my energy, I couldn't even ask Jangbu what had happened. Apparently, in anticipation of bad weather, he had sent them up ahead to set up Camp 4 for our arrival as they could cover ground faster. Jangbu kept climbing at a ridiculously fast pace, with Sam just managing to keep up, some 20 m below. However, the gap between Sam and me steadily began to increase, and it was impossible for me to convey a message to slow down. Fortunately, Vikas was right behind me and I could turn to him for any help I needed. When we arrived at a bend in the fixed ropes, I had to stop for a short break and asked Vikas to pass my thermos from my rucksack for a sip of water. As he opened my bag, my helmet slipped off and went flying down the wall, almost 1,000 m below. Luckily, it didn't hit anyone, and I could see it landing somewhere around the bergschrund.

The climb to the Yellow Band was very steep, nothing like I'd ever done before. I was getting increasingly frustrated at the growing gap between us and the fact that Vikas and I were practically alone. Strong winds were constantly blowing down the Lhotse ice wall, forcing us to fight for every step. Up on Everest, a long plume of snow blowing off the summit indicated that the weather had taken a turn for the worse. Later, I learnt that Tendi Dai and Uta, seeing these conditions, had turned back down the mountain, descending all the way to Camp 2 to wait it out.

After a gruelling ascent, we finally arrived at the Yellow Band, a challenging and technical section of the climb that demands careful navigation across a steep expanse of rock rather than ice. This distinctive geological feature, composed of sedimentary sandstone, cuts horizontally across the mountain face at an altitude of approximately 7,600 m and serves as a crucial landmark on the route to Camp 4. The band is crisscrossed with multiple fixed ropes, a stark reminder of the countless climbers who have passed through this demanding stretch before us. This made it extremely difficult and dangerous to distinguish the new ropes from the old. As I attempted to cross over a sharp ledge on the Yellow Band, my jumar ascender device got jammed in one of the knots at the rope at the anchor point. Vikas was still twenty minutes behind me, and my frustration was fuelling my anxiety. As much as I tried, the situation just kept getting worse with no one around to help. For twenty minutes, I kept struggling until a Sherpa descending the Yellow Band stopped and helped release my ascender. With immense relief, I clipped onto the higher rope, by which time Vikas had also caught up with me.

Together, as we pushed up the mountain, we could see Sam in the distance, all alone, precariously climbing up the Geneva Spur, struggling and scrambling on loose snow as he tried to get up the vertical face. He, too, looked like he was having a very hard time. Jangbu, having finally stopped to check on us, was closer and waving his arms frantically, urging us to hurry up. He stood near some tents (which I later learnt were part of Lhotse Camp 4). It had been six hours of non-stop climbing, and despite Jangbu's estimate, we were nowhere near South Col.

I began to experience an unnatural feeling of exhaustion with everything – the weight of the equipment, the layers of clothes and even the heat of the sun. I was convinced that the oxygen cylinder I had used during the night at Camp 3 had been faulty. Coupled with the lack of sleep, it must have been the reason I was feeling so drained.

In front of us towered the huge rock of the Geneva Spur, located just under 7,900 m and the final obstacle on our approach to South Col. The first Swiss Everest expedition of 1952 named this distinct and massive rock formation, and that team eventually had to turn back from this point. With a Herculean effort, Vikas and I, led by Jangbu, began climbing the Geneva Spur, a steep 150–200 m ascent with soft snow that caused us to slip back a step for every three we took. Like previous sections on the route, it was also very difficult to discern between the new ropes and the old ones. If the rope broke, we would fall at least one vertical kilometre – straight into Camp 2. The dangers of crossing this section were frightening, and I felt justified in my disappointment with our Sherpa team for leaving us alone to manoeuvre across these patches despite the decision to stay together, especially if there had been an emergency.

Somehow, we scrambled over the Geneva Spur after thirty minutes of climbing and made our way, completely exhausted, towards Camp 4 at South Col, the highest camp in the world, located at 7,925 m (26,000 ft). As we arrived at South Col at 2 PM, we witnessed complete mayhem as winds blowing at over 100 km/hr tore across the exposed Col. In freezing temperatures, amongst the scattered debris of previous expeditions, our team of Sherpas and Sam had managed to set up one tent and were struggling to set up another. Holding down the corners of the tent, they wrestled to anchor it to the ground as it flapped violently, threatening to fly away. Scared of losing the tent in the wind, we saw Sam scramble inside to weigh it down, while the Sherpas scurried to secure the corners. Vikas and I reached the tent Sam was in and bundled in with all our equipment and bags, hoping to get some respite from the force of the cold wind. I lay in a heap like that for fifteen minutes, breathing heavily through the mask, trying desperately to calm the pounding in my chest. I only moved when Jangbu came into the tent to check our oxygen regulators, discovering that my cylinder was completely empty. Somehow, I knew I had run out of oxygen around Lhotse Camp 4, below even the Geneva Spur, which explained the feeling of exhaustion I had never experienced before. The moment he replaced my cylinder, I immediately felt better. He cautioned us to breathe slowly and told us he would return shortly with some hot tea.

The three of us sat in a state of shock. We had reached the Death Zone and, true to its name, we felt completely spent. I was so exhausted that I could now understand how my body could slowly start dying without the supplementary oxygen from our cylinders. In another six hours, we were planning to leave for the summit and needed to make sure we had recovered. I was tired and thirsty. I needed to hydrate, eat and rest so that I could recover enough to begin the final leg of the climb. After an hour of waiting for Jangbu, we tried to shout, but our voices could not carry over the sound of the wind. Though desperately thirsty, the water in our bottles had frozen, and I didn't have the heart to leave the tent. Sam, having had the most time to recover, volunteered and climbed out of the tent without his mask and oxygen cylinder. He returned ten minutes later with a single thermos of hot tea and collapsed onto the tent floor, gasping for breath from this small exertion as if he had run a mile. Once he had strapped on his mask and had a chance to catch his breath, he told us that the team was struggling to melt snow, but Jangbu would bring some more water and food rations in a while. We had painstakingly set aside a separate stash of food supplies specifically for this moment, which was to have been carried up by Pasang. After twenty minutes, we suddenly heard the zip of the tent being pulled open, and Dawa Sherpa stuck his head in with a single packet of sweets. 'Dai!' he said. 'Sorry. This is all we have.' I stared at him in complete shock. Apparently, Pasang had forgotten to bring the rations, and they were lying in a tent at Camp 3. Fortunately, Sam had a decent reserve of dry fruits and chocolates, which he had hauled all the way up to Camp 4. Along with some emergency rations Vikas was carrying, we made do with whatever little we had and settled into our sleeping bags to wait out the storm. The winds started blowing with more force, making it hard to even talk to each other inside the tent. Things were progressing from bad to worse, and I wasn't getting a very good feeling about this day.

13

The Death Zone: In the Eye of the Storm

> When you come out of the storm, you won't be the same person who walked in.
> Haruki Murakami, *Kafka on the Shore*
> (translated by Philip Gabriel)

Sam

The storm raged on, pummelling our tents with hurricane-force winds. Often, the howling gusts would push down the tent walls onto our sleeping forms. Occasionally, a stronger blast would lift the entire structure, despite the combined weight of Sauraj, Vikas and me lying in it. My senses had now been completely dulled by the wind constantly pounding against the tent fabric. Time dragged on, and we felt like we were trapped inside a never-ending beating drum.

A few hours later, as I looked around the tent, it was very dark and freezing cold. I checked the illuminated dial on my wristwatch just to be sure, but in my heart, I already knew it was well past our ETD (estimated time of departure) – 8 PM Ordinarily, we should have started from Camp 4 at South Col and been well on our way, making the final push for the summit. I looked at Jangbu questioningly. He had shifted into our tent earlier in the evening from the adjoining one he was sharing with Samden, Pasang and Dawa when the storm had threatened to blow our tent away. He looked at me, wordlessly shook his head and then shrugged his shoulders. His gesture said it all: 'Kei karne? [What to do?]'

I took a deep, laboured breath from my oxygen mask and tried (in vain) to discern who was where amongst the four of us squashed together in the confines of this 6 x 4 ft space. Despite us being in our respective down suits, it was bloody cold with night-time temperatures possibly touching −40°C! Vikas and Sauraj had squeezed into their sleeping bags and had tried to optimise space by lying down opposite each other. Jangbu and I sat diagonally across them with our legs pushed into our sleeping bags, hoping to find some warmth amidst the mass of bodies inside the tent. Our equipment and shoes were inside as well, lest they be blown off the face of the mountain. Each of us was wearing a face mask connected to an oxygen cylinder with a hose that had to be placed close by. A constant eye had to be kept on the pressure gauge and the rate of flow controlled to make certain that oxygen was constantly flowing. In case the flow was disrupted either due to freezing of the regulator/hose or the cylinder becoming empty, a climber would not realise it unless they could see the pressure gauge.

Since I was positioned closest to one of the entrances, despite the wind, I stuck my head outside to look for any signs of movement. I drew comfort from the fact that no other team was trying to venture out in these conditions. Though there were no clouds, it was difficult to focus. The icy winds, still blowing at speeds of 70–80 km/hr, were making my eyes water, blurring my vision as I squinted through the dark of the night past the wreckage of the neighbouring camps. Anything not securely anchored had either been ripped, destroyed or blown away by the storm.

As the weather wasn't allowing us to go anywhere, we did a quick oxygen check. Surprisingly, Vikas was going through his cylinders much faster than we had calculated, which either indicated a problem with his breathing or possibly one with his mask and regulator. We all changed over to fresh cylinders, and with the reassurance of not running out of oxygen in our sleep, we hunkered down to wait out the wind and the long night.

It was approaching midnight, and it felt like I had waited out every single minute of the night. I knew Jangbu was also awake as he would kick us every hour just to make sure we had not fallen into a deep slumber. Well aware of the dangers of people dying in their sleep due to a combination of hypoxia and hypothermia, I readily forgave him this breach in social decorum.

Slowly, I became aware of a change, one that I couldn't quite put my finger on at first. I realised it was the wind. It felt like it had eased off a bit. My spirits rose, clinging to what I was certain was a glimmer of hope in this otherwise hopeless situation. I braved another look outside the tent and noticed some movement from the Chinese camp, which seemed to add credence to my presumption. I instantly relayed the information into the tent and was greeted with mixed reactions. Sauraj sat up immediately, eager to go, but Jangbu put a firm hand on my shoulder. He took off his mask and said, 'No, Dai! Wind still too strong. Climbing no good. Very dangerous.' Vikas didn't respond immediately during this exchange, which got me concerned. I reached out and shook him, after which he answered through his face mask, 'Yeah! I heard. We should wait. I agree with Jangbu.'

'You OK?' I asked him, genuinely worried.

'Yeah! I think so. Just feeling really cold!'

19 May 2017

The dial on my watch showed 1:30 AM when I heard movement outside. I peeked out of the tent entrance to see a row of white headlights moving up the slope, out of South Col and towards the summit. I spent the rest of the night intermittently watching the slow progress of these climbers as they tried to push past the elements and weather the storm, but sheer exhaustion had me drifting seamlessly between sleep and some form of semi-conscious vigil over the next few hours, hoping against hope for a sign that the storm was abating. By 4 AM, the winds seemed to have slowed down, and darkness gradually gave way to the smoky grey of dawn. I looked out, expecting to see climbers high above us on the mountain, but I was shocked to see their headlights glinting off the snow at almost the same location as where I had last seen them. They appeared to be coming down. I watched them descend slowly down the mountain, and as the sun peeked over the horizon at 5 AM, I saw them stumble into the Chinese camp.

I was restless and needed to move, not just because I had been stuck waiting through the long, relentless night but also because I desperately wanted to find out what had happened to those climbers. I strapped on my boots and, using my safety cord, put together a makeshift sling that allowed me to hoist my oxygen cylinder onto my back. As I stumbled out of the tent in my down suit and face mask, I suddenly felt circulation return painfully to my feet. I staggered forward through the howling wind and snow, making my way to the Chinese camp, avoiding the debris of wreckage and ripped tents from the neighbouring camps.

Despite the gusts of wind pushing me off balance, I paused, taking a minute to look around and appreciate the spectacle around me in the light of day. In spite of the early hour, the sun blazed over the horizon of Tibet to my right, forcing me to squint and shield my eyes from the brightness. To my left, the vistas of Nepal were covered in an angry haze, indicating the direction of the storm we had endured through the night. South Col was nothing more than a small basin cradled on the ridge between Everest and Lhotse, funnelling the wind from one country to another. As I looked up at the summit of Everest, so tantalisingly close, I was awestruck by the long plume of snow being blown off the face, shrouding the entire peak in an ethereal mantle of misty white.

As the cold cut through my senses, shattering my thoughts, I made my way across whatever was left of Camp 4 to speak to the climbers. What I saw would haunt me for the rest of my life. The climbers looked exhausted and half-frozen, as if they had narrowly escaped death. The Sherpa guide's fingers looked like they had been frozen into claws, while one Chinese climber looked like half his cheek (the side facing the wind) had been chewed off to the bone. The team that had stayed back was working furiously, trying to warm up these climbers and give them first aid. They had paid a very heavy price for attempting to push upwards in the storm. Given their predicament, I thought it best not to harass them any further with pointless questions and made my way back to our tent to give our team a report of what I had seen.

My feet were freezing, but after spending an entire night doing little other than sitting, I just did not want to get back into that godforsaken tent. Jangbu came out and we made our way to the bottom of South Col to try and patch a radio connection down to Everest Base Camp. We needed help and had to inform them of our situation. Fortunately, despite the winds, Jangbu was able to get through and, speaking in Nepali, proceeded to fill Ghanshyam in. After he was done, I took the radio, pressed it close to my ear and said, 'Dai! Namaste.' I heard Ghanshyam's voice through the static.

'Bhai!' I shouted back. 'Big winds. Bad weather. Kei karne? [What to do?]' I asked.

'Just be patient. Do you have oxygen? Can you wait one more night?' he asked.

'I don't know,' I yelled. 'We will check. I will get Sauraj Dai and call you again.'

As we made our way back to our tents, holding on to the fixed rope for support, Jangbu kept talking, telling me how he had never experienced weather like this, how dangerous this situation was and that we should head down for the safety of the team. With my freezing feet occupying my thoughts, I listened with only half a mind to what he was saying, walking behind his bulk in an attempt to gain some respite from the cold wind. By the time we reached our camp, my hands and feet were completely numb. I stumbled in, finally allowing myself to give in to the exhaustion of having moved around Camp 4 for the past few hours.

I could feel my feet freezing and ripped off my boots and began to rub my toes vigorously. Sauraj handed me all his 'hand and foot' warmers, which I used immediately to restore some circulation despite the pain. I had always been told that pain is good. 'It lets you know you don't have frostbite.' My feet hurt like hell. Meanwhile, Jangbu proceeded to update the others on our conversation with Ghanshyam and tried to convey the gravity of the situation to us.

'Dai! I'm so sorry!' he implored. 'We must go down.'

This became his mantra for the next hour, punctuating our discussion at regular intervals as we deliberated over the various options available to us. Sauraj and I were both angry. Going down was just not an option for us, not now when we were so close! We realised then that Vikas was out of oxygen. Again! Jangbu changed his cylinder and, as he did so, began to use this as the main point for persuasion.

'Dai! We don't have enough cylinders! Please! Let's go down,' he pleaded.

Sauraj vehemently refused, wanting to discuss the available options at the very least. Vikas listened patiently as he tried to weigh our odds and options carefully.

'Jangbu must be scared,' I thought. 'Why else would he be acting so silly?'

My emotionally distraught, angry, oxygen-starved brain had completely discounted the advice being given by this man who had accomplished twelve summits of Everest. At this altitude, even talking was exhausting and left us all breathless. Our discussion was made more frustrating by the interspersed pauses required to take a couple of breaths from our oxygen masks just to sustain the conversation.

We kept talking about two options: stay and climb, or everyone descends to safety. I kept wondering why we couldn't look at an alternative. I tried to calculate how many cylinders we had left, but performing simple maths at this height had begun to feel like I was trying to solve a differential equation. I ran the numbers again and was reasonably confident. We actually had enough oxygen to sustain a summit attempt for two climbers and two Sherpas, but who would it be? I began deliberating on the rationality of this possibility. In my mind, Vikas had come on board this expedition because he trusted Sauraj and me. As our first Everest client, he was our responsibility, and his success was paramount. He should go.

That left Sauraj and me. Both of us wanted to go. We had trained hard and given up so much for this. Both of us deserved it, but we only had enough resources for one. While difficult to accept at first, I eventually reasoned that it didn't matter which of us it was, because at the end of the day, it would still be an Adventure Pulse team on the summit of Everest. That was the big picture. It was not a sacrifice but an opportunity for our team, and a successful outcome overall would certainly be better than all of us turning back on account of limited oxygen. 'Sauraj and Vikas can go up with two Sherpas. I will go down,' I said determinedly. 'That will work. We will have enough oxygen then.'

There was a heavy pause as everyone considered this possibility. The awkwardness was unceremoniously broken by Sauraj, who responded emphatically, saying, 'No way! Absolutely not. We aren't doing this without you!'

Though it was I who had made the offer and had accepted the possibility of turning back while the others climbed, I will always be grateful to him for saying that, for in doing so, he had further cemented our friendship.

I shook my head, knowing how important this was to us and worried that if we didn't try for the summit, there was no way we would be able to get Sauraj off South Col. I remembered how difficult it had been to convince him to leave Everest Base Camp two years ago after the avalanche. 'It's the only thing that makes sense,' I persisted. 'Either we all go up, or we all go down,' Sauraj insisted. Jangbu interjected. 'Dai! I'm so sorry! I climbing sirdar. We go down now, Dai. Please!'

'I'm with Jangbu,' said Vikas. 'What he says, goes.'

As this discussion went back and forth, we realised we were at a stalemate. 'I want to talk to Ghanshyam,' said Sauraj. 'Yes!' I said. 'He's expecting your call. I'll come with you.'

I pulled on my climbing boots once again and led Sauraj back down to the radio point at the head of South Col. The wind had eased a little, making communication a lot easier.

'Can you get us more oxygen, Ghanshyam?' yelled Sauraj into the radio.

'I don't know, Dai! But I can try,' came Ghanshyam's distorted voice over the radio.

'Okay. That's good,' said Sauraj.

So we are staying, I thought with some relief.

'But what's the weather prediction for the next twenty-four hours?' asked Sauraj suddenly, something I had not even considered until then.

'No good, Dai! Not good. Very difficult to predict,' replied Ghanshyam over the radio, thus casting a fresh shadow of doubt over our newly renewed hope for the summit.

'Okay! We will call you before we leave and update you on our decision. Over and out!' said Sauraj as he signed off.

We stood there in silence for a minute, not knowing what to say. 'Let's stop at Kishore's tent on the way and check what they are doing,' suggested Sauraj. Though the Satori team had also gone through a rough night, they had planned for the possibility of having to spend two or perhaps even three nights at Camp 4. Kishore and Mingma Tenzi Sherpa (their climbing sirdar) confirmed that their team was staying despite the uncertainty of the weather.

Back in our tent, it was finally time for us to take a call. We had discussed, analysed and considered all the possibilities, and had unwittingly gone through the first three stages of grief as we battled denial and anger and attempted to bargain with a relatively unyielding situation. However, Sauraj's questions about the weather had raised serious doubts about the sense of trying for the summit, let alone the logistical feasibility. Despite Jangbu's constant appeals and all the evidence we had in support of the decision, I just didn't have the courage to say the words. It was Sauraj who finally made a reluctant, resigned call. 'I don't agree with it, but if everyone feels we should go down, let's go.' That was the final nail in the coffin. It was done.

It was 11 AM when we began the process of securing our campsite and tents. We tried to postpone the disappointment we were all feeling by taking some pictures with the banners of our sponsors and well-wishers before heading down, but it was an exercise in futility. The storm had picked up again, and we couldn't get through to anyone on the radio. Jangbu had managed to sell our remaining oxygen cylinders to the Chinese expedition, who desperately needed them to revive their team.

I looked up at Everest in pure despair. After fifty-one days on the mountain, we needed just twelve more hours to reach the summit. I was heartbroken and I could only imagine what

At 2860 m above sea level, Lukla is the deadliest airstrip in the world – just 527 m long with a sheer drop at the end

A climber on the Everest Base Camp trail at around 4000 m

Namche Bazaar, also referred to as the capital of the Khumbu region, nestled in the clouds

Yaks carrying supplies to Everest Base Camp

A typical team set-up at Everest Base Camp

Everest Base Camp after the avalanche, 2015

The dining tent after the avalanche, 2015

Tents in ruin at the base camp after the avalanche, 2015

The team at a pooja with a senior lama from the Tengboche Monastery performing the pooja

Equipment to be blessed at the pooja ceremony

Prayer flags hoisted immediately after the pooja ceremony, signifying that the team is ready to climb

A precarious ladder over a crevasse in Khumbu Icefall

An exposed crevasse between Everest Base Camp and Camp 1

A team of climbers making their way across the expanse of Khumbu Icefall

The team with Camp 1 in the background

Sauraj and Vikas were feeling. After we had taken the call, we had all walked away to separate parts of South Col to grieve. Facing away from the camp, I wept, feeling the tears freeze against my face. I was desolate and had no outlet for my sorrow. Since we couldn't get through to the team below, I called Kay on the sat phone. I vaguely remember the conversation, trying to sum up the situation and doing my best to maintain a brave front. My resolve soon cracked, and I wept as I told her the expedition was done. We would be descending as we didn't have oxygen. It was all over.

Later, when she recalled the conversation to me, she said that it was one of the most frightening things she had ever heard. 'Kay, we are at Camp 4. The weather is really bad, and we've been here all night. We've run out of oxygen. It's over. It's all over.' Then she heard me weeping through the noise of the wind. She imagined horrific scenarios, fearing the worst.

At 12:30 PM, we were finally ready to start our descent. We clipped onto the fixed line out of South Col in the opposite direction from the summit, making our way to the Geneva Spur. I descended the rocky outcrop of the spur, a stretch that had filled me with such terror just twenty-four hours ago. This time, I could only feel a sense of crushing sadness. Just as we reached Lhotse Camp 4, we passed Ravi Kumar sitting alone, taking a break as he made his way up to South Col. He was climbing ahead of his team, who were still struggling up the Lhotse Face. He was thrilled to see us and congratulated us with a lot of enthusiasm, presuming we had already summited Everest. I didn't have the heart to say it, but Vikas told him that we hadn't summited and were going down. As we briefly shared our experience, I remember Sauraj distinctly cautioning him about the weather and asking him to be careful. The storm was possibly going to get worse.

After our brief interaction with Ravi, I was done. I just didn't want to talk to anyone else and tell them about our failure. I saw Dawa accelerate his pace and start rappelling down the Lhotse Face. With Dawa ahead of me and the rest of the team following slowly behind, I spent that long descent alone with my thoughts of anger, hatred and betrayal. I cursed myself for coming back to Everest, cursed Sauraj for having talked me into it and cursed Adventure Pulse. But most of all, I cursed this godforsaken mountain for having plunged my life into a living hell of heartache, frustration, exercise, fatigue and destitution, attempting to scrounge every single penny towards these ridiculously expensive expeditions.

I had put my life on hold for the last four years, attempting to climb Everest, and I was done – done with this lifestyle, done with adventure and done with the mountains. That day, 19 May 2017, was the worst day of my life. I climbed down from the mountain feeling like a complete failure.

14

The Aftermath of Failure

> The world breaks everyone, and afterward, some are strong at the broken places.
> Ernest Hemingway, *A Farewell to Arms*

Sauraj

My head was still reeling from the shock of failure as I climbed down from Camp 4. I kept replaying the events of the morning, wondering if I could have done something differently, if there was still a way to turn things around before it was too late.

The events of that morning already felt like a lifetime ago. I remember glancing at my wristwatch, even though I knew exactly how late we were. The dial read 6:30 AM, and the four of us – Samir, Vikas, Jangbu and I – had just endured a sleepless night in the suffocating confines of a single tent at Camp 4. Had things gone according to plan, we would have been nearing the summit by now, standing on top of the world.

Instead, we lay there in silence, drifting in and out of a restless sleep, each of us battling the bone-chilling −40°C cold that gnawed at our bodies. The wind howled like a beast outside, rattling the fragile walls of our tent, a cruel reminder of the storm that kept us pinned down. The air inside was thick with unspoken dread – the kind that clings to you, growing heavier with each passing hour. We all knew the inevitable choice that loomed ahead: risk another night at Camp 4, gambling on the weather to grant us one last chance or begin the long, heartbreaking descent back to Everest Base Camp. After my radio call with Ghanshyam, the answer became painfully clear – time was no longer on our side. Jangbu, our climbing sirdar, had already made his decision. His voice, usually calm and measured, now carried an urgency that sent a fresh wave of unease through me. 'We go down,' he said firmly. Vikas, weakened by a faulty oxygen regulator that had left him struggling through the night, nodded in agreement. He was in no condition to debate, deferring to Jangbu's experience and the mountain's unforgiving reality. However, I wasn't ready to surrender yet.

I turned to Jangbu, desperation clawing at my chest. 'We should at least try to get more oxygen and attempt the summit tomorrow,' I insisted, grasping at whatever sliver of hope remained. Other teams were still waiting it out, believing the weather might turn in their favour. Ghanshyam hadn't ruled it out either – he had promised to try. It wasn't much, but it was something. However, Jangbu shook his head. 'No oxygen at Camp 4,' he said flatly. He was right. Finding extra oxygen here was as unlikely as finding gold. Any climbers who had stayed behind would be guarding their limited supply fiercely. Yet, I couldn't let go of the possibility that if Ghanshyam could secure oxygen from a team at Camp 2, we might still have a chance. The real question was how we could get it up to us in time.

The odds were slim – maybe a 20–30 per cent chance at best – but even that felt better than outright surrender. I pressed on, but Vikas leaned towards Jangbu's side. Sam remained neutral, unwilling to take a stance. The futility of it all settled over me like a heavy fog. After a long, suffocating silence, Sam finally broke it with a suggestion that sent a chill down my spine – he would descend without oxygen, accompanied by a single Sherpa.

'No,' I said instantly. That was not an option. Jangbu, too, dismissed it outright. Splitting up at these altitudes was a death sentence.

It came down to three against one. Jangbu, Vikas and Sam were ready to descend. I was the last holdout. I could see it in their faces – they were exhausted, drained and unwilling to gamble with their lives any further. In that moment, I knew I had no choice. I swallowed the lump in my throat, forcing myself to accept the brutal reality before us. If we somehow secured the oxygen but the storm didn't relent, we would be trapped at Camp 4 for another night, exposed to the elements, inching closer to the thin line between survival and disaster.

In a few short hours, we prepared to descend. Before I could leave Camp 4 behind, I had to make one final, crushing call. My family and friends were waiting for an update – from the summit. I knew my parents hadn't slept, holding their own anxious vigil, desperate for news.

With a heavy heart, I dialled my mother's number on the satellite phone. As soon as I heard her voice, the weight of everything threatened to break me. My throat tightened as I forced out the words: 'We didn't make it. We're turning back.'

A long silence. Then, her voice – gentle and steady, trying to mask the heartbreak I knew she was feeling – came through. 'Come home, beta. Do what's best.'

Just like that, it was over.

By 12:30 PM on the morning of 19 May, our team began the descent towards Camp 2. Disheartened, all of us trying to come to terms with our predicament, we were in no mood to talk to anyone. By an unspoken agreement, we all walked some distance from each other to avoid conversation. Samir had sped ahead of us all, maintaining an unrelenting pace, followed closely by Jangbu, while Vikas and I made up the rear, a considerable distance behind them. I remember very little of our journey to Camp 3. I was numb from disappointment and consumed by trying to process what had transpired in the last twelve to fourteen hours. I was shocked beyond belief at having to turn back a mere 800 m from the summit, and I refused to accept that this could very well be the end of our 2017 expedition and possibly the end of our Everest dream. As soon as we reached Camp 3, I noticed a crackling over the radio, which had been entirely silent since we had left Camp 4 earlier that morning. This was not unusual in the mountains, and I figured we must have lost the radio signal somewhere between the Geneva Spur and Camp 3. Hearing the radio static, I tuned into our frequency used for communicating with each other. As soon as I tuned in, I heard Ghanshyam and Jangbu arguing. They were both agitated to the point of hurling abuses at one another. Ghanshyam was clearly upset and with reason.

'Where are you guys?' I heard Ghanshyam demand angrily of Jangbu. 'I have been trying to reach you for the last six hours. I am trying to arrange the oxygen. I hope you guys are okay at Camp 4.'

'We are already at Camp 3,' Jangbu informed him.

This upset Ghanshyam even more as he reminded Jangbu that, as base camp manager, he should have been informed before we left Camp 4, and he was right. After our gut-wrenching decision to descend and our disinclination to linger in the cold winds at South Col any longer than necessary, we had entirely forgotten to update Ghanshyam on our movements. Although this had not been explicitly agreed upon, as our base camp manager, he should have been informed about our whereabouts at all times. Despite the fact that this conversation was between Ghanshyam and Jangbu, I was certain that all of us in the team had heard the argument. By now, however, Samir was halfway down to Camp 2, and we had no opportunity to reconvene and discuss whether it made sense to wait for Ghanshyam to arrange oxygen.

By 4:30 PM, we arrived at Camp 2, and I called Ghanshyam on the radio. I proposed that we spend a couple of days at Camp 2, which is relatively safer than the higher camps, rest for a few days and then once more make our Everest bid. This would also give Ghanshyam enough time to procure more oxygen for us, I reasoned. Once again, though, Jangbu disagreed. He pointed out that the Sherpa team was tired and needed time to rest before returning to Camp 2 with oxygen and food supplies. He proposed that we all go back down to Everest Base Camp, and Ghanshyam, too, was unable to make him change his mind. The discussions between Ghanshyam and Jangbu over the radio quickly devolved into arguments, and they just didn't seem able to see eye to eye on how we should proceed as a team. I was beginning to feel very uncomfortable about the entire situation. I was afraid that once we reached Everest Base Camp, we would not be able to return to make a summit attempt this year. The time spent at Camp 2 was extremely depressing and nerve-wracking for me as I couldn't get rid of the nagging feeling that we weren't trying hard enough to make our expedition successful.

On 20 May, as we trekked down to Everest Base Camp from Camp 2, news from the summit trickled in, each update relayed by Ghanshyam over the radio. We learnt that the Satori team, who had chosen to wait it out at Camp 4, had successfully reached the summit. A wave of disappointment crashed over me, and I cast a baleful, accusing glance at Jangbu. He met my gaze with a resigned shrug, his expression mirroring my dejection. But just twenty minutes later, Ghanshyam radioed again – this time with terrible news. Our friend Ravi, whom we had last seen heading towards Camp 4 as we began our descent, had lost his life.

The grief and heartbreak were overwhelming, but I couldn't shake the realisation that our team might have shared Ravi's fate if we had pressed on. When I met Jangbu's eyes again, no words were needed. We both understood the grim reality: there had been a 50–50 chance we might have summited if we had stayed, but it was just as likely that we could have perished in the attempt. These were odds I had been willing to gamble with, but as our climbing leader, Jangbu couldn't accept that risk. Our team was worn down to the bone, our nerves frayed by the relentless emotional rollercoaster of the past few days.

On 20 May 2017, Ravi reached the summit of Everest despite terrible weather conditions. On the way down, he disappeared off the face of the earth. His body was discovered two days later. It was an unfortunate and terrible tragedy.

Back at Everest Base Camp, a sombre atmosphere hung over our tents. Everyone, including our base camp team, was visibly upset about our failed attempt, and we didn't really want to talk much to anyone. Physically, the altitude and inclement weather had taken their toll. We even had chilblains on our faces. We spent much of the remaining day resting in our own tents in the relatively balmy −5°C temperatures of our glacial base camp home after the prolonged exposure to −40°C at the higher camps. We slept for hours, waking up intermittently only to eat and then going back to sleep again. News of other climbers' Everest expeditions continued to reach us, once again putting us in the throes of emotional turmoil as we constantly relived the events of Camp 4. It had been a very difficult season, chequered with reports of continued high winds, summits and deaths.

On 21 May, Ghanshyam informed me that Tendi, whom I had consulted on weather updates prior to our own summit bid, had successfully climbed along with his client. My resolve to go back up and try once more had not wavered, and I was beginning to worry that we were spending too long at

The Aftermath of Failure

Everest Base Camp. Ghanshyam and I brought up the topic of heading back up with Jangbu, but he stubbornly refused to entertain the suggestion. He told me, 'Dai, mountains give you only one chance. Either you reach the summit, or you go home. We have had our chance to summit, and now you go home.'

I couldn't believe what I was hearing. On the morning of 21 May, we called for a team meeting in the dining tent. We had barely spoken to each other since our last discussion at Camp 4, and we all needed to come to a consensus on how to proceed as a team. Jangbu was once again very vocal about not wanting to lead us back. Over the past couple of months, we had realised that Jangbu was extremely superstitious and placed a lot of faith in portents and auspices. He reiterated his belief that the mountain allows only one chance at the summit and that we would die if we went back again. He then informed us that his Sherpa team had refused to go back up. I had expected this since all the Sherpas on the team were related to Jangbu – he was not only their climbing leader but also the head of the family. They would not go against his wishes.

Despite not being in the least bit superstitious, I still knew the perils of this mountain with the familiarity we had now gained and so it was hard not to feel shaken by his prophecies of certain death if we climbed again. Vikas, who had already said he wanted to back out the previous night, also made it clear that he was not going back up. He did not like the odds and wasn't willing to take any chances. Sam had remained neutral up to this point. I had been concerned, though, about his cough – a condition called the Khumbu cough, which has been known to jeopardise many mountaineers' Everest expeditions. By that evening, Sam's cough had worsened. He told me, 'I would have loved to go back up, but I can feel the congestion in my chest.' Our discussion at Everest Base Camp was giving me a horrible sense of déjà vu. It appeared to resemble the Camp 4 conversation from only two days ago. Once more, it came down to three versus one in favour of aborting the expedition – just like two years ago.

I couldn't bring myself to give up. I knew it was a long shot, but I had to know I had done everything possible to make it happen. I turned to Ghanshyam and asked him what my options were. Ghanshyam started telling me that it was difficult but we could try when Jangbu once again chimed in, 'Dai, if you go, you die.' I could see that Jangbu really believed it and nothing I could say would convince him otherwise.

Ghanshyam and I stepped out of the tent to talk. Ghanshyam said, 'Dai, it's impossible to climb without Sherpa support and our team won't go.'

'Can we try to arrange for one or two Sherpas from another team? We still have four or five days before the weather window closes. We can fly oxygen and food up to Camp 2 and then take it from there,' I persisted.

Although not really convinced, Ghanshyam promised to try. It was an extremely long shot as we both knew. There are no Sherpas simply waiting around to be engaged by climbers at Everest Base Camp. All Sherpas are assigned to climbing teams. Our only hope was getting in touch with Sherpas still at Everest Base Camp whose clients might have aborted the expedition due to sickness or had gone back home.

By afternoon, Ghanshyam came back and said, 'Dai, it's not possible. I can't find any free Sherpas.' With that, I knew that it was all over. I would not be climbing in 2017. Although Ghanshyam had been extremely supportive, I realised that at this point, even he was showing some hesitancy. When I asked him about it, he admitted that with the rest of the team backing out, he, too, was beginning to have his doubts. He told me that while no Sherpas were to be found at Everest Base Camp, he was, in any case, sceptical about engaging new Sherpas this late in the season. As climbers, our very lives depend on the partnership with the climbing Sherpas. It made him extremely uneasy that I should undertake the climb with someone I was not well acquainted with. I realised how valid his point was, and with Ghanshyam too not entirely supportive of the scheme, I knew I could not carry on by myself.

The rest of the day went by in a haze of depression. I couldn't shake off the grief of failure and didn't know how to move on from here. All of us spent our remaining time at Everest Base Camp as far away from each other as we could. I kept analysing and re-analysing what had happened during the expedition and the mistakes that we had made. I called up my parents from Everest Base Camp and told them that it was all over and we were coming home. Sensing the mental anguish and the toll this expedition had taken on me, my parents decided to fly out to Kathmandu the next day and meet me there.

I was in no mood to undertake the long trek down to Lukla. There was nothing new to see after having done this trek dozens of times already, and I really wasn't looking forward to spending more time walking in the mountains alone with my thoughts, agonising over our failure. I proposed we charter a helicopter from Everest Base Camp to Lukla and head back home. Vikas agreed immediately, eager to get back to Mumbai and resume work. He figured that at least this way he would be able to save on some leave. Sam took a little more convincing but eventually agreed. The chopper arrived the next morning, and I turned to look at Everest one more time – the last time that year. I promised myself that this wasn't over and that I had to come back to conquer the peak.

From Lukla, we reached Kathmandu by plane that same afternoon. At Kathmandu airport, we were received by our logistics partners who had helped us organise the expedition.

Despite not being at all in the mood, we left directly from the airport to have lunch with the team. Lunch was a grim and sombre affair. Usually when mountaineers return to civilisation after sixty days of what can only be described as the most basic of facilities and physical hardship, a good, hearty meal is all that is on our minds. This time around, things were very different. Despite being at our favourite restaurant in Kathmandu, Vikas, Samir and I realised that we had no appetite for food. Our disappointment ran so deep that we could barely face each other, let alone make polite conversation with other people. After a perfunctory glance at the menu, Vikas and I ordered a few dishes so as not to disappoint our hosts. Sam, I noticed, just couldn't bring himself to look at the menu. By this point, I guess we all just felt numb and wanted to put this entire ordeal behind us as soon as we could. Vikas was already talking about wanting to leave for Mumbai the next day, back to his family, work and normalcy.

My parents, anxious and concerned about us, had already arrived in Kathmandu to spend some time with me. After lunch, we checked into a hotel, and after resting for a bit, we met with my parents, who shared in my disappointment and realised how crushed I was after coming so close to the summit and then having to turn back. My mother tried her best to comfort me. My father, while extremely supportive, commiserated with our ordeal, but somewhere, he also shared the conviction that we should have waited at Camp 4 for the weather to improve and tried again.

We were exhausted. Summit or not, the mountain takes its toll, and we went back to our hotel early that evening. After more than two months of sleeping on cold, hard ice, we were grateful for the clean comfort of our hotel beds. The next day, the entire team, including our organiser Ganesh and Jangbu, met once more over a meal. Everyone was trying to console and reassure us, yet the atmosphere remained tense. My parents also joined us, and my dad initiated a conversation with Jangbu to understand what had happened during the expedition. A retired officer of the Indian Army, my father has spent a lifetime dealing with complex life-and-death situations where failure is not an option. With his military instincts kicking in, he tried to conduct a root cause analysis of how, despite being skilled mountaineers, we had turned back barely 800 m from the top.

After spending nearly two months with Jangbu, we had grown accustomed to his terse communication style and limited English. For my dad, however, it was a new experience, and it was somewhat comical to watch him grow increasingly frustrated as he tried to understand Jangbu, who would offer only brief sentences like 'What to doing?' and 'How to going?' punctuated by eloquent shrugs. Beyond this amusing exchange, very little was said, and an uncomfortable silence settled over us as we went through the motions of eating and making small talk. The next day, reassured that we were managing as well as could be expected, my parents flew back to Delhi from Kathmandu. We spent most of the day in our hotel, resting and sleeping. Although our bodies were beginning to recover, our spirits had not. Each day, we read news of more successful summits in the Kathmandu papers and felt even more disheartened. Shortly after we arrived in Kathmandu, eight members of the Indian Navy team successfully summited.

Failure is a relentless, crushing force. It seeps into every corner of your mind, whispering doubts and feeding insecurities until you're left hollow. Back at Everest Base Camp, the weight of our failed summit attempt felt unbearable. The hope and determination that had fuelled us for weeks dissolved into an overwhelming sense of helplessness. Each moment was a replay of what went wrong – every choice and every hesitation dissected endlessly in the quiet of my thoughts. Failure wasn't just a setback; it was a storm that left me battered, forcing me to confront the glaring gap between aspiration and reality.

The worst part was the helplessness – knowing I could do nothing to change the outcome. The mountain was indifferent to my dreams, my efforts and my suffering. The futility of it all weighed more heavily than the physical exhaustion. Each breath at Everest Base Camp had seemed laboured not just from the thin air but from the crushing realisation that we had come so close, only to fall short. Failure had a way of gnawing at me, making even the comfort of the hotel bed in Kathmandu feel undeserved. No meal, conversation or reassurance from loved ones could quiet the gnawing voice inside: What if I had pushed harder? What if I had waited just a little longer?

Failure didn't just hurt; it lingered, forcing me to sit with it, learn from it and, somehow, make peace with its relentless shadow.

In Kathmandu, we were surprised to receive an invitation from Jangbu to have dinner at his home one evening. That night, we met his family, including his children, and his wife prepared a sumptuous meal with Nepali delicacies such as momo for us. As the beer flowed freely, we finally began to relax and speak openly with each other for the first time in almost seven days. Seeing Jangbu at home, surrounded by his family, I started to understand and appreciate his perspective. As we talked, I realised that not leading us to the summit had been a disappointment for him too. But as our lead Sherpa, he believed that his foremost priority was to keep us safe. To him, the success of an expedition wasn't just about reaching the summit – it was about ensuring that everyone returned home safely. In that respect, he had fully succeeded, making decisions that very well might have kept us all alive.

Admittedly, over the past few days, I had resented his role in what I saw as a failed expedition. I had argued with Jangbu and questioned his decisions more than anyone else. That night, I finally found the closure I needed to put this chapter behind me and start looking forward. I was going home defeated but determined to return – and this time, I would reach the top.

PART 3
PERSEVERANCE

15

Resurrection

> Do not judge me by my success, judge me by how many times I fell down and got back up again.
> Nelson Mandela, *Long Walk to Freedom*

Sauraj

In the summer of 2017, we were back home sooner than expected. June is always extremely hot in Pune, and it is a lean period for Adventure Pulse with most of our clients and corporate engagements suspended during the warm months. Sam and I struggled to get back into some semblance of routine, going to our office and looking into the operational side of the business. But our hearts were still in the mountains. I was miserable. I couldn't sleep at night, my mind replaying over and over again the events that had taken place on Everest and asking difficult 'what if' questions. What if we had started for the summit a day later? What if we had not turned back? This mountain and I had unfinished business. I realised that until I returned and successfully reached the top, I wouldn't find peace of mind.

Over a couple of drinks one evening, I confided in Sam about my inability to sleep. Sam shared that he, too, was having trouble coming to terms with things. Like me, he lay awake in bed for hours. Like me, he, too, felt that until we scaled this mountain, an undercurrent of failure would continue to haunt us. Encouraged that we both were on the same page,

I told Sam that I believed we should go back and try again the very next year. Sam wasn't convinced it would be possible for us to raise the ₹70 lakh required, that too with less than a year to go. I had given the financial aspect some thought as well. Raising money would be tougher than ever this time around, but I had come to realise that not being able to summit would continue to gnaw at my soul. I was no longer able to enjoy the comforts of home. The way I saw it, there was no point in owning a house and property if I could not be at peace. As raising money was the major concern, I had made up my mind to sell some land that I owned near Pune. The sale proceeds were unlikely to cover the entire expedition cost, but they would provide a much-needed boost to our fundraising effort.

I could see that Sam was moved by my appeal and agreed that pooling in our personal resources would be a good start. I knew he was still not entirely convinced. He again asked me if I was sure I wanted to sell my property and dip into my personal savings. I reiterated that I was very sure and was even prepared to take a loan if it came to that to make Everest happen. He was increasingly warming up to the notion of trying to go back in 2018 but was still not sure if we could pull it off. Worryingly, he had started talking about how perhaps only one of us should go back to climb Everest if we weren't able to raise enough funds for both of us. I didn't even want to hear about it. We had started this journey together, and I was determined to reach the summit with him. I let the subject drop for the time being, although for both of us, the question of when we were going back occupied most of our waking thoughts.

As it happened, in July, we drove down to Mumbai for work and planned to catch up with Vikas. We met at the Oberoi Mall in Goregaon and were pleasantly surprised to learn that Vikas was as enthusiastic about returning to Everest. He already had some ideas about building a sponsorship proposal, and after quickly dispensing with the pleasantries, we were all soon engrossed in discussing how to make the 2018 expedition happen. We acknowledged that seeking sponsorships would require more persistence than ever. Yet, his positivity was contagious, and I began to see a glimmer of hope. The three of us agreed to have monthly calls to review the progress of our preparation as well as discuss our fitness and training plans. As Sam and I drove back to Pune, we felt more upbeat than we had in the entire preceding month. We talked about our training and altitude acclimatisation plans. I was glad to see that finally Sam had begun to believe we just might be able to make it in 2018.

Both Sam and I had been missing the mountains and were keen to get on with our preparations for Everest. My friend Greg, who had accompanied us on our Elbrus climb, had been wanting to climb again with me for some time. Greg, an avid climber and ultra-marathoner, is a French national, and his hometown is very close to Mont Blanc, the highest peak in France.

In July, I was hosted by Greg and flew out to Lyon. From Lyon, on a Saturday morning, we drove to Chamonix, a popular ski resort in the Alps and the starting point for our Mont Blanc climb. We were going to climb the peak Alpine-style, just the two of us carrying our supplies. Being the highest peak in western Europe, the mountain attracts a large number of climbers and has refuge buildings with dorm-like rooms available to trekkers to rest in. We had started from Lyon on Saturday morning and were at the base of the mountain by 5 PM that same evening. We made good time and, by 6 PM, had reached Refuge 1. Despite the fairly long drive, both Greg and I felt strong and were eager to continue climbing. Instead of spending the night at Refuge 1, we decided to rest for a couple of hours and then resume later the same evening.

We started from Refuge 1 at 11 PM and continued to make good progress, reaching Refuge 2 at 3 AM the next morning. We decided not to halt here and to push for the summit.

But another fifteen–twenty minutes into our climb, the weather turned, and we were pounded with gale-force winds. We continued trekking for some more time despite the storm when Greg, who had climbed Mont Blanc earlier, decided to turn back due to the deteriorating weather. With memories of having had to turn back from the Everest summit only three months ago still fresh in my mind, I was loath to give up on another peak. Mont Blanc was at a relatively lower altitude at 4,800 m compared to the Himalayan peaks I generally climbed in preparation for Everest. The Everest Base Camp itself is at 5,364 m above sea level. With all our climbing experience at 5,000 m and 6,000 m altitudes, often facing inclement weather, I was pretty confident of my ability to summit solo. I also knew that I was unlikely to return to France to climb anytime soon if I turned back now. I took the water bottle and rope from Greg and continued on while Greg headed back to Refuge 2 to rest and wait for me. We agreed to hike back down together from Refuge 2 after I returned from the summit.

The winds continued to rage on, and the temperature dipped below −20°C. The mountain was almost completely deserted with most of the climbers having decided to wait out the storm. This was of slight concern to me since I wasn't familiar with the route, and without Greg accompanying me, this could mean more time spent figuring out the trail. As I scanned the mountain, I spotted two other climbers making their way towards the summit, about five minutes ahead of me. Keeping them in my line of sight, I followed their trail for the next four–five hours.

When I reached the summit later that morning, there were only three climbers at the peak – me and the other two climbers whose trail I had followed. We acknowledged each other with nods as they didn't speak any English. Despite the language barrier, they were able to help me by taking a picture of me at the top of Mont Blanc. I spent some more time at the summit, allowing a wave of contentment to wash over me. This time, as a solo climber, I had felt more in control, having pushed on despite the bad weather, and I was beginning to regain my confidence, which had taken a beating during the 2017 Everest expedition. Climbing down from the peak to Refuge 2, I caught up with Greg, and together we continued to descend. We made it to Refuge 1 later that afternoon and took the train back to Chamonix village. By 11 PM that same night, we were back at Greg's apartment in Lyon.

With Mont Blanc under my belt, I was now raring to go and get on with climbing other peaks. In September, Sam and I were to go back to Ladakh to lead a climb to Stok Kangri, a mountain familiar to both of us. As an added challenge for ourselves, we decided to arrive in Leh ahead of our climbers' group and climb Kang Yatse 2 before their arrival. Standing tall at over 6,000 m, both peaks are known to be difficult climbs. We planned to accomplish them back to back within a span of six days. This is no mean feat and is something akin to running full marathons on successive weekends. Despite being a somewhat audacious target, we were both well prepared to undertake the challenge.

In Leh, we met up with Pasang Sherpa, whom we knew from Nepal, another Everest veteran. Together, we travelled to Chokdo, located near the Hemis Monastery, and onwards to the base of Kang Yatse 2. On the first day, we climbed steadily for ten to eleven hours, crossing the Kongmaru La pass at 5,000 m the same day. It was a busy season at Kang Yatse 2, and we noticed quite a few teams with around twenty-five other mountaineers climbing towards the summit. In the distance, Kang Yatse's twin peak Dzo Jongo gleamed invitingly in the sunlight. Very few climbers attempt Dzo Jongo, and seeing how crowded Kang Yatse 2 was that year, after a quick team consultation, we decided to quit the trail and climb Dzo Jongo instead. Speaking to a few Sherpas familiar with the terrain, we identified the face we would be climbing and made our way towards the point that would serve as our base camp for Dzo Jongo.

We set up camp with three of us in a single tent, rested for some time and then began the climb from the base camp at 10:30 PM We could see the summit up ahead. As we walked further, we realised we had not accounted for the snow conditions. With no other climbers, we had to open up the route ourselves, navigating through deep, untrodden snow reaching up to our knees and even thighs in many places. We made slow progress, struggling to find our foothold, sinking into the softly yielding ground below us. We trudged on in these conditions until 3 AM at which point Sam noticed that his shoes were completely drenched in ice-cold water. In temperatures as low as −10°C and −12°C, we knew that this meant a very real risk of frostbite, which has cost many mountaineers life and limb. With no clear idea of how far we were from the summit, disappointing as it was, we knew that Sam had to turn back towards the shelter of base camp immediately and get out of his wet shoes.

Having come so far, Pasang Sherpa and I decided to continue. It was a clear, dark night, and we were surprised when, after just another hour of climbing, we reached the top. After Dzo Jongo, Sam and I successfully summited Stok Kangri with our group of climbers less than a week later. Although Sam was a bit disappointed at having had to turn back so close to the summit at Dzo Jongo, completing Stok Kangri helped boost our morale tremendously.

After a quick stopover at Delhi, where I met with my family who were happy to note our confidence and preparedness to take on Everest, we were back in Pune by the end of September. The good cheer after our success in Ladakh was short-lived. Our hearts sank as soon as we were back in Pune and we realised that with less than five months to go for our expedition, we were far off our funds target with no significant sponsorship offers yet.

The lack of funds was especially demotivating for Sam, who once more proposed that perhaps only one of us should go for Everest this time. I knew that Sam was right, but I was not prepared to talk about this just yet. In the meantime, we started looking at consolidating some of our earnings from Adventure Pulse and began the process of applying for personal loans. While I had been trying my best to appease Sam's fears, the months sped past. By December, with still no significant movement on the funding front, I was beginning to get very anxious.

Early on in our monthly planning calls with Vikas, we briefly considered climbing Everest's north face – that is, from Tibet. While the expenses incurred and difficulty levels are pretty much the same in approaching the summit from either side, in the last couple of years, we had noticed more successful expeditions completed from the north side. In 2014, for instance, when the avalanche at the Khumbu Icefall claimed the lives of many Sherpas and conclusively put an end to most expeditions from Nepal, there had been no impact on the north in Tibet, and many expeditions reached the peak successfully. Once again, in 2017, when the weather conditions on the south face had put a spanner in the works of the dreams of so many mountaineers, including ourselves, conditions on the north side had remained stable. A big factor in favour of approaching Everest from Tibet is the absence of the deadly Khumbu Icefall.

In the end, though, we decided to climb the south face from Nepal, given our familiarity with the terrain and our experience of reaching Camp 4, which constitutes almost 75 per cent of the entire expedition. In taking on the formidable peak, this experience gave us a significant leg-up. Despite being different routes to the same summit, the experience of climbing from each face is so dissimilar that, from the climber's perspective, they could be two different mountains altogether. The only point of convergence for the two routes is the summit itself.

Another change from previous years that we agreed on was to engage a professional company called Satori Adventures to manage our 2018 expedition instead of our previous attempts to organise it ourselves. Once we had decided to climb from the south face again, our unanimous choice was to hire a professional Nepalese company to coordinate the logistics of the expedition.

Satori Adventures was a relatively new company, but over the years, they had built an excellent track record of successful expeditions, which we had witnessed first hand. At Camp 4 in 2017, right before we had to make the difficult call of turning back, I visited this team's camp. There I learnt that they would be staying on for another night to wait for the weather to improve, having planned for just such an eventuality. They were meticulously well-organised with the provisions and logistical support needed to stay longer if required. I was also impressed by their Sherpas' calmness under pressure.

We had been in discussions with them for the 2018 expedition since October 2017, and in December, we had to start making payments to them as per the agreed schedule so that they could initiate the process of procuring the permits and making other logistical arrangements. We paid them an initial advance, advising them that this payment was provisional for either two or three climbers – in the event that we were later able to arrange funds for only two of us instead of three, either Sam or I, plus Vikas. By 15 January, they were following up relentlessly with us to confirm and pay the next instalment as per the payment schedule as applying for the climbing permits needs to be initiated well in advance. We continued to negotiate with them for more time, and finally, they agreed to defer payment by another month and wait for our confirmation on the number of climbers. Even with the deferment, we knew our position was precarious. It was beginning to look like, between Sam and me, only one of us could make the 2018 expedition.

16

Summiting Possibilities and Unexpected Alliances

> You have to take risks. We only understand the miracle
> of life fully when we allow the unexpected to happen.
> Paulo Coelho, *By the River Piedra I Sat Down
> and Wept* (translated by Alan R. Clarke)

Sauraj

At Adventure Pulse, it was business as usual. Work couldn't stop just because we were close to a crisis mode. In the cooler winter months, our local hikes and expeditions had picked up pace, and we both often accompanied a few of the group treks in the Western Ghats. During one of these treks, we were joined by Sejal Firodia, wife of Prasan Firodia, managing director of Force Motors, and her two children. As we walked alongside her, we got talking, and Sam and I spoke about how we also led groups of trekkers to Everest Base Camp. She was very keen to know more and asked us a lot of questions. We shared some of the details of the treks we organised and specifically about the Everest Base Camp trek. A few days later, she once again reached out to us for another hike, along with their eleven-year-old twin boys who also enjoy the outdoors. Once more, we spoke about

Everest Base Camp, and this time, Mrs Firodia expressed an interest in planning this for her family with us.

Two weeks later, we received a call from Mrs Firodia, who invited us over to her residence to discuss more about the Nepal trek. She mentioned that her husband, Prasan Firodia, would also be joining us. Sam and I arrived at their bungalow at the appointed time and were greeted warmly. Some time later, Mr Prasan also joined us and showed a keen interest in understanding more about Adventure Pulse and our plans for their Nepal trek. We showed him some of the pictures of our expeditions in Nepal, and soon, we started talking about the details and the logistics involved in planning the trip. Over the next few weeks, we worked very closely with them, going over all the trip details.

Sejal and Prasan Firodia were both keen trekkers. By January 2018, it was decided that we would lead Mr Prasan, Mrs Sejal Firodia and their two sons on the Everest View trek. In one of our conversations with Mrs Firodia, she asked us if that we planned to climb Mt Everest ourselves. We told her our story about our failed attempts in 2015 and 2017, and also that while we were keen to go back and try again in April, given the financial constraints we were facing, it seemed unlikely that we would be able to make it. She was extremely moved and empathetic towards our predicament and suggested that since Force Motors supports sportspeople from various fields, we should share our sponsorship proposal with them. For us, this was a welcome ray of hope. As soon as we were back in our office, we sent out our sponsorship proposal to Mrs Firodia. A few days later, as we were concluding another meeting with Prasan Firodia, Sam spoke up. It was 12:30 AM, and Sam asked him if he could talk to him for another five minutes. Despite the late hour, he graciously acquiesced and heard us out. In the next two minutes, Sam detailed our Everest story and then made a strong pitch, highlighting the salient points of our sponsorship proposal. Mr Firodia asked us how much we needed to make it happen and then, giving us the details of the Force Motors marketing head, asked us to send him our proposal. We were now beginning to feel cautiously optimistic, but as the days passed and we had still not heard from the marketing team, we tried not to get our hopes up too much.

In mid-January, Sam and I were both out of town. I was leading a Chadar trek group in Ladakh, and Sam was in Africa, leading a group of twenty climbers up Mt Kilimanjaro. The trek to Kilimanjaro, a first of its kind, was a huge success for Adventure Pulse, and we received a fair bit of media coverage for being the largest Indian contingent to climb the highest mountain in Africa. For the most part of those two weeks, neither Sam nor I had network coverage. On the morning of 25 January, I was in Leh when I got a call from Cyriac Jacob, the head of the marketing team at Force Motors, asking if either of us could come down to their office the next day. I explained that I had a group of fifteen trekkers with me in Ladakh for the Chadar trek and that I would be able to come down and meet them only the following week.

The entire week, I was wracked with anxiety, hoping that our unavailability had not cost us the sponsorship. I even considered heading back to Pune from Leh immediately but then decided to complete the trek first so as not to let down the group I was accompanying. In the first week of February, as soon as I was back in Pune, I went down to the Force Motors office for a meeting with the marketing team. Mr Jacob himself, a very well-respected industry stalwart, was at this meeting with the rest of his team, and I was quite nervous going into the discussion. All my apprehensions were quickly dispelled once I met the team and especially Mr Jacob, who was not only very helpful but genuinely invested in the success of our expedition. The team even helped us go over and refine the sponsorship proposal.

We had a series of discussions around the public relations campaign, tying in the sponsorship proposal with their Himalayan Trails campaign for the Force Motors Gurkha SUV brand. We accepted sponsorship from them in exchange for giving them the expedition naming rights. We would be representing the company as the Force Motors Everest Expedition. With the Force Motors sponsorship, we had raised enough money to comfortably cover the expenses of one climber. Feeling much more positive, we diverted some of the Adventure Pulse profits, put in our own savings and finally applied for a personal loan to cover the shortfall. It was March by the time the sponsorship money and the loan finally came through, with just a few weeks to go before we left for Nepal once again.

Meanwhile, Vikas, too, had been able to raise funds just in time for the 2018 expedition, partly through some sponsorships and the rest by investing his personal savings. With everything finally falling into place, we heaved a sigh of relief. Having gone through long periods of uncertainty, we had more than once almost given up hope of finding the necessary funding. Still, all three of us had managed to keep up with our training and preparation. On 1 April 2018, Sam and I headed to Nepal from Pune with the Firodia family. We would lead them on the Everest View trek until 10 April after which they would fly back from Lukla and we would continue on to base camp for our Everest expedition. In the preceding fortnight, everything for our expedition had miraculously fallen into place. Yet, this time around, for both Sam and me, the stakes were even higher. This was our third attempt, and there was immense pressure on us to reach the top. We were glad, therefore, to have the Firodia family with us in those first few days in Nepal, their enthusiasm and positivity helping us overcome our fears of reaching the summit.

The trek with the Firodias turned out to be a memorable experience for us even though we had been trekking in this region for years. The Firodias had generously booked rooms for us to stay with them at the luxurious Hotel Everest View, which we normally never book for ourselves. A beautiful property built by the Japanese in 1970, the hotel overlooks Mt Everest, offering guests breathtaking views of the world's highest mountain. On our Everest Base Camp group treks, we frequently bring our trekkers here for coffee and to take in the view, but this was the first time we were actually staying in the hotel. Over the next few days, as we spent time with Mr and Mrs Firodia and the kids, relaxing in the comfort of the world's highest-placed luxury hotel, I could feel the vestiges of the tension and stress of the past year melt away. We were here, looking out of the picture windows at the imposing vistas of Mt Everest. I felt quietly confident. I was beginning to feel certain that in about two months, we would be standing at the top of the world.

17

In the Shadow of Everest: A New Odyssey Begins

> It is not the mountain we conquer, but ourselves.
> Sir Edmund Hillary, *High Adventure*

Sam

Standing beside the ancient monastery of Tengboche, Sauraj and I watched the Firodias' departing helicopter vanish into the distant Kathmandu skies. For them, their journey had come to a successful end, but for us, the adventure was only just beginning. The last few days of travelling with them through the pine and rhododendron forests of the lower Khumbu Valley had been an amazing experience and, in many ways, a busy distraction from the daunting expedition that lay ahead. As the helicopter became a tiny speck against the backdrop of colossal, snow-clad peaks, I began to realise the harsh reality of why we were here: to resume the pursuit of our quest for Everest.

Unlike the fervour of our previous Everest attempts, we embraced this expedition with cautious optimism and an underlying sense of apprehension. In addition to the understandable burden of accountability to family and friends (who had financially supported us in our past attempts), this time we also had a sponsor. The fact that this would be our third attempt, coupled with the pressure to fulfil our commitment

A steep ice wall between Camp 1 and Camp 2

The team between Camp 1 and Camp 2 in the Western Cwm

Camp 2 with Lhotse in the background

Tents on an incline at Camp 3

Climbers approaching the Yellow Band, a well-known feature between Camp 3 and Camp 4

The team climbing the Lhotse wall

Camp 3 in the distance, as seen from a point on the Lhotse wall

Sauraj after crossing the Geneva Spur, approaching Camp 4, as the summit of Mt Everest towers in the background

The team approaching Camp 4

Sauraj (*left*), Vikas (*centre*) and Sam (*right*) at Camp 4 on supplementary oxygen waiting for the winds to reduce

Sauraj (*left*) and Sam (*right*) at Camp 4 at 8000 m, right after taking the decision to retreat down to safety and give up the summit attempt in 2017

An oxygen stash at the Balcony at 8400 m

Climbers crossing the South Summit towards the final summit of
Mt Everest, 2018

The final ridge to the summit of Mt Everest as seen from the South Summit

Samir Patham (*left*), Sauraj Jhingan (*right*) and Vikas Dimri (*centre*) hoisting the Indian flag at the summit of Mt Everest on 18 May 2018

to Force Motors as the title sponsor, left no doubt as to how high the stakes were. We were putting everything on the line, not just the future of Adventure Pulse and our reputation but also, once again, our lives.

As the sun ascended above the peaks, thawing the morning chill from the crisp mountain air, we slung our rucksacks across our backs and trekked back to Namche Bazaar, anticipating the arrival of the Satori expedition team. It was 10 April, and we found ourselves three days ahead of our schedule, a rare luxury that afforded us time to rest and acclimatise comfortably at 3,400 m. Amidst the tranquillity of this picturesque mountain village, we aimed to find solace, allowing ourselves to mentally and spiritually prepare before the expedition unfolded. Little did we know how distant this peace would remain.

An old saying claims, 'An idle mind is the devil's workshop.' This adage was proven true as we spent the following day in endless discussions about past setbacks and fretting over worst-case scenarios. The charming Tibetan shops and inviting Italian cafés of Namche Bazaar held no allure as we drowned in our apprehensions and fears. By the next day, a pervasive sense of despair engulfed us. Memories of avalanches, storms at 8,000 m, shattered knees and broken backs haunted us, intensifying the ominous feelings of what fate might have in store for us.

Our escape from the looming shadows of disaster arrived in the most unexpected guise. Our pause in Namche Bazaar coincided with the return of one of our small trekking groups from the Gokyo Lakes. Bursting with delight, they insisted on a celebration, and we found ourselves, quite surprisingly, perched at the counter of our cherished haven, The Irish Pub in Namche Bazaar.

As we shared tales of our trekking and climbing escapades, the group's wide-eyed fascination mirrored their unbridled enthusiasm. They were captivated, hanging on to our every word. Urging us to join them in a drink – a simple pleasure we'd refrained from during the six months of rigorous training – they cheered to their triumphs and our shared joy.

Whether it was the ambience of the bar, the brilliant company or just the spirits consumed, for that moment, we shed our doubts and enjoyed the thrill of being alive. Who knew what the future had in store for us? But for the moment, we were in the middle of the Himalayas, setting forth on another incredible adventure.

The following evening, nestled in the warm confines of the Namche Bakery and enveloped in the aroma of freshly baked bread, we noticed the expedition team passing by the window, led by Mingma Tenzi Sherpa. Stepping outside, I greeted them, eager to familiarise myself with the team and alleviate my apprehension about climbing with strangers. Among the team members, the sole familiar face was Kuntal Joisher, who had faced the avalanche alongside us in 2015. He had returned in 2016 to successfully climb Everest and was now leading a team to attempt Lhotse, the world's fourth-highest peak.

Given that both Everest and Lhotse shared much of the climbing route, we anticipated spending the next forty-five to sixty days in shared quarters at Everest Base Camp. Initial introductions were made, but with a large accompanying trekking group, it was challenging to discern the climbers from the trekkers. We hoped for more opportunities in the coming days to acquaint ourselves with their climbing team. However, our chance to do so was delayed as we opted to stay in separate teahouses owned by our friends along the trek route to Everest Base Camp.

As Sauraj and I journeyed up the valley at an unhurried pace, our path intertwined once more with Melanie Barnett Southworth. Fondly known as Mel, she had returned to the Everest Valley, this time as a trek leader for a team comprising

Afghan war veterans from the Canadian Army under the guidance of the renowned climber and mentor Peter Hillary (son of Sir Edmund Hillary, the first man to summit Everest). We had maintained regular contact with Mel over the years, and it was delightful to enjoy her company during these days of trekking towards Everest Base Camp. In the tranquil setting of our teahouse in Deboche, she introduced us to her trekking group, and together, we shared our experiences of dealing with the aftermath of the Everest avalanche. For many of these veterans, this trek marked a poignant journey of self-healing and reconciliation with the trauma they endured during the war.

Encountering Peter Hillary in the same room was nothing short of a momentous occasion for me. An incredibly accomplished mountaineer and philanthropist, Peter Hillary has devoted a lifetime to continuing the extraordinary legacy established by his father, Sir Edmund Hillary, in both mountaineering and the 'Himalayan Trust', dedicated to aiding the people of Nepal. I found it surreal that he moved around the room, engaging with the group, right before my eyes. Despite spending the entire evening with Sauraj psyching ourselves up to approach and greet him, our nerves got the better of us. The fear of making a fool of myself if I attempted to talk to him held me back. As dawn broke the next morning, I watched his team depart, filled with profound regret at having missed the chance to meet a living legend.

Upon reaching Deboche, we found ourselves joining the Satori team once more. This was more due to a lack of alternatives than any desire to appear sociable. We were acquainted with the three climbers accompanying Kuntal, only to realise they were part of the Lhotse expedition. Sylvine and Caroline hailed from Quebec, the French province of Canada, and had previously climbed Manaslu alongside Kuntal. Joining them was Brijesh Sharma, an Indian Everester and esteemed ultra-marathoner who preferred the moniker 'Breeze'. While Brijesh remained reserved, Sylvine and Caroline exuded warmth. Despite English not being their primary language, they made consistent efforts to engage with us in conversation, exchanging playful banter and jokes.

Initially bewildered by the size of the team, we discovered the expedition comprised four climbers for Lhotse and six for Everest. Alongside us, some climbers were already stationed at Everest Base Camp, while others lingered in Kathmandu. The magnitude of this combined expedition was becoming apparent, seeming vast and somewhat unwieldy. Despite relinquishing some of our independence by joining Satori, we clung to the hope of leveraging their expertise and logistical support, particularly crucial above 8,000 m in the 'Death Zone'. Only time would reveal the implications of this pivotal decision to opt for a commercial operator over organising our expedition independently.

Two days later, bidding farewell to the tranquil village of Deboche, we ascended the valley, leaving the tree line far below at 4,500 m. Sparse clusters of juniper stubbornly clung to the rugged Himalayan terrain. Traversing the Thukla Pass, we paused briefly to honour the memorials of Everest climbers, pressing on beneath the imposing shadow of Lobuche Peak. Glancing upward, I discerned faint silhouettes of climbers descending from the summit. In a matter of days, that would be us, climbing Lobuche Peak as an integral part of our acclimatisation strategy to gain height and reduce our exposure to the dangers of the Khumbu Icefall.

Our night's rest awaited us in the settlement of Lobuche, named after the peak itself. At 4,900 m, it wasn't quite a village but rather a settlement of teahouses bustling only during the trekking season. As we entered Lobuche, luck brought us face to face with Mel once more. Her warm embrace and invitation for dinner at their lodge thrilled us. Swiftly changing into fresh attire, we expressed apologies to Mingma and made our way to the Oxygen Lodge in Lobuche. Another delightful evening unfolded, swapping tales with military veterans and gleaning valuable insights from their experiences.

Later, huddled at a table with Mel over hot chocolate, we were startled by a composed, gentle voice asking, 'May I join you?' We looked up and saw, with a shock, Peter Hillary pulling up a chair and taking a seat across the table with his cup of coffee. Mel chuckled at our flustered reaction and swiftly introduced us, recounting our past encounter during the Everest 2015 expedition and the subsequent avalanche. Once we overcame our star-struck awe, conversation flowed. For nearly an hour, Peter shared stories from various mountain expeditions. As the evening waned, his keen inquiries led us to admit our insecurities about our experience in relation to Everest. As we sat in embarrassment, he looked at us with a smile and said, 'That's unusual, because the way I look at it, you probably have the most experience on the mountain compared to any other aspirant. You've already reached 8,000 m. You have only 900 m more to go.' We looked at him in complete bewilderment. His words struck a chord, reminding us of an overlooked truth. That evening was one of the most surreal experiences of our lives and a definitive turning point in our enthusiasm and motivation to climb Everest – an invaluable personal endorsement from Peter Hillary.

On 14 April, we re-entered Everest Base Camp, reclaiming our 'home away from home' in this unique and remote habitat. The campsite felt unusually crowded with a multitude of climbers and support personnel. Takeshi Nakayama, a thirty-year-old Japanese climber embarking on his maiden Everest ascent, warmly welcomed us as we walked into camp. Despite lacking experience above 6,000 m, Takeshi's exceptional fitness, evident in his lean physique, allowed him to effortlessly match our pace during subsequent forays up the mountain. With his limited English proficiency, we often found ourselves interpreting Mingma Sherpa's instructions for him, thus forging an unexpected friendship along the way. Sauraj, with his protective nature, swiftly took Takeshi under his wing, offering guidance and camaraderie, especially as this was his first attempt to scale Everest.

Takeshi appreciated the companionship, particularly as he struggled to communicate with Wojtek Gawron, the Polish climber also stationed at Everest Base Camp. Our brief encounter with Wojtek during lunch at the dining tent revealed his reserved nature, primarily attributed to his limited English proficiency rather than any innate disposition. This being Wojtek's second Everest attempt, he harboured a distinct approach to the climb, evident in his self-sufficient expedition. Accompanied by his own Sherpa, Phurba Sherpa, and following a personalised acclimatisation plan, Wojtek operated almost independently. Consequently, our interactions with him over the following days remained limited.

Life settled into a rhythm at Everest Base Camp as we gradually familiarised ourselves with fellow climbers, accommodating each other's habits and idiosyncrasies. Building this camaraderie was essential to avoid friction in the future, when waiting for an uncertain summit window could result in agitation and constant irritation. The sheer size of this expedition team stationed at Everest Base Camp was still overwhelming, and I struggled to adjust to it.

On 17 April 2018, under a bright sun and brilliant weather, we had our base camp pooja ceremony. Mingma had taken great pains to ensure that this was a very special event. The pooja ceremony was conducted by the lama from Pangboche and accompanied by several traditional musical drums and trumpets to complement the recitation of Buddhist prayers.

Our ceremony was also attended by the liaison officers from the Nepal ministry who were at Everest Base Camp, along with the doctors from the Everest ER clinic. After the customary blessing of the Sherpas, climbers and all the equipment, there was a huge celebration in the camp. The colourful prayer flags hoisted over the entire camp beautifully complemented the overall merriment and bonhomie of the day, marking an auspicious beginning to the climbing season and hopefully a successful expedition.

18

Unpredictable Paths

> History unfolds itself by strange and unpredictable paths. We have little control over the future; and none at all over the past.
> Winston Churchill, *The Second World War*

Sam

On 19 April, we found ourselves heading back down the valley in our attempt to climb Lobuche Peak. Here, we met Vikas, who had been making his way up the Khumbu Valley. Though delayed due to work commitments, Vikas was finally back, and it felt good to have our team together again.

An unexpected addition to our group was Ricky Singh, an Indian settled in America, whose climbing aspirations aligned with ours, or so we thought. Surprisingly, Ricky had diverged from our Everest quest, aiming only for Everest Camp 2 as a preliminary step. His strategy to navigate the Khumbu Icefall on a reconnaissance mission this year rather than via another peak was a bold yet intriguing move, drawing interest for its directness and single-minded focus on climbing Everest. In this way, he could gain elevation and build the experience of actually climbing Everest without the exorbitant expense of undertaking a full Everest expedition.

As we had done in the past, we were attempting to acclimatise to a height of 6,000 m (roughly the same height as Camp 1) without actually going through the Khumbu

Icefall, thereby also avoiding the dangers of the constantly shifting ice on the glacier. Lobuche Peak, standing at a height of 6,119 m, provided us with the perfect opportunity to do so. It would also be a testing ground, allowing Mingma and the Sherpas to assess our skills and to give the team an opportunity to work together. The four Lhotse climbers, namely Kuntal, Caroline, Sylvine and Brijesh, were joined by our Everest team, which comprised primarily Sauraj, Vikas, Takeshi and me. The Polish climber, Wojtek, had chosen to stay on at Everest Base Camp and climb through the Khumbu Icefall later as part of his acclimatisation plan, rather than expend energy on Lobuche Peak. The climb went brilliantly well as we powered up the steep slopes, holding our own and egging each other up the mountain.

On 20 April, we reached the summit of Lobuche, and over a cup of hot tea from our thermos flask, we stood on the top and patiently listened to Mingma point out the distinct features of the climbing routes for both Everest and Lhotse from one of the best vantage points in the entire valley. We returned to Everest Base Camp two days later, brimming with confidence. Witnessing the strength of our team and the success of attaining the summit of Lobuche had done wonders for our morale. I was especially happy to see the ease with which Takeshi had been able to keep up with Vikas, Sauraj and me, despite it being our first climb together. On our return to camp, we learnt that Phurba Sherpa had taken Wojtek and even Ricky up to Camp 1 as part of their rotation. I could see that this was a surprise even to Mingma, but he accepted it without any resentment, maintaining his usual calm demeanour.

As we settled into Everest Base Camp, we took the opportunity to meet some of the other climbers in the neighbouring teams. In the last few years, due to our frequent Everest attempts, we had developed a good sense of who the other climbers were on the mountain. We crossed over the moraine separating the camps and dropped by to visit Bhagwan Chawale, who was also back this year to complete his Everest aspirations from 2017. During his attempt the previous year, he had tried for the summit a few days after us, reaching all the way up to the South Summit at 8,748 m before strong winds forced him to turn back. In his team was Sangeeta Sindhi Bahl, who was also attempting to climb Everest for the second time after 2017. If she were successful this year, she would be the oldest woman from India to have reached the summit of Everest. Appreciating their company, we would often stop by their camp to say hello or enjoy a cup of tea, a pleasant distraction during our period of rest and acclimatisation.

The success of the Lobuche climb, the friendly nature of the camp staff and the brilliant weather over the next few days had lulled us into a false sense of security. However, Everest has a cruel way of reminding you of the ever-present danger lurking just below the surface. Once again, on 25 April, disaster struck. A massive ice serac in the Khumbu Icefall collapsed during the early hours of the morning, grievously injuring two Sherpas. One of the injured, Dawa Sherpa, was part of our Everest team and suffered serious head trauma despite wearing his helmet. Due to his injuries, he had to be immediately evacuated to Kathmandu for treatment. His departure cast a shadow over the mood of our entire camp. Having seen this sudden ferocity of Everest in the past, we were once again reminded never to underestimate this extremely hostile environment.

This reality was further reinforced when Ricky returned with Phurba Sherpa to Everest Base Camp from their rotation at Camp 1. Ricky had developed a chest congestion known as the Khumbu cough due to the cold, dry air and was having trouble breathing normally without coughing. I would often lie in my tent, listening to his bouts of coughing through the entire night. Wojtek, who was in a much worse condition, was forced to take a medical helicopter evacuation from Camp 2 back to Kathmandu. Having decided to push further up to Camp 2, Wojtek had stayed at high altitude longer than Ricky and Phurba Sherpa, hoping to accelerate his body's adaptation to the environment. However, he had not been able to acclimatise to the higher altitude and had progressively become extremely weak. On his return to Camp 2, his condition deteriorated further, and eventually, he had to call off his expedition. For Wojtek, this marked his second departure from Everest without reaching the summit.

On 27 April, Mingma Tenzi Sherpa led our four-member Everest team and the Lhotse team through the Khumbu Icefall up to Camp 1. Phurba Sherpa, after being relieved of his responsibilities with Wojtek, joined our group of eight climbers for this rotation while other Sherpas worked on the logistics of higher camps. The icefall doctors' route through the Khumbu Icefall was marvellously set this year, guiding us across high seracs, narrow snow bridges and deep crevasses. Though precarious and a vigorous test of our technical skills, the crossing was faster than all our previous expeditions. Takeshi was able to comfortably keep up with us, much to our relief, firmly establishing his technical climbing credentials on the mountain.

Favourable weather allowed us to progress further up the mountain, spending days at Camp 2 and even climbing up to Camp 3 for acclimatisation. Being part of a larger team meant opportunities for engaging conversations and competitive sessions of Uno with Sylvine, Caroline, Kuntal, Vikas and Takeshi. At those altitudes, we often crossed paths with Bhagwan and Sangeeta Bahl, offering moments for chats over steaming cups of chai at 6,500 m above sea level.

After five days at high altitude, we returned to Everest Base Camp on 1 May, having acclimatised well to the higher camps. Everest Base Camp now welcomed us with comforts unimaginable at the higher camps – warm dining tents, private sleeping areas and the chance for a hot bath. As we recovered over the next few days, I was impressed by each climber's performance and their rapid recovery. The expedition had been progressing smoothly in terms of our physical and mental readiness. But I knew from experience that the hardest part lay ahead: waiting for the summit window.

Mingma Tenzi Sherpa, as the expedition sirdar, meticulously checked all logistics, ensuring oxygen and food provisions at the higher camps. We frequently checked in with Mingma, particularly about the availability of extra oxygen tanks at Camp 4 in case we needed to wait for forty-eight hours before the summit window. His calm assurance, often followed by, 'No worry, Dai. I also with you at Camp 4', significantly boosted our confidence, knowing Mingma would be there with us.

Next was the allocation of Sherpas to each climber. Mingma introduced Dawa Temba, Pemba Tashi and Lakpa Tenzi as part of the Everest support team that would assist us from Camp 4 to the summit. Although the Sherpa team would aid with the load ferrying during the final push, reaching 8,000 m was our own responsibility. The shortage of one Sherpa climber due to the accident concerned us slightly, but Mingma assured us that he would address it if necessary by requesting someone to join us from Kathmandu. Meanwhile, Brijesh announced that Phurba Sherpa would be his personal Sherpa for his Lhotse expedition, which seemed to cause some tension within the Sherpa team, although I paid it little mind. As we prepared our gear for the summit push, our main concerns were the route opening to the summit and the weather window. Typically, the Everest route opens between 11 May and 16 May, followed by the Lhotse route. About a week before the expected opening, instead of waiting around at Everest Base

Camp, I urged Sauraj and Vikas to descend with me to the treeline for further recovery, similar to what we did in 2017. Takeshi was eager to descend, but Sauraj was hesitant given the Lhotse team's decision to stay in camp.

On 4 May 2018, our Everest team – Sauraj, Vikas, Takeshi and I – departed Everest Base Camp, descending the valley to Pheriche for an overnight halt. The next day, as we continued to Deboche at 3,650 m, seeking solace in the Rivendell Lodge within the dense rhododendron forest, an eerie sense of impending challenge settled on us. The oxygen-rich air was a temporary respite, a brief pause before the storm.

Our refuge at Deboche was abruptly disrupted by a call from Everest Base Camp. Reports spoke of improved weather conditions higher up, hinting that the Lhotse team might forge ahead. Lingering rumours whispered of the route to the summit of Lhotse opening before Everest, which was very rare. This compelled us to hastily pack and ascend the valley on 8 May.

That night at Pheriche, the darkness seemed more menacing, haunted by memories that refused to fade. Startled awake by a thunderous storm, my heart raced, fear gripping my chest. The echoes of past avalanches and storms mingled with the rolling thunder, shaking the very core of my being. When morning broke, the landscape had been transformed, shrouded by a thick blanket of snow – an absurd blend of winter in the heart of summer.

Pressing on, we halted for the night at Lobuche, the air thick with an unsettling anticipation. Reaching Everest Base Camp on 10 May, our elation upon arrival swiftly dissipated in the eerie silence that blanketed our camp. The absence of familiar sounds – the bustling energy of climbers and staff – left an unsettling void, a prelude to the unknown.

Sauraj's urgent call to Rishi Bhandari in Kathmandu, the owner of the expedition company, gave only partial clarity.

The Everest Sherpas were redirected to bolster the Lhotse expedition, set to attempt a summit by 14 May. This update left us feeling abandoned, to say the least. Though we were assured that the Sherpas would rendezvous with us at Camp 2, led by Mingma, we could not shake the feeling of yet another expedition spiralling out of control. The fog of uncertainty and the lack of communication cast an ominous shroud over Vikas and me. Takeshi, frustrated by the language barrier, was caught in the confusion as he attempted to grasp the unnerving conversations. For Sauraj, the sense of déjà vu fuelled his anger, which added to the palpable tension. Amid this, we sensed a creeping dread, understanding that these looming days would demand more than our patience – testing our resolve in ways we never foresaw.

19

The Western Cwm Beckons

The oldest and strongest emotion of mankind is fear. And the oldest and strongest kind of fear is fear of the unknown.

H.P. Lovecraft, 'Supernatural Horror in Literature'

Sam

I opened my eyes to complete darkness, escaping what was, at best, a fitful sleep. It was a few minutes before 2 AM, an early hour (even for me), but I felt alert and ready to take on the new day. After months on the glacier and multiple rotations on an unforgiving mountain, 14 May 2018 had finally brought with it our long-awaited summit push. At last, we were leaving Everest Base Camp for the summit. A heady mix of trepidation and excitement had left me little room for rest, and sleep had chosen to evade me for most of the night. I could hear Sauraj and Vikas restlessly tossing in their tents through half the night as well and knew that I was not alone.

I braced myself against the bitter cold as I crawled out of the warm cocoon of my sleeping bag, reaching for the small solar-powered lamp that stood stoically on the tent floor beside me. My breath fogged up as it met the torch's white beam of light, and I shivered involuntarily, my body struggling against the sub-zero temperatures inside the tent. When my head accidentally brushed the roof, I was showered with a flurry of tiny icicles. What had once filled me with wonder – this incredible white layer of ice forming nightly on the inner roof of the tent due to the rapid condensation of our breath – had by then lost its novelty, leaving me largely indifferent to the phenomenon.

Despite the frigid temperature, I resisted the urge to retreat into the seductive warmth of my sleeping bag, opting instead to meticulously prepare my gear. In the quiet privacy of my tent, I patiently dressed, layering each piece of clothing like a suit of armour – the only defence I had against the elements. I then reorganised my bag, committing the position and order of each item to memory, carefully weighing its importance against its weight and potential utility on the climb. I knew without a doubt that every hundred grams would feel like a kilogram. Once I had completed my preparations, I steadily laced up my boots and donned my climbing equipment, finding a sense of meditative calm in this familiar process that I had repeated countless times before. In these moments before a summit attempt, I often felt like a gladiator preparing for battle before stepping into the Colosseum. The parallels were always clear to me; though our arena was far larger, a single misstep could, much like in ancient times, mean the difference between life and death.

An hour later, Sauraj, Vikas and I stood in a silent circle around the makeshift altar at the centre of our camp, patiently waiting for Takeshi and Lakpa Sherpa. Words felt unnecessary. The three of us had been here before, at this defining moment in our quest for Everest. Now, exactly one year later, we were once again setting out from Everest Base Camp before dawn, preparing for our summit push in the endeavour to stand on top of the world. There were no guarantees of a successful summit or any illusions of grandeur this time, for that matter even over life and death – just an acute awareness of the moment and a touch of cautious optimism.

At 3:30 AM, along with Takeshi, we followed Lakpa Sherpa out of Everest Base Camp into the Khumbu Icefall. It was eerily quiet, barring the sound of the inexorable ice crunching under our boots. Up ahead, we could see flickering lights, twinkling in the glacier like stars, emanating from the torches of climbers who had set out a few hours before us. As we reached the fixed ropes, the four of us kept up with Lakpa Sherpa rather effortlessly, dogging his every step so that we could get through the icefall as fast as possible. Our destination for the day was Camp 2 (6,450 m), nestled at the foot of the Lhotse wall, promising a long, arduous day of climbing. Along the way, we briefly caught up with Sangeeta Bahl, exchanged pleasantries and then pushed ahead, weaving our way through the maze of ice walls and crevasses.

As darkness gradually gave way to the grey of dawn, we crested the final massive crevasse and caught sight of the yellow tents of Camp 1 (6,100 m), strategically perched at the top of the Khumbu Icefall. We had completed this section in a remarkable three and a half hours – a record time by any standard – reassuring us that we were well conditioned to the altitude. After a brief stop for snacks and water, we were ready to push through the Western Cwm toward Camp 2. I was eager to traverse this section before the day's heat turned the vast snow-covered basin into a giant solar cooker. As we prepared to move on, Lakpa suddenly expressed a desire to rest a bit longer as he was feeling a little tired and wanted to have a cup of hot tea at one of the camps. Since Lakpa had just been flown into Everest Base Camp two days before as a replacement Sherpa, we did not really know him well enough to merit a longer discussion. He asked if we were comfortable going ahead without him, and after assuring him we were, we set out on our own. However, this did add to our concerns, especially as we were moving from Camp 1 to Camp 2 on the highest mountain in the world without guided support.

The trek through the Western Cwm was a long, flat and seemingly never-ending slog. The sun's reflection off the snow was like that of a polished mirror, making the featureless crossing even more arduous. Sauraj and Takeshi arrived at Camp 2 first, and within twenty minutes, Vikas and I reached our tents as well. As we entered the camp, our team of Sherpas greeted us. They had been staying here for the past few days, assisting the Lhotse expedition team. By 12 PM, we had gathered in the kitchen tent, sipping on a well-deserved cup of tea and catching up on news about the progress of our Lhotse team. However, this news was far from promising.

As the famous adage goes, 'The best-laid plans of mice and men often go awry', and so it seemed that our fate was sealed. As we huddled over lunch, digesting updates from our Sherpas, the gravity of our predicament became chillingly clear. The Lhotse team's summit bid had been halted by relentless bad weather, leaving them trapped at a high camp, 7,800 m up, enduring brutal winds. Among them were Mingma Tenzi Sherpa and Dawa Sherpa, who had originally been part of our Everest team. Their ability to rejoin us after their Lhotse ascent – a perilous endeavour on the world's fourth-highest peak – now loomed as an uncertainty. The weather's volatility threatened to extend their delay, and with it, our own Everest expedition hung in the balance. The stark reality was that we might be condemned to wait indefinitely at 6,400 m in Camp 2. Our plan to ascend to Camp 3 the next day was now suspended, overshadowed by the ominous wait for an update from Mingma, who was still trapped in the storm with the Lhotse team.

With mounting apprehension, we strained to extract a plan from Pemb Dorje. Yet, since Mingma was the climbing sirdar, the only response we received was, 'Don't know! Ask Mingma Dai.' As we grappled with the escalating challenges and their potential impact on our summit bid, another blow struck us. Lakpa Sherpa, who had guided us through the Khumbu Icefall earlier that morning, staggered into our Camp 2 nearly three hours after us. He was utterly spent and severely dehydrated. We rushed him to his tent for urgent rest and set up an oxygen cylinder to aid his recovery. The relentless ascent from Kathmandu to Everest Base Camp and the forced march through the icefall had taken a brutal toll. Despite his assurances, Lakpa was visibly succumbing to acute mountain sickness. Now, another Sherpa team member was incapacitated, deepening our concerns. Sauraj voiced serious doubts about the reliability of our support team. Our meticulous preparation and readiness seemed to crumble beneath the weight of escalating uncertainties that were threatening our expedition. That night at Camp 2, we were haunted by nightmares of a possible repetition of our ill-fated 2017 attempt.

The following day was consumed by our desperate attempt to recover as much rest as possible. Lakpa had managed to get some restful sleep with the aid of supplemental oxygen, but he remained in no condition to continue the ascent. Regardless of the expedition's progress, he would soon have to descend to Everest Base Camp for medical treatment.

At midday, we were greeted with an exhilarating update: the entire Lhotse team – Kuntal, Caroline, Sylvine and Brijesh – had successfully reached the summit. They had battled through fierce winds to achieve their goal and were now safely descending back to their high camp. A few hours later, Japanese climber Matsumoto Tatsuo, at the age of seventy-nine, made history as the oldest person to summit Lhotse. This remarkable news brought a wave of optimism and shifted our focus back to our Everest team. The worries and uncertainties of the previous day seemed to fade into the past, and we were poised to resume our ascent with renewed determination.

Excited by the news from the Lhotse expedition and eager to speak with Mingma, we patched a radio call to the team camped at 7,800 m on the Lhotse wall. From Camp 2, their tents appeared as mere pinpricks of yellow against the vast white expanse of the mountain high above us. As we extended our congratulations, Kuntal greeted us with a chilling indifference, delivering the shocking news that Mingma had refused to speak with us. Stunned, we listened as Kuntal expressed his disappointment in us over our perceived lack of faith in Mingma's leadership, whom he held in the highest regard.

Apparently, Phurba Sherpa, who was climbing with Brijesh Sharma, had conveyed to the entire Lhotse team that we had requested him on Everest. Phurba then left the Lhotse team at high camp that very same evening just after the summit and had begun his descent with Brijesh down to Camp 2. As the climbing sirdar, Mingma was deeply upset and felt his authority had been undermined. Consequently, he had decided to withdraw from leading the Everest team, presuming that we wanted Phurba Sherpa instead.

As Sauraj stared at the handset in stunned silence, I took up the radio transmitter and said, 'Kuntal! Sauraj and I never had such a discussion with Phurba. Our entire reason for choosing Satori was to climb with Mingma. We're genuinely concerned since we did half the climb yesterday on our own. The Sherpa who guided us through the Khumbu Icefall is unwell and may need to return. Now, we're being told Mingma doesn't want to climb with us. We are in complete shock.'

To his credit, Kuntal began to grasp the gravity of the miscommunication and empathise with our distress, despite being at a remote camp at 8,000 m after having just completed the climb of the fourth-highest mountain in the world. We discussed the communication gap and clarified the situation to Mingma, who was listening in. It turned out that Phurba had offered his services to Vikas as his personal Sherpa for the summit. Although this was merely an initial discussion,

Phurba's enthusiastic communication had caught Mingma off guard. With his leadership in question and assuming that Vikas, Sauraj and I were united in our preference, Mingma had decided to withdraw from leading our expedition. I reiterated multiple times during the call that Phurba Sherpa was not even a consideration for us, waiting anxiously for Kuntal's response.

Sauraj took up the radio and, for the first time, spoke directly to Mingma, 'Dai! If you are not with us, I will not climb this mountain. We want only you.' After a minute of silence that seemed to last forever, Mingma's voice finally crackled through the receiver, filling us with instant relief. 'Okay, Dai! No problem. I'm with you!'

20

Entering the Death Zone

> It is not death that a man should fear, but he should fear never beginning to live.
>
> Marcus Aurelius, *Meditations*
> (translated by George Long)

Sam

In the early hours of 16 May, the Everest climbing team departed from Camp 2, heading towards the bergschrund at the base of the Lhotse wall. We made good progress, with Sauraj leading us efficiently up the gruelling, 70° incline of the ice wall. Along the way, we encountered climbers being escorted down on oxygen and ropes, assisted by a dedicated rescue team. We were aware that Seven Summit Treks had stationed a ten-person rescue team at Camp 2 this season. Their careful, methodical work left us impressed by their commitment and efficiency.

As we neared Camp 3 (7,450 m), we crossed paths with the Lhotse team who were descending from the mountain. They looked utterly spent, having endured fierce winds and the relentless strain of extreme altitude. We offered our heartfelt congratulations, then approached Mingma with a mix of apprehension and hope. To our immense relief, his demeanour was free of bitterness or resentment. He reassured us that he would indeed be our expedition leader. Despite descending with his team, he promised to return early the next morning and ascend to South Col with us. Buoyed by his reassuring words, we reached Camp 3 and spent another restless night in our tent, precariously perched on the steep incline of the Lhotse wall.

The morning of 17 May dawned quietly, without much ordeal. Despite the biting cold, the awkward angle of the tent and the extreme altitude, I had slept relatively well, wrapped in my down suit and breathing from an oxygen tank. After lacing up my boots, packing my sleeping bag and strapping on my climbing harness, I stepped out of the tent to allow Sauraj to get ready in the cramped space. That day's ascent to South Col required us to use supplementary oxygen to survive in the thinning atmosphere. We were about to enter the 'Death Zone'.

Outside, chaos reigned. Teams scrambled around their tents, and climbers jostled to get onto the main fixed line running through Camp 3 which led up the mountain. The sub-zero temperatures turned every task into an agonising struggle. Replacing oxygen cylinders, managing regulators, adjusting crampons and packing up the tents became Herculean efforts, each task taking twice as long as usual. By the time we were set to start at 6:30 AM, my hands were painfully frozen despite wearing gloves. My only thought was, 'Let's move.'

Spotting Pemba clipping onto the main fixed line, I followed, hoping the act of climbing would relieve the burning cold in my extremities. We began the slow ascent up the ropes, confident that the rest of our team would be just minutes behind. As we reached the first crest, about twenty minutes out of Camp 3, I noticed a climber ahead, sitting in the snow with his down suit half unzipped and his hands bare despite the extremely cold temperatures, which was a shocking sight. Pemba and I reached him to find him dazed and struggling with his oxygen mask. A Sherpa climber was attempting to assist him, but he seemed disoriented. I voiced my concern to Pemba, who quickly communicated with the Sherpa and then turned to me, translating: 'Russian climber going down. Needs rescue!' Pemba immediately radioed Camp 2, and we received confirmation that the rescue team was aware of the situation and on its way.

As Lakpa Tenzi led Sauraj, Vikas and Takeshi up to us, I saw the shock and alarm etched on their faces as they took in the sight of the incapacitated climber. 'Oh God! Are you okay? Is he okay?' Vikas shouted through his face mask. 'Let's help him,' said Sauraj, taking a few steps towards the climber. But Lakpa and Pemba quickly stopped him, emphasising that the rescue team was already on its way. Though we were eager to assist, Pemba insisted we keep moving. The rescue team would arrive any moment, and we were ill-equipped to handle a medical emergency of this scale.

Visibly shaken, we resumed our ascent. The encounter had left an indelible mark on our minds, starkly illustrating the perilous nature of high-altitude mountaineering. As we climbed the Lhotse Face, each step felt like a heavy, painful reminder of the danger we faced. My thoughts drifted into a dark chasm of anxiety and fear, overshadowing the once glorious summit aspirations. The focus of my solemn prayers shifted from 'Dear God, please let me succeed' to 'Please, just let me survive'.

We must have been climbing for another sixty minutes when we heard Mingma Tenzi Sherpa's deep, commanding voice behind us. He had started his ascent all the way from Camp 2 early that morning after a good night's sleep. Having joined the rescue team, he had caught up with us, bringing with him the reassuring news that the Russian climber was being evacuated. With Mingma's presence and the rising sun, our earlier fears began to dissolve, and our spirits were renewed. Mingma directed the Sherpa team to advance at their faster pace, while the four of us followed him up the Lhotse wall.

I stayed close behind Mingma, constantly in awe of his strength and resilience. Here was a man who had just led an expedition up Lhotse, the fourth-highest mountain in the world. After descending the previous day and getting only one night's rest, he was back on the mountain, leading us up the Lhotse wall as if it were a morning stroll. Acclimatised to the high altitude, he wasn't even wearing an oxygen mask. Watching him effortlessly stride ahead, occasionally looking back with a reassuring smile, filled me with immense gratitude and admiration. His superhuman strength and unwavering calm were a beacon of hope amidst the daunting climb.

It took us nearly six hours to ascend the Lhotse wall. With a final, strenuous push, I hauled myself over the rock ledge marking the top of the Geneva Spur and secured myself at the anchor point before sinking into a well-earned rest. It was just 12:30 PM, and we had already conquered the most challenging section of the day. Our tents at South Col were now only a short twenty-minute walk away. As I took in the breathtaking panorama of the Western Cwm below, I marvelled at the fact that we were back here at 8,000 m above the world. Despite the uncertainties of the next twenty-four hours, we had defied the odds and reached this pivotal point where only a brave few had ventured.

Sauraj climbed up to the Geneva Spur, his eyes locked on the Everest summit, where a fierce white plume of snow trailed from its dark, jagged edge. His face was a mask of intense focus and unyielding determination, capturing the summit that had eluded us for four long years. When he turned towards me, I captured the moment on camera: Sauraj, resolute and powerful, with Everest's pinnacle daring us to test our resolve against its towering heights. We took a breath to appreciate the significance of our achievement before Takeshi and Vikas arrived. Once they had caught their breath, we pushed onward together, tackling the final few hundred metres to our camp. As we emerged from the shadow of Lhotse and entered the exposed basin of South Col, a powerful gust of wind hit us. I looked up at the peak, dismayed to see that the snow plume was a stark reminder of the fierce winds at the summit. Despite the forecast of clear weather, we were once again battered by icy winds at Camp 4.

The support team of Sherpas was impeccably organised. Arriving an hour earlier, they had already pitched most of the tents and started heating water. We, utterly spent from the gruelling climb up the Lhotse wall, bundled into a single tent with immense relief. The tent, shielded from the relentless wind, surprisingly offered warmth, which began to aid our recovery. Inside, we adjusted our climbing gear and found solace in the confined space, which now felt like a sanctuary. Mingma came by with a flask of hot water, checking on each of us and ensuring we were okay. He took a quick inventory of our oxygen regulators and advised us to change into dry clothes. He even insisted we remove the insoles from our boots to prevent frostbite – a crucial piece of advice that later proved invaluable. One of the Sherpas, who had neglected to do this, later suffered severe frostbite and had to be evacuated.

As we huddled in our tent, preparing for the long, arduous night ahead, we drew immense comfort from each other's presence. After enduring the harsh conditions of the past two months together, our shared experiences had forged a bond of strength. Words of caution and advice were received with grace, and even moments of silence were filled with a profound sense of camaraderie. Vikas's calm demeanour, Takeshi's inadvertent humour and Sauraj's unwavering determination each contributed to a renewed sense of confidence. Despite our diverse personalities, we drew strength from one another.

Outside, the winds raged on, tearing at anything not securely anchored. Memories from a year ago haunted us, but we kept them at bay. The tent, packed tightly with the four of us in our down suits and sleeping bags, became our fortress. With easy access to oxygen, hot tea for hydration and a generous supply of chips, chocolates and dried fruits fuelling us, our bodies began to recover and our spirits lifted. Sauraj had even managed to bring a pack of Uno, resulting in perhaps the highest game of Uno in the world.

With the unwavering support of our Sherpa team and Mingma's vigilant care, we managed to recover well during the seven hours we spent at South Col. As the sun dipped below the horizon, the ferocious winds began to ease. The weather forecast had proven accurate, offering a brief respite from the relentless elements. With our departure set for 8 PM, we made the most of the final hours, retreating into our sleeping bags and mentally bracing ourselves for the gruelling night ahead.

Everything above us was uncharted territory, an alien expanse of ice and rock. We had no inkling of the trials that lay in wait, only the daunting knowledge that the coming hours would test our limits in ways we could scarcely imagine. The anticipation was palpable, mingling with the cold, as we settled in, preparing for the unknown challenges that awaited us in the darkness.

21

The Final Push

> It is not in the stars to hold our destiny but in ourselves.
>
> William Shakespeare, *Julius Caesar*

Sam

I struggled to keep up with Pemba Tashi, his bright orange climbing suit a beacon in the pitch darkness as I stumbled behind him. It was 8:30 PM on 17 May, and we had just left our tents at Camp 4, already racing ahead to overtake the ghostly figures in puffed-up down suits who were queuing up on the route leading out of South Col. I gasped for air, fighting to draw oxygen through my mask as my heart pounded frantically in my chest. In the chaos, I lost sight of our entire team and found myself blindly following Pemba up the snow slope as he led us to the fixed ropes. This was the highest I'd ever climbed in all my years of mountaineering.

We finally slowed down when we clipped onto the ropes, taking our place in the line of climbers trudging up the snow-covered slope towards the summit. Pemba Tashi urged me to go ahead so I could climb at my own pace. As my breathing gradually returned to normal, I took my first real look around to assess my surroundings. The slope's gradient had increased substantially, but fortunately, the route had been well-prepared, and I felt the firm, compact snow beneath the spikes of my crampons. I moved steadily, keeping pace with the climbers ahead of me in the line. Pemba was right behind me, and though we climbed in silence, his constant presence was a source of reassurance – a familiar face in this dark, desolate and alien world.

My confidence grew with each step, and I soon settled into the steady rhythm of the climb. The repetitive movement allowed my mind to escape the despair of my surroundings, transcending the cold and fear gripping my heart. After the first hour, time began to lose its meaning, and my thoughts wandered, reflecting on the years of patience, frustration, disappointment and stubborn perseverance it had taken to reach this far. The darkness of the night pervaded everything, enveloping not just the physical space around us but also unapologetically invading the edges of my thoughts. Everything was precariously balanced on the edge of a knife – or in this case, on a ridge 7,924 m high, towering above the world – where a single misstep would not just mean failure yet again, but this time would also spell certain doom.

As Pemba and I attached our safety ropes and manoeuvred around slower climbers on the fixed line, I suddenly recognised the pair ahead of me. Despite the initial logjam, we had covered a decent distance and had caught up with Dawa Temba and Sauraj. We patiently followed them for a while until they acknowledged our presence with a nod and a wave, each of us focusing our energy on the Herculean task of just lifting one foot and placing it in front of the other. We were now proceeding as a team of four. Somehow, knowing that Sauraj was only a few paces ahead filled me with a tremendous sense of relief. The dark night seemed less oppressive, and my overwhelming sense of foreboding began to ease.

As the hours dragged on, the cold started to creep in, infiltrating the many layers of my insulated clothing. I felt it most in my feet, forcing me to consciously wriggle my toes and kick my boots against the hard snow to stimulate better blood circulation. I contemplated pulling out my Nikon 160 ASW point-and-shoot camera to take a few pictures now and then, but the thought of removing my mittens in −40°C, unzipping my down suit and retrieving it from the warm confines of my inner pocket was overwhelming. I reasoned that the darkness and reduced visibility would make any attempt at photography futile. Besides, it was more important to conserve the batteries – especially in these frigid temperatures – for pictures on the summit, which was a justified excuse. Having read several accounts of climbers in a hypoxic state, especially above 8,000 m in the Death Zone, I found myself anxiously checking my watch from time to time. The luminous dial glowed green, subtly announcing the time as I tried to calculate our rate of progress and the estimated time of summit – my way of testing my mental faculties. Feeling no signs of confusion or hypoxia, I pushed forward, still experiencing every single step of the climb with a constant sense of anxiety.

About four hours into the climb, the gradient gradually eased, and ahead of Sauraj, I saw a small cluster of headlights. As we approached the group of climbers, Pemba tapped on my shoulder and, through his mask, uttered just two words: 'Balcony! Rest.' I hesitated to sit, afraid of the effort it would take to get up again. Instead, I took off my rucksack and accepted Pemba's help to exchange my depleting oxygen cylinder for a fresh one. I watched wordlessly as he stashed the extra oxygen cylinders at the Balcony. I then tried to take a drink from one of the small plastic Coke bottles I had placed in the inner pockets of my down suit. This unique geographical feature on the way to the summit was called 'the Balcony' as it was the only relatively flat section on the entire climbing route, giving climbers a much-needed pause from the relentless steep gradient up the mountain face. It was also a good place to leave extra cylinders to be used on the way down.

My hands reached down absently, struggling to find the zip. After failing a few times, I looked down in confusion to see a thin layer of ice coating the front of my suit. Over the course of the climb, my warm breath had condensed upon contact with the cold rubber of my face mask, dripping down the front of my suit and freezing immediately in the sub-zero temperatures. Icicles had formed on the lapels and along the zip's channel. As my shocked mind tried to process this, my gloved hands worked frantically to break away the ice and free the trapped zip. With some relief, I finally unzipped the front of my suit and accessed the water, which was still warm from being nestled against my chest. The effort required to take even these few sips was formidable, leaving me both shaken and acutely aware of the implications of even the smallest tasks at this altitude.

During this episode, I realised with a start that I had lost sight of the entire team. To my relief, Pemba suddenly appeared in front of me, giving a thumbs-up, which I interpreted as a signal that we were good to go. Once again, a crowd had formed to get back onto the fixed lines. Pemba navigated his way around the climbers, and we clipped onto the ropes a few metres ahead. Despite the brief break at the Balcony, the sudden scramble to overtake the crowd had left me breathless. I willed myself to proceed steadily upwards, letting my breathing settle into the rhythm of the climb.

As we progressed, the route curved to the left, and with the darkness, I could now feel the wind tugging at the fabric of my suit as we climbed onto an exposed ridge. The snow tapered off onto steep slopes on either side, plunging into a pitch-black abyss where the pull of gravity was ever-present. Looking down, the light from my headlamp seemed to vanish into the depths of obscurity – a frightening reminder of the dangers posed by a misplaced foot or an unconscious wobble.

As I paused to change my safety line at one of the anchors, I turned around and saw Sauraj and Dawa a few metres behind us. Below them, at regular intervals, I could see a line of tiny lights marking climbers along the fixed rope all the way down to the Balcony. The lights resembled a stunning string of pearls set against the marble-white backdrop of the snow, each climber faintly illuminated by torchlight – a stark contrast to the blackness of the night. For a brief moment, the cold, anxiety and discomfort all faded away as I stood at 8,500 m on a snow ridge under the night sky, taking in the beauty of the scene and feeling a thrilling sense of being alive.

As Sauraj approached me, I noticed his headlamp was distinctly dimmer than when we started – a sure sign that the batteries were draining from the cold. He struggled to see the trail, so I called out through my mask and gestured for him to move ahead. Dawa Temba took the lead, with Sauraj shadowing him closely. I stayed right behind, my torch set on high beam to illuminate the path for both of us. We soon developed an effective system, with Sauraj climbing in the relative brightness of our combined headlamps. The anchor points were tricky, requiring me to focus my torch on the line so Sauraj could see clearly as he clipped himself onto the next rope. Pemba Tashi brought up the rear to assist in case we encountered any issues.

After a long and steady climb, at around 2 AM, I noticed the terrain's incline had increased dramatically. The easy snow ridge suddenly gave way to a sheer rock face. We had arrived at the Triangular Face, a distinct feature below the South Summit, marked by large rock slabs and several ropes from previous expeditions. Climbers struggled and skidded on these rocks, slowing our ascent and creating a bottleneck over 8,000 m above sea level. Seizing the opportunity, Dawa Temba and Sauraj navigated around the struggling climbers, bracing themselves against the cold, exposed rock face and occasionally using older ropes to pull themselves up. Once they bypassed the slower climbers, they clipped their safety lines back onto the main fixed rope.

Afraid of being left behind, I followed their lead, manoeuvring around a pair of climbers in bright fluorescent-green down suits who were unsuccessfully scrambling up a steep rock outcrop. However, the extra effort to overtake them while pulling myself up the near-vertical rock face left me breathless and dizzy. Loose rocks, kicked free by climbers higher up, hurtled down like high-altitude missiles, adding to the danger. Though I wasn't putting any weight on the fixed rope, I felt a tremendous amount of tension on the line. Looking down, I saw a long queue of about twenty climbers using the fixed rope to haul themselves up the rock face. Occasionally, a single climber pulling hard on the rope would dislodge everyone else in the process. Calming my mind and regulating my breathing, I tried to establish a new rhythm, pacing myself to conserve energy.

Having overtaken a few of the slower climbers, I scrambled over the top of the Triangular Face, exhausted but relieved to find both Sauraj and Dawa waiting on a narrow section of the route. As they began to move ahead, Pemba tapped my shoulder gently, cautioning me to rest. I stood breathing heavily and fumbled once again to access the water bottle in my down suit. While the water's warmth had dissipated long ago and I could now taste small icicles in it, those few sips felt incredible. Refreshed, I reached for some dried fruit from my pocket and slipped it under the mask into my mouth while staring vacantly into the night and at the darkness that surrounded us.

I barely registered it at first, but it was there: an unusual interruption in the vast sea of black that we struggled through. It tugged at my attention, departing from my peripheral vision and slowly creeping into focus. The pitch darkness of the night appeared to be divided by a thin, straight line of orange below us, set against the distant horizon. Confused and unable to process what I was seeing, I rubbed my squinting eyes with my mittens in disbelief, certain that my mind was beginning to play tricks on me. I blinked, closed my eyes and blinked again, but it was still there. I could have sworn that the orange line looked perceptibly thicker and brighter. With a start and the unmistakable surety that accompanies the clearing of a blinding mental fog, I realised that it was 3:30 AM and that I was witnessing one of the rarest sights on the planet – the breaking of dawn from Mt Everest, with the sun still well below the eastern horizon. I retrieved my camera from my down suit, casting all my earlier misgivings aside, and attempted to capture this spectacular and awe-inspiring phenomenon, confident that this was a moment that only a chosen few would ever be lucky enough to experience.

Revitalised by this break and brimming with the renewed hope that only sunrise can bring, I set off after Sauraj and Dawa, trudging up the snow slope until I caught up with them. As I looked around, I noticed the sky brightening on the right, while everything on the left side of the mountain remained shrouded in darkness. It was as if I were standing on the axis of the world, on the intangible yet very real line dividing night and day. From this vantage point, I could simultaneously witness the breaking dawn on one side and the impressive night sky on the other. As the darkness around me gradually turned to a faded grey, I saw a distinct snow pinnacle on the mountain ahead of Dawa and Sauraj. We pressed onward and upward, breathing hard and staying focused even during our breaks. On one such brief respite, I turned around and was surprised to see Vikas and his Sherpa behind us, followed closely by Takeshi and his Sherpa. Despite the constant manoeuvring around other climbers, we had managed to stick together as a group.

My relief at being reunited with the other members of our team was somewhat short-lived. The steep gradient, rarified atmosphere and long hours of climbing had finally begun to take their toll on me. I could feel the mind-numbing icy temperatures and fatigue weighing me down. From past experience, I knew that this part of the climb would be the toughest, since my senses would be dulled by the cold and exhaustion I was feeling. I plodded on in a daze, literally counting out ten steps before allowing myself to take a five-minute pause (which seemed far too short) to catch my breath. I inched my way to the top of the snow pinnacle at an inexorably slow pace, hoping that it would mark an end to this torture.

At 4:15 AM, I finally crested the pinnacle, only to be hit by a fierce gust of ice-cold wind that jolted me awake with all the subtlety of a slap in the face. Staring in shock, I struggled to comprehend what lay before me. My cold-addled brain had expected to see prayer flags and jubilant climbers celebrating their successful summit. My eagerness to join them had driven me through the gruelling ascent, but the climb was far from over. We had not reached the top yet. Pemba and I were standing on the South Summit of Everest, a few paces behind Sauraj and Dawa. From this vantage point, the true summit of Everest loomed tantalisingly close in the dawn light, just above eye level, sitting proudly above a gentle, inviting slope. However, as my gaze traced back from the summit, my heart sank. Below this slope stood a steep, nearly vertical 15-ft rock wall, a resolute barrier blocking our final approach. Worse still, the path to this wall merged seamlessly into an incredibly precarious ridge, barely wider than a knife's edge, with sheer drops on either side promising a swift, certain demise. No amount of prior theoretical knowledge could prepare me for what lay ahead of us. A strong wind blew across the ridge, whipping up snow and creating spindrift in a taunting dance.

The ridge appeared too narrow to traverse, and I would have declared it impossible if not for the three climbers balanced precariously on the edge ahead of us, attempting to navigate it. As I stood on the South Summit, the route seemed to vanish, with no visible path down to the knife-edge ridge. My heart raced, and for a brief moment, I was overwhelmed with terror.

The strong crosswind made it difficult for us to stand upright. The path ahead looked too dangerous and too narrow to cross. In that moment, just for a second, I was ready to give up and turn back. I froze, mentally revolting against the thought of running the gauntlet. I was almost certain that attempting to do so would be absolutely fatal. Then, it happened! Dawa Temba took a firm, surefooted step and disappeared over the edge. I stared in shock and horror as Sauraj followed him with grim determination and disappeared over the edge as well.

22

Triumph Written in Snow and Sky

> Through perseverance many people win success out of what seemed destined to be certain failure.
> Benjamin Disraeli, *Coningsby*

Sam

I staggered towards the edge of the ridge, my heart pounding against my chest. The void below seemed to stretch endlessly, the sound of the wind deafening my senses, which were already numb with the cold. Then, with a surge of relief so overwhelming, I spotted them – Dawa and Sauraj – emerging right below me. They had descended onto a narrow, precarious ledge of ice that was clinging to the right side of the mountain, leading down to the treacherous knife ridge just below the South Summit. Until now, it had been hidden from view, shrouded in the swirling snow and angles of the mountain. The sight of them filled me with a renewed sense of hope and courage, cutting through the fear that had threatened to overwhelm me.

I took a minute to calm my nerves, taking the opportunity to capture a few more pictures and document our progress before donning my snow goggles and descending to the ridge. While it was still not very bright, I figured that the goggles would at least prevent the wind and, with it, tiny particles of snow from going into my eyes, which, in turn, would hopefully allow me to see the route more clearly. My fear kept me vigilant, and I stayed as close to Sauraj as possible as we shuffled along the ridge.

The path was barely wide enough to accommodate both my feet, and some sections offered a sheer, precipitous 1,800 m drop all the way down to Camp 2! Despite the cold, I could feel the clammy sweat of fear building up under all the layers of my clothes. I held on to the fixed line with a death grip. A few minutes felt like an eternity as we crossed the ridge and came face to face with the vertical wall of rock and snow.

Focusing all my energy on suppressing the rising fear that threatened to overwhelm me, I failed to recognise the feature before me as the Hillary Step. Instead, I viewed it as just another rock formation and obstacle to overcome. I didn't even pause to appreciate this historic landmark in the annals of Everest climbing. The fixed ropes guided us to the right of the wall, leading us through a steep, narrow gully that had previously been out of sight.

Using the ascender on the fixed rope and any available rock purchase, I painstakingly climbed the wall behind Sauraj. Gasping for breath and struggling to find a foothold with my crampons, I pressed on with relentless determination, fearful of being left alone on the exposed ridge. My lungs burned from the strain of climbing at high altitude, and I struggled to draw each breath. For the next twenty minutes, every ounce of my focus was devoted to the monumental effort of hoisting my body up the 5 m gully, manoeuvring between rock and ice.

As I finally pulled myself over a massive boulder, a wave of relief washed over me. I realised with a profound sense of accomplishment that I had just climbed The Hillary Step and was now at the base of the snow slope leading to the summit.

In my struggle to navigate this challenging section and with my snow goggles obscuring my view, I hadn't noticed the sky brightening. When I finally stood up on trembling legs, I was struck by the sight of the sun-drenched blue sky. The realisation that dawn had arrived hit me with exhilarating force. Driven by the adrenaline still surging through my veins, I climbed the slope, following the path marked by the rope.

At the other end of the rope, Sauraj and Dawa Temba were closing in on the final pinnacle. I attempted to catch up, but sheer exhaustion forced me to pause. The climb up The Hillary Step had drained me, and I needed a few minutes to recover. I pulled out my camera and began recording as Sauraj, with Dawa Temba close behind, made his way towards the summit. Overcome with joy, I laughed and cheered through my mask as I watched Sauraj ascend towards the white peak illuminated by the morning sun and adorned with colourful Tibetan prayer flags against the stunning blue sky.

Sauraj moved slowly, his steps measured as he neared the summit. He came to a standstill just before reaching the top and then, in a moment, he fell to his knees, bowing his head in front of the prayer flags adorning the summit. Worried for his safety, I immediately stopped recording and mustered a final burst of energy to cover the last few metres separating us. I knelt beside Sauraj and placed my hand on his back, feeling his shoulders tremble. As I heard the soft sound of his sobs, the enormity of the moment overwhelmed me, flooding me with emotions I hadn't anticipated. With our heads together, kneeling in the snow just a few feet from the prayer flags, we wept, releasing all the anxiety and fear we had bottled up for so long. In that pure release of energy, we allowed ourselves to fully embrace the joy and elation of finally reaching this pinnacle. Just five steps ahead of us was the summit of Mt Everest, the highest peak in the world.

Sauraj

Just a few steps now separated me from the summit – a dream I had carried for years, one that had burned itself into my soul through endless days of training, sacrifice and struggle. Every breath felt like an eternity, every heartbeat an echo of the countless moments that had led me here. This was it. The moment I had envisioned a thousand times, but now that it was here, it felt even more surreal than I had ever imagined.

Crossing the Hillary Step, I had felt an overwhelming sense of relief as the mountain seemed to relent, its fierce winds easing as if granting permission for this moment to unfold. But Everest is never truly conquered – it allows passage only on its own terms. There was a moment before the Hillary Step when the breaking dawn sky threatened to shift, the wind gathering speed in ominous gusts. The potential consequences of strong winds at this altitude, denying us the summit when we were so close, struck me with a force stronger than any physical exhaustion. Yet, just as abruptly, the winds faltered – as if the mountain itself had made its decision. It would let us pass.

Ahead of me, prayer flags fluttered in the now-gentle breeze as a testament to those who had stood here before, their bright colours vibrant against the vast, white snow. Just beyond them, a small group of climbers stood in silent embrace, their bodies trembling – not from the cold but from the sheer, unfiltered emotion of standing atop the world. The final crest lay before me, impossibly close yet still feeling like the edge of a dream.

It was perfect – exactly as I had imagined yet infinitely more profound. I turned, my vision blurring with exhaustion and emotion, to see Sam, Vikas and Takeshi slowly cresting the last ridge. Their figures were resolute against the boundless skyline, their slow, steady steps carrying them closer to a destiny we had fought so hard to reach. In that instant, an unshakable certainty surged through me – we were going to make it. We would stand here, together.

Just like that, the floodgates broke. My knees buckled, and I collapsed onto the ice, overcome by a wave of emotion so intense it threatened to consume me. I pressed my forehead to the frozen ground, overwhelmed with gratitude, with reverence, with the sheer weight of what we had done. I had imagined triumph, exhilaration – but not this. Not this uncontrollable outpouring of relief, humility and surrender to the moment.

Later, I would learn that Sam had captured it – the exact moment I fell to my knees, just metres from the summit, a frozen snapshot of the most raw, unguarded second of my life. Then, moments later, I felt a hand on my shoulder. I looked up and saw the same storm of emotions that raged inside me. No words were needed. We wept together, not just for the victory but from relief and the struggle, for the years of pain and persistence that had led to this very second.

Finally, after what felt like a lifetime and no time at all, we stood. Together, side by side, we took the final steps forward.

At 6:17 AM on 18 May 2018, four years after embarking on this relentless pursuit, we stepped onto the summit of Everest.

We were there. At the very top of the world.

Moments later, Vikas and Takeshi reached us, and suddenly, we were four men standing literally at the pinnacle of our ambition. We congratulated each other, arms wrapped tight around each other, with cheers of sheer joy to share this moment, to feel the warmth of our camaraderie in the coldest, highest place on earth. The happiness of it all beat loudly in our chests – a wild, unfiltered mix of triumph, disbelief, exhaustion and pure, unadulterated joy.

Then, as if by silent agreement, we simply sat – just sat, letting the silence speak for us. No words were necessary. The mountain understood.

Nearby, Dawa Sherpa, who had been assigned to support me, stood respectfully behind us, his presence steady yet unobtrusive. He didn't rush us or intrude on our moment. Instead, he quietly raised his radio and whispered into it, his voice carrying down the mountain to Mingma Sherpa and the rest of our team at Camp 4: 'Summit *Boyo* [We reached the summit].'

With those two simple words, the world below knew.

The year 2018 had been very fortunate for Everest aspirants. The weather had held, and there had been successful summits every day from 10 May to 24 May. When we reached the summit at 6:17 AM, there were only four or five other climbers apart from our team. The day was bright with winds lower than usual, and I was literally standing at the top of the world. This was the moment I had dreamt of for years. I had tried to picture the view in my mind's eye countless times. But now that I was finally here, I felt a deep sense of peace with myself and the world. All the times I had come so close yet fallen short, the years of wondering if it was worth the pain and effort – all those doubts melted away completely. I was fully present in that moment, my mind clear and sharp, absorbing everything around me. That was all that mattered. Every image from that morning is still etched vividly in my memory, as it was when I looked around in awe.

It was a cloudless day, and as we gazed at the horizon, we could see hundreds of miles in every direction, stretching into Nepal and Tibet. The vast expanse of the planet lay below us, with the curvature of the Earth visible to the naked eye. Directly ahead, I could see the peaks of Mt Lhotse, the fourth-highest mountain in the world, and towards the southeast, Mt Makalu, the fifth-highest peak. Looking northeast, I could just make out Kangchenjunga's summit jutting above the landmass.

After about ten to fifteen minutes of absorbing the breathtaking view, we quietly got to work, taking photos with the banners we had carried – those of our sponsors and, of course, our national flag. Capturing the moment was not only important for us but also a crucial part of our agreement with our sponsors. Taking pictures on Everest is far more complex than simply snapping selfies and requires careful planning. All three of us – Sam, Vikas and I – carried banners bearing the Indian tricolour, made of lightweight, wrinkle-free silk, folded carefully inside the inner pockets of our down suits. Sam and I also carried the Adventure Pulse and Force Motors banners. This way, even if only one of us made it to the summit, we'd have pictures with the banners. Vikas carried banners from his sponsors, and Takeshi had the Japanese flag and other banners from his sponsors to photograph.

We spent the next twenty to thirty minutes in companionable silence, arranging the silk banners and taking pictures – a task made more complex by the need to stay clipped to our safety ropes at all times. Between us, we carried four extra cameras, knowing that digital devices often malfunction in the frigid 'Death Zone'. I also had my iPhone 7 in an inner pocket of my down suit, hoping it would stay relatively warm against my body. When I reached the summit, I unzipped the suit and pulled out my smartphone. The battery was almost drained, showing just 1 per cent charge. To my surprise, it was still on, and I managed to take a few selfies before it finally powered down.

I had often imagined myself at the summit of Everest, making a phone call to my family and proclaiming, 'I'm here, standing at the top of the world.' So I turned to Dawa Sherpa and asked if I could make a call home using the satellite phone. Unfortunately, the battery had drained considerably, and we realised we needed to conserve the remaining charge for emergencies. Thrilled as we were to have reached the summit, we were keenly aware that this was only the halfway point of the expedition. The equally treacherous descent still lay ahead, and we knew from experience that many accidents happen on the way down. Even the most seasoned climbers can collapse from exhaustion during the descent. Still, I couldn't help but feel disappointed about not making that call. Often I jokingly tell Sam that the desire to return to the summit remains strong – perhaps via Tibet next time – so I can make that call and capture even better photographs of Everest.

Once we had taken our formal pictures with the banners, we spent some time capturing our moments together on the summit as a group, along with photos of our Sherpa team. For the Sherpas, each successful summit is a momentous event, meticulously recorded in the Himalayan database and invaluable to their climbing resumes. A short while later, another expedition reached the summit, and we were overjoyed to see our friend Tendi Sherpa leading the Tag Nepal team. We took more pictures with him, and Dawa Sherpa radioed Mingma Sherpa at Camp 4, where he was stationed with the backup rescue team, to share our success.

Standing on the summit of Everest, I was struck by the realisation that this was not just the culmination of years of training, planning and relentless pursuit – it was the pinnacle of everything I had poured into this dream. The years of perseverance had finally paid off. So often, people ask me what it was like to stand on top of the world, but words fall short of describing the enormity of the experience, especially after so many failures. It is often said that it is not who you are that defines you but what you do. Everest was everything to me. It was the ultimate test of endurance, character and willpower. It gave me direction, focus and a sense of becoming something much more. As an ordinary person, I had achieved the extraordinary. As I stood there, I realised that reaching the summit wasn't just about conquering a mountain but also about conquering the doubts, the fears and the limitations that had once held me back. This was a moment of pure transformation that made every setback, every moment of pain and every sacrifice worth it.

23

The Return

A man travels the world over in search of what he needs and returns home to find it.
George A. Moore, *The Brook Kerith: A Syrian Story*

Sauraj

As I stood on the summit taking in the moment, Sam started gently nudging us to begin our descent. I was surprised by his urgency and glanced at my watch, only to be shocked by the time – it was already 7:10 AM. We had arrived at the summit around 6:17 AM and had spent nearly an hour up there. For me, time had seemed to stop when we reached the top. Typically, climbers spend no more than fifteen to twenty minutes at the summit, aware of the dangers of prolonged exposure at this altitude. With another ten hours of gruelling descent ahead to Camp 4, we knew we needed to leave soon. Sam was the first to get moving, swiftly taking the lead. By the time I got my gear together and was ready to start, Sam was already about a hundred metres ahead.

After climbing together for so long, we were intimately familiar with each other's pace, and we had more or less reached the summit together. Now, as we headed back down, even as Sam quickened his pace, I wanted to hang back a bit, savouring the majestic panorama before me. I was mesmerised by the stark, rugged beauty of this impossibly high mountain and didn't want to miss a thing. I felt light-hearted and brimming with confidence – confidence in my skills that had brought me this far and in the experience of our Sherpa team. The days of incredible weather had allowed the mountaineering expeditions to pace out the summit pushes, so there were fewer people than usual this high up on the mountain that morning. As I walked along the narrow ridge from the summit, I encountered barely four people descending and a couple more on their way up. I was grateful for this bit of good fortune as I quickly crossed over the ridge, a dreaded feature during peak season that could hold up climbers for hours, exposed to inclement weather and winds.

This knife-edge ridge is so narrow that whenever you encounter another climber coming from the opposite direction, you need to unclip from the main line to make room, go around them and then clip back onto the line. Depending on the volume of traffic, this can cause significant delays. I continued at a comfortable pace, enjoying the clear, crisp morning until I reached a rocky section and rappelled down to the relatively flat feature called the Balcony. I checked my watch again and was pleasantly surprised to note that within two hours of leaving the summit, I was already at the Balcony and could see the tents of Camp 4 clearly visible below me.

I took out a bottle of water from my down suit and sipped it. It was still early in the day, but as the sun climbed higher in the cloudless sky, I noticed that the water in my bottle was beginning to melt. I stood there at the Balcony for another moment – I could see Vikas and Takeshi some paces away – and took some more pictures. Eventually, I hoisted an oxygen cylinder into my pack that had been previously stowed by Pemba and continued on. The sun beat down on the mountain face, intense in the rarefied Death Zone air. I felt completely at home on the mountain, and with the summit behind me, my head was clear, and I was enjoying the technicality and physical effort of the descent. I rappelled down almost 60 per cent of the remaining distance to Camp 4.

In another two hours, I reached Camp 4. It was 11 AM, and Mingma was delighted to see us. We had made good time and had the entire day ahead of us. Sleeping at Camp 4 is always dangerous – the human body is not meant to function at these altitudes. Yet for most Everest mountaineers, resting for the night at Camp 4 on the way back is unavoidable. Even the most experienced climbers often take considerable time to descend from the summit back to Camp 4, depending on the weather conditions and their levels of fatigue. Despite the exhaustion, there was an unspoken sense of celebration among us – a quiet acknowledgment of the incredible feat we had achieved and the relief of being safely back at Camp 4, which felt almost like a second summit. It had been almost fifteen hours since we had left Camp 4 the previous evening.

Since we had made it back to Camp 4 by late morning and were all in good physical condition, Mingma suggested we rest for a couple of hours and then head down to Camp 3 for the night. We had the rest of the day to make it there. As we sat outside our small Camp 4 tent, sipping the hot Tang the Sherpa team had prepared for us, I asked to use Mingma's satellite phone. He agreed, and I finally made that call home to my mom. She must have been surprised to see an unknown number flash on her phone screen, answering with a confused 'Who's this?' I could only speak with her for about thirty seconds, just long enough to update her that we had summited and were already making our way down to Camp 3. Hearing the relief in her voice, I was glad I could make the call.

We went inside our tent at Camp 4 and lay down for a bit, too keyed up from the rush of summiting to sleep. We spent our time lying down, resting and hydrating. None of us wanted to spend the night at Camp 4, so we called Mingma to tell him of our decision to head down to Camp 3, possibly even Camp 2. Mingma was pleased to see us in good spirits and excellent physical form. We packed up our sleeping mats and replaced our oxygen cylinders, and by 12:30 PM, we were ready to leave Camp 4.

We started off at a good pace, keeping each other in sight, never more than twenty minutes away from anyone in the team at any point. The climb down to Camp 3 was relatively challenging and involved a lot of rappelling. Around 2 PM, I began to feel uncomfortably hot in my down suit and the thermal layer underneath it. I had visibly slowed down, and Sam, who was the closest to me, called out, 'It's hot. Take off the top of your down suit.' Hearing him, I stopped for a few minutes to remove the top of the down suit, rolling it up under my backpack, and sipped some more water. Feeling much better, I resumed climbing down.

It was 3:30 PM when I reached Camp 3. Sam and Vikas, who had been slightly ahead of me, had already started their descent towards Camp 2. I allowed myself a brief pit stop, resting for a few minutes and sipping some more water. The descent from here to Camp 2 would be gruelling, involving nearly two hours of constant rappelling down the steep mountainside. After an hour of hard rappelling, I finally saw Camp 2. It was at this point that the exhaustion truly hit me. I slowed down noticeably, feeling extremely dehydrated. With the safety of Camp 2 now in sight, I began to get complacent. I knew I would make it, and there was no longer any need to rush. I started to lean into my exhaustion, realising what we had just accomplished. Not only had I summited the highest peak in the world, but here I was, less than twelve hours later, already near Camp 2 – a feat in itself.

For Everest mountaineers, Camp 2 represents safety and the promise of relief. It's the highest camp from which helicopter rescues on the mountain are possible and is usually well-appointed with kitchen setups and other comforts that are unavailable higher up. It was around 5 PM, and I was rappelling down a steep rock wall with another 100 m to go. At the foot of the wall, Takeshi, Vikas and Sam stood waiting, shouting words of encouragement. From the foot of this wall, Camp 2 was just a one-and-a-half-hour walk on relatively flat ground. We had made it. In my tired state, it took me another fifteen to twenty minutes to reach the bottom.

Our support team had been our greatest cheerleaders during the expedition, and our successful summit was the cause for celebration back at our team's support camp at Camp 2. The team at Camp 4 had already relayed the message to Camp 2 that we were on our way down, and the camp was bustling with activity, ready to receive us. Depending on the weather, it's often difficult to communicate with Everest Base Camp from Camp 4 but easier to relay messages to Camp 2. The walkie-talkies we all carried didn't always work on every part of the mountain, but our Sherpa and cook had come out to meet us, having been informed we were on our way.

Knowing how tired we would be, they had trekked out to the point where the steep rock face plateaued into flat ground, waiting for us with Coca-Cola and apples. At 6,500 m, we felt at home and once again hugged and congratulated each other. We had held our own until this point, but the sight of these comforts and the warmth of our team was overwhelming. At the sight of Coke, Takeshi burst into tears of joy, speaking incoherently to us in Japanese. The only word we caught was 'Coke'. We could see our camp lights glimmering in the dusk, beckoning us.

When I saw our team there to greet us, I was so relieved and exhausted that I snatched off my oxygen cylinder and mask and shrugged the heavy backpack off my shoulder. At 6,450 m above sea level, Camp 2 felt like home. Despite the relentless climbing, rappelling and mental fatigue of the last twenty-two hours, we felt immense gratitude towards our support team, the weather and this incredible, momentous journey. We sat down right there, overjoyed. For me, the sight of our tents in the distance was almost as joyous a moment as reaching the top of Mt Everest a mere twelve hours earlier.

Statistically, most Everest tragedies occur on the way down. Nine out of ten summiteers reach Camp 4 exhausted, often later in the day, and are forced to spend the night there with supplemental oxygen. This is especially stressful and dangerous in a climber's already fatigued state. We had rationed our oxygen, prepared to spend the night at Camp 4, but it was a great comfort to me that I would be going to bed relatively warm and without an oxygen mask strapped to my face at Camp 2 instead.

From the base of the steep rock face, we watched the sun dip below the horizon, casting a classic, golden light that sharply outlined the peaks of Lhotse and Everest. It was a glorious sight, perfectly commemorating what I consider to be my greatest achievement. We sat in silence, absorbing the moment, feeling energised and ready to tackle the last one-and-a-half-hour trek to our tents. But as we rose, the thought of hauling my rucksack, goggles and sleeping bags any further was unbearable. I was ready to leave it all behind. Thankfully, the Sherpas who had trekked out from our camp offered to carry my gear, sparing me the burden.

For me, the best moments of the entire expedition came after summiting when we were safely settled in our tents at Camp 2. We had a relatively comfortable setup there, with a fully equipped kitchen, a dining tent and our personal two-person sleeping tents. As we neared our camp, I saw Vikas and Takeshi entering the dining tent and calling for me to join them for hot Tang. But all I wanted was to head straight to my sleeping tent and get out of my down suit and mountaineering gear – a task that's anything but simple in the cramped confines of a small tent where you can't even stand up.

As I wriggled out of my gear, Mingma came by to check on me to make sure I was all right. I reassured him that I was just tired. During the expedition, we were particularly fortunate to have Anup as our cook. Having been part of Indian expeditions before, he made excellent Indian cuisine. He had even accompanied us to Camp 2, and Mingma now told me that he had prepared aloo parathas. Realising I was hungry but too exhausted to head to the dining tent, I gratefully accepted Mingma's offer to bring the food to my tent. After I finished changing, I slid into my sleeping bag, and soon after, Mingma arrived with a paratha and pickle, which I devoured within minutes. I asked for another, and as I sat in my tent at 6,450 m, eating my second paratha, tears of joy and gratitude welled up in my eyes.

I have never felt a greater sense of well-being and satisfaction than I did at that moment, sitting in a small, cramped tent, eating a simple aloo paratha. No gourmet meal could ever compare.

As I savoured that moment of peace, the journey of the past three years flashed before my eyes, and I had a sudden realisation. In what felt like a spiritual epiphany, I knew I had achieved my greatest dream, and if I were to die right then, I would die with no regrets. I felt completely light and fulfilled. It was my nirvana moment, right there in our spartan tent at Camp 2. Whatever life may bring, I doubt I will ever experience the deep contentment of that moment again. Seconds later, as my head hit the pillow, I was fast asleep.

I slept so deeply that when Sam, who was sharing the tent with me, came in from the dining tent at around 8 PM, I didn't even notice. He went through the entire process of taking off his boots and down suit barely 5 cm away from my sleeping bag. The space was so small that usually one of us had to step outside while the other got in or out of the down suit. But I slept dreamlessly, oblivious to the world, until 7 AM the next morning. And it was, hands down, the best sleep of my life.

The morning of 19 May 2018 was another clear, bright day on Everest. As we leisurely packed up camp to begin our descent to Everest Base Camp, I couldn't help but reflect on the significance of this date. Exactly one year earlier, on 19 May 2017, I had made this same trek back to Everest Base Camp, utterly dejected and despondent. That date was etched in my memory as the worst day of my life – the day we had to turn back just 800 m from the summit of Mt Everest. Yet here I was, a year later, on the same mountain, making the same journey, feeling like the luckiest man alive. It had only taken a year – a year of hardship, inner turmoil and more anxious moments than I care to recall – to completely turn things around. A date previously associated with sadness was now to be remembered only for joy and a deep sense of satisfaction.

By 9 AM that morning, we were on the final leg of our journey, making our way towards Everest Base Camp, our home away from home in Nepal. We were in high spirits, enjoying each other's company as we playfully flicked snowballs at one another. The three-hour trek to Camp 1 was easy, and we took a brief five-minute break for a quick snack. Our hearts were light, and I wanted to savour every moment as we basked in the glory of our achievement. Mingma, who had descended earlier that morning, was already at Camp 1. Ever the true leader, he was ensuring all safety protocols were met, even as he allowed us to enjoy our descent. The dreaded Khumbu Icefall still lay ahead, and Mingma was glued to the radio, getting updates on the melting ice and terrain changes.

We all knew that until we reached Everest Base Camp, it was crucial to observe every safety measure, especially as we approached the icefall with the bright sun overhead, increasing the risk of ice chunks breaking loose. Despite the dangers,

I found myself enjoying the concentration and challenge of crossing the icy glacier. Earlier that day, we had radioed Everest Base Camp to announce our imminent arrival. Our team, overjoyed by our success, promised us a hero's welcome – and they didn't disappoint. As we removed our crampons at the safe point on the icefall, we saw two figures approaching from Everest Base Camp, carrying boxes. As they drew closer, we recognised them as members of our support team bringing two crates of Everest beer, a popular and delicious Nepalese brew. It was only fitting that our first toast to celebrate our achievement was made with Everest beer. We stood there drinking beer, reminiscing about our expedition and relaxing at the crampon point on the Khumbu Icefall for almost thirty minutes.

Life had come full circle for me over the past year. On this exact day last year, I had hit rock bottom, and now, here I was, celebrating the most important victory of my life with some of my closest friends on a precarious, temperamental glacier. We laughed, drank more beer and, of course, took more pictures right there before finally heading back to Everest Base Camp – our home away from home.

By noon, we were back at our camp, making long-overdue calls to our families and being congratulated by our loved ones. The base camp team, who had stayed in touch with us via walkie-talkie throughout the expedition, had also kept our families updated on our progress. They already knew about our successful summit in real time and had been eagerly waiting to hear the full story from us.

It felt good to be back at camp. After speaking to my family and finally taking off my shoes and climbing gear, I made my way to the dining tent around 1 PM. As I approached the entrance, I could hear raucous laughter and the sounds of merrymaking. Our celebratory party was already in full swing, and I joyfully joined my comrades. The kitchen staff had outdone themselves in catering for our little party, and all the liquor in camp was brought out.

As luck would have it, since our climbing season was winding down after our successful summit, we were now sharing camp space with a group of Bulgarian ultra-marathoners. Every year in May, marathoners from around the world come to Everest Base Camp to participate in the annual Everest marathon from Everest Base Camp to Namche Bazaar. The race was scheduled for 29 May, ten days later, and some of the runners, including the Bulgarian contingent, were already at Everest Base Camp. They joined us at our little mountain soirée.

We were exhausted and sleep-deprived but buzzing with adrenaline. Climbing Mt Everest is one of the most extreme challenges the human body can endure. Over the last four days alone, from 16 May to 19 May, during our final push for the summit and then back to Everest Base Camp, I had lost 4 kg. Yet, there at Everest Base Camp, I felt completely alive as we ate and drank prodigiously from 1 PM that afternoon until about 10 PM that night.

Despite the constraints at Everest Base Camp, we managed to gather an eclectic supply of liquor, ranging from whiskey and cherry liqueur to the potent Nepalese Khukri rum. Around 7 PM, in the midst of our partying, Mingma came over with an exciting proposition. Bibek, another client with the company, had suffered frostbite and was scheduled to be evacuated by helicopter from Everest Base Camp the next morning. Mingma informed us that the chopper had space for a few more passengers and asked who would like to fly back to Kathmandu.

Years ago, as an amateur trekker to Everest Base Camp, I was fascinated by Everest climbers who would summit, return to Everest Base Camp and then fly out by helicopter. To me, they seemed like glamorous, sporting demigods. The idea of summiting the highest mountain in the world and then nonchalantly flying out epitomised coolness. Over the years, during our Adventure Pulse treks and almost annual visits to Nepal, I had taken the chopper ride from Everest Base Camp on numerous occasions. While the novelty of flying out by helicopter had worn off slightly, I couldn't quite shake the youthful fantasy of summiting Everest and then exiting in a chopper. So when Mingma suggested that the helicopter could accommodate us, I jumped at the opportunity and immediately agreed.

Vikas also decided to fly out to Kathmandu. He was eager to return home to his family and figured he could save some of his vacation time and get back to work sooner. Sam and Takeshi, on the other hand, chose to trek back to Lukla. Sam was looking forward to the trek down and the chance to spend time with our friends in the Khumbu Valley who had been part of our Everest journey over the years. He wanted to celebrate with them and express our gratitude.

After our night of revelry, I passed out in my tent, and the next morning, the chopper arrived by 8 AM. I took one last look at Everest Base Camp for the year and boarded the helicopter. Within forty-eight hours of summiting, I was comfortably settled in Kathmandu, awaiting Sam's arrival. I checked into our hotel and indulged in simple creature comforts – a proper hot shower for the first time in sixty days and some junk food. For the next nine days in Kathmandu, I fell into a routine of having pizza every single day, followed by two scoops of ice cream. The ice cream vendor near my hotel came to expect me like clockwork twice a day – once at noon and again at 7 PM – for my regular scoop.

During my week in Kathmandu, waiting for Sam and Takeshi, I had time to reflect on the journey we had just completed. As I strolled through the bustling streets of Thamel, a sense of validation settled over me, like a proverbial cape draped across my shoulders. Finally, I could fully embrace the title of

Everest summiteer. Yet, the transition back to normalcy wasn't as smooth as I had imagined. On some mornings, waking up in the comfort of a hotel bed, it was easy to forget the freezing nights spent on hard, uneven tent floors at 8,000 m. It almost felt like a distant dream, a surreal memory that could vanish with the morning light.

At times, the peace and calm I felt looking back on our years of struggle and perseverance was overwhelming. But there were also moments when I would wake in a panic, gripped by the fear that I was still on the mountain, that this was all a dream and the summit was yet to be reached. It was a strange and unsettling mix of relief and disbelief, as though my mind had yet to catch up with reality. In those moments of doubt, I had to remind myself that it was over and that we had succeeded. The expedition was behind us, and the summit was ours, but the emotional roller coaster continued. I knew it would take time to settle and fully process the last few years of my life.

Throughout the years of anxiety, self-doubt and heartache, the one mantra that had kept me going was: 'This, too, shall pass.' Now, having returned from the mountain, having survived once again, and this time with success, I knew it was true. The journey had tested me in ways I had never imagined, but in the end, it was all worth it. I had not conquered the mountain but had conquered the fears and doubts that had plagued me for so long. As I walked through Kathmandu, I carried with me the knowledge that I had faced Everest more than once and had lived to talk about it.

24

Finding Purpose

> The mystery of human existence lies not in just staying alive, but in finding something to live for.
> Fyodor Dostoevsky, *The Brothers Karamazov*

Sam

I stood nervously on a stage set up in one of Force Motors' vast factory workshops, addressing an audience of over 700 employees. Standing on this stage felt like being back on the summit. The lights shone bright, almost blinding, casting long shadows across the sea of faces. I could hear the buzz of excitement in the room, a soft hum of murmurs and whispers that only intensified the nervous energy in my chest. We had been invited by the managing director, Prasan Firodia, to share our Everest experience upon our return. Having successfully raised the Force Motors banner on top of the world, we had expected a small gathering. Instead, we found ourselves staring into a sea of faces, more than 700 managers – an overwhelming sight that only magnified the grandeur of the moment. The only saving grace was that I wasn't alone. I glanced at Sauraj, who flashed me a wide grin. It was a grin of brotherhood, of having survived the unimaginable. The way he stood tall beside me, confident and calm, grounded me. He was the reminder that we had stood atop the highest peak in the world. This was nothing compared to the wind, the ice and the biting cold of Everest.

Coming home had felt surreal, as though we were living someone else's life. Family and friends welcomed us as conquering heroes, hosting celebratory dinners and gatherings where we presented pictures and videos of our latest expedition and recounted the years of struggle that had led us to Everest. Local media covered our story, and we even appeared on national TV. My awkward attempt at answering interview questions in Hindi on Doordarshan remains a source of amusement among friends to this day.

As Sauraj and I took centre stage at Force Motors and recounted our adventures, something remarkable happened. As we began to speak, the initial nerves started to dissolve. With each word, we were drawn back to the towering heights, the biting winds and the sheer adrenaline of the climb. The more we talked, the more it felt like we were back on that mountain, standing at 8,849 m. The audience was hanging on to every word, their rapt attention pulling us deeper into the memories. We relived every step – from the treacherous Khumbu Icefall, with its deep, crevassed labyrinth of shifting ice, to the perilous final ascent, where every step took us closer to the top of the world.

As the presentation neared its climax, the tension in the room mirrored the tension we had felt in those final moments before reaching the summit. The image of the Indian flag fluttering on the summit of Everest filled the screen, followed by the Force Motors banner, and the room erupted in a standing ovation. Deafening, thunderous applause ricocheted off the walls. The force of it was overwhelming, a physical wave of energy that washed over us. In that moment, it felt as if we were invincible. The thrill of being celebrated, hailed and praised for an achievement that had consumed our lives for years was intoxicating.

Then came the shock – the announcement that would etch itself into our memories. Mr Firodia, standing tall at the podium, smiled proudly and said, 'For this incredible achievement, though I can't gift you a Sherpa, we at Force Motors would like to gift you this Gurkha.' The words echoed in my ears as he gestured towards the gleaming off-road beast parked beside the stage, the flagship jeep produced by the company. The magnitude of the gesture left us both speechless. It was as if the summit had followed us down from the mountain, another peak of excitement right here on solid ground.

After the ceremony, we were swept into a whirlwind of congratulatory handshakes, back-patting and hugging. The warmth of the crowd and the sheer volume of well-wishers were exhilarating. Every handshake felt like an affirmation, every cheer like fuel for our fire. We were carried by the excitement, lifted by the smiles and words of admiration that seemed endless. It was a triumphant high, the kind that leaves you giddy and breathless.

In that moment, we were not just Sauraj and Samir – we were heroes, modern-day explorers returning from the edge of the earth who were being celebrated for having conquered the unconquerable. The euphoria was palpable. We were riding the wave of admiration, basking in the glow of public adulation. It felt like the grand culmination of every moment of struggle we had experienced.

However, as the echoes of applause faded into silence and the bright lights of celebration dimmed, a stark reality set in. The jubilant atmosphere that had once enveloped me began to dissipate, leaving behind an unsettling stillness. As weeks gave way to months, the accolades and the proud smiles of colleagues and friends began to feel like distant memories, as if they belonged to someone else. In the quiet that followed the storm of triumph, I found myself grappling with an inexplicable emptiness. The high of public adoration quickly gave way to an alarming realisation: I had climbed the highest peak in the world, yet I felt more lost than ever. The void that replaced the euphoria was disconcerting – a chilling silence that echoed in my mind.

Our endeavour to climb Everest – what had begun as a four-month projection – had consumed four years of our lives. Four years of single-minded determination, planning, training, heartbreak, frustration, physical injury and emotional agony, all of it culminating in one explosive moment of triumph. And then ... nothing. The obsessive fire that had fuelled me through it all had gone out, leaving a void so deep, I wasn't even sure who I was without it. I had trained myself to exist with tunnel vision, focusing only on the summit. But when that tunnel finally ended, what lay beyond it was not the vast horizon I had imagined. It was an endless expanse of monotony, suffocating and oppressive. Friends had moved on, changed jobs and had children. Babies born while I was chasing Everest now called me 'uncle'. Time, it seemed, had passed while I was frozen in place, and I could no longer relate to the world that kept moving forward without me.

I did not recognise what was happening to me at first. I couldn't name the strange numbness that began creeping into my daily life. There was no longer a mountain to climb and no need to maintain the physical and mental conditioning that had shielded me from distractions. Yet, even though I was free to re-enter the world, I found myself recoiling from it. Social interactions that had once been rare due to my training now became something I actively avoided. Late-night gatherings with friends felt pointless and draining. The laughter and conversations that once brought joy now grated on my nerves. I began pulling away, not just from friends but also from my life. I didn't realise it at the time, but I was slipping into a state of depression. It crept in like a slow poison, dulling my senses and making the world around me seem colder and darker. The things that had once driven me – the desire to explore, achieve and push the boundaries – no longer ignited the same passion. I couldn't understand why nothing seemed to matter anymore. I had climbed Everest. I had conquered the ultimate challenge. Yet, in the aftermath, I felt more lost than ever.

Karishma, who had stood by me through years of obsession and sacrifice, was suddenly confronted with a version of me she could not recognise. Despite her love and support, she was helpless, unable to stop the slow unravelling of the person she had known. I became a shadow of myself, withdrawing further and further into an internal world of despair. I found no solace in work, no joy in the personal milestones that once excited me. Even the smallest tasks felt insurmountable, as though I were trudging through a fog that never lifted.

The hardest part was that I didn't understand what was happening. I didn't have the vocabulary for the darkness I was sinking into. How could I explain to anyone, let alone to myself, that after climbing the highest peak in the world, I felt so low? Depression wasn't something I had ever prepared for – it wasn't something I had ever thought I'd face.

I wondered if it was normal to have these feelings or if it was even safe to express them. Was this void real or just a figment of my imagination, a byproduct of overthinking? I found myself ridiculing my thoughts, calling it a First World problem. After all, I had achieved something remarkable – something few people dream of and fewer still attempt. How could I, of all people, feel lost? But the reality of mental health is undeniable. It's an invisible weight that presses down, and no summit or achievement could lift that weight from my mind.

This sense of a sudden loss of purpose isn't just a personal flaw or weakness – it is a well-documented phenomenon in psychology, often referred to as post-achievement depression or goal withdrawal syndrome. Many high achievers, especially athletes, encounter what is colloquially known as the post-Olympic blues, where the euphoria of victory gives way to emotional collapse. Research by psychologists like Dr Shane Murphy, a leading figure in sports psychology, explores how athletes and mountaineers experience an emotional void after achieving their life's pinnacle goal. Their sense of identity becomes intertwined with their journey, and once the goal is achieved, they face a destabilising loss of purpose that feels akin to emotional free-fall.[1]

This void, which I now recognise as part of the same phenomenon, was more than just an emotional slump – it was the dismantling of the mental architecture I had built around Everest. I had dedicated four years to this one objective, and suddenly, with no greater height to climb, I was adrift. The psychological toll of achieving long-term goals is far more profound than one might expect, and it's documented in various studies on goal disengagement and achievement loss. Psychologists refer to this as a form of grief, not for a person but for a purpose. I now realise this was exactly what I was experiencing – the loss of the one thing that had defined me for so long.

However, I wasn't alone. Though it might have helped to seek psychological support, I found solace in Sauraj – someone who had stood with me through every high and low of the last four years. Instead of dissecting my feelings, we instinctively chose to take a deep breath, embrace the uncertainty and focus on the next small step forward. Without even realising it, we began to set our sights on our next Everest, slowly redefining our purpose in the process.

For far too long, our venture, Adventure Pulse, had faded into the background, with our Everest aspirations being the main focus. Yet, as time passed, it became evident that reviving this purpose was essential. Invitations began pouring

Finding Purpose

in for us to share our story in corporate settings, where our tale of resilience resonated deeply. It became a beacon of hope for many – not only as an example of perseverance but also as a narrative of confronting and overcoming failure. In these moments, we discovered a new purpose: to inspire others to believe that they, too, could reach their peaks, no matter how insurmountable they seemed.

Gradually, life regained its vibrancy. What I had failed to recognise was how profoundly my existence had become devoid of purpose. Yet, with Sauraj by my side, we started taking small, meaningful steps towards defining our mission for Adventure Pulse and seeking our next Everest. Our journey wasn't solely about conquering peaks; it was about empowering ordinary individuals to pursue extraordinary adventures.

As we reflected on our journey to Everest and beyond, we began to see that the challenges we had faced weren't just isolated moments of hardship – they were lessons in disguise. These lessons, when examined closely, would become invaluable both in our personal lives and in running Adventure Pulse. These insights became the foundation of how we approached the future, shaping the way we lead and inspire others.

One of the most profound realisations we gained from this journey was the necessity of passion and conviction. We had to believe in our ability to climb Everest with an almost obsessive focus. On the mountain, there was no room for self-doubt – every step we took had to be grounded in absolute certainty because second-guessing ourselves could be fatal. This lesson extended beyond climbing. We realised that dreams, no matter how daunting, demand not just passion but total commitment. Whether scaling Everest or leading Adventure Pulse, we had to cultivate an unwavering belief in what we were doing. When doubt inevitably arose, it wasn't something we could ignore – we had to confront it immediately, just as we had done on the mountain.

However, passion alone wasn't enough. Another critical lesson we learnt was the power of a strong team. Too often, we become consumed by the need to prove ourselves, silence the naysayers and conquer our challenges alone. But there were days on this journey when I felt utterly dejected and demotivated, and it wasn't my willpower that lifted me – it was the strength of those around me. Sauraj, our families, friends and supporters were the reason I could get back up when I fell. We realised that no one could do it alone. In climbing and in life, the brilliance of your strategy doesn't matter if you're going up against challenges by yourself. You need a team – a group of people who believe in you and are ready to lend a hand when the climb becomes too steep. This is a truth we carry with us in Adventure Pulse, where we've built a community that uplifts and supports one another.

Perhaps the most profound lesson we took away from Everest, though, was the importance of overcoming the fear of failure. The fear of failing can often be more paralysing than failure itself. Throughout our journey, failure seemed like a constant companion, a shadow that followed us with every step. But it was those failures that forced us to innovate, go back to the drawing board and reassess our approach. Failure, we learnt, wasn't the end of the road – it was a chance to start again, this time with more insight and experience. It's true that 'fear kills more dreams than failure ever will', as stated by Dale Partridge in *People over Profit*. Everest taught us that success is not about avoiding failure but about having the persistence to keep going when failure seems inevitable.

In a world where mountains stand as silent sentinels of our dreams, Adventure Pulse has become a beacon of inspiration for those daring enough to rise to the challenge. Our purpose is not merely to guide individuals up rugged terrains but to ignite a spirit of adventure that transcends the physical. We aim to inspire people from all walks of life to embrace the thrill of exploration and experience the transformative power that lies in the heart of nature.

As we continue our journey with Adventure Pulse, we are going beyond simply reaching for summits. We are rediscovering the essence of who we are. We step into a realm where the extraordinary becomes attainable, where mountains become metaphors for the challenges we can conquer in our own lives. With Adventure Pulse, in addition to witnessing breathtaking landscapes, we help others uncover the depths of their potential.

This journey began as a thought in 2008 as we stood at the foot of the largest mountain in the world, fuelled by a desire to climb it and stand on its summit. That dream took shape and became a reality a decade later. At some point in your life, you will face an incredible ambition that will compel you to rise to the challenge and redefine your existence – your own proverbial 'Everest'. The question you must ask yourself is: What's your Everest? More importantly, do you have the passion, the team and the courage to conquer it?

Epilogue

So what's your Everest?
                    Sauraj Jhingan and Samir Patham

Has life come full circle for us? Not quite. It has been more of a progressive journey, navigating the highs and lows of life and always hoping for the best while preparing for the worst. After summiting Everest, our speaking opportunities expanded, culminating in Sauraj and me being invited to share our story on the prestigious TEDx platform. Interest in trekking steadily grew across the Indian subcontinent, and Adventure Pulse began leading more and more people from all walks of life, expanding our expertise not only in Nepal but also to the far reaches of the Arabian Sea in Tanzania, summiting Kilimanjaro, climbing Mt Elbrus in Russia, opening up the Western Himalayas in Kashmir and Ladakh, and exploring the Eastern Himalayas in Sikkim.

In line with our experiences in the mountains, we designed an innovative training programme called the Avalanche Simulation Workshop. We recreate an earthquake–avalanche scenario in the controlled setting of a banquet hall or office, forcing participants to react and survive, thereby honing crisis management and decision-making skills during times of uncertainty. This unique offering became a highly effective tool for corporate training in crisis management, taking us from Kerala to Kalimpong to conduct these workshops. In later years, we even had the opportunity to conduct this programme across Europe and Southeast Asia.

Just as we started gaining momentum, however, the world came to a sudden standstill in 2020 with the outbreak of the global pandemic. COVID-19 redefined reality, forcing each of us to retreat into our homes, paralysing industries and bringing travel and tourism to a complete halt. In a world that suddenly grappled with maintaining even essential services, where the simple act of a hug or a handshake became a life-threatening risk, the idea of travel – let alone adventure travel – seemed remote, if not impossible. The ripple effects on our industry were profound. Our guides and staff were stranded in remote villages, reaching out for help, and like so many others, we found ourselves navigating a crisis for which no one had a playbook.

The pandemic wasn't just a health crisis – it was a crisis of connection, purpose and livelihood for millions. The travel and tourism industry was hit especially hard, with mass cancellations, financial ruin for small operators and an overwhelming sense of uncertainty about what the future held. The fear of contagion, travel restrictions and the general sense of vulnerability brought the world to a halt.

Amidst this despair, we had to adapt. When a friend mentioned how restless his children were becoming in lockdown, it sparked an idea. If we couldn't bring people to the mountains, why not bring the mountains to them? Thus began the Junior Mountaineering Course, a virtual workshop that allowed children to explore the world's highest peaks from the safety of their homes. For seven days, we took children on virtual expeditions across the continents, teaching them about climbing, mountain survival and the spirit of adventure. The joy of watching kids from across the world – logging in from Hong Kong, Mumbai, Dubai and even Chicago – engage with our content was an unexpected reward. These sessions were filled with hands-on experiments: teaching about hypothermia by holding ice cubes for sixty seconds or explaining the effects of hypoxia by asking them to hold their breath. By the end, we had inspired over 2,000 children, creating a ripple effect of curiosity and passion that extended far beyond what we had initially imagined.

At a time when isolation and fear defined so much of life, these virtual adventures provided a sense of escape and connection, reminding us all that the human spirit can adapt and endure even in the most challenging times. Our online programmes became a bridge between the lockdown and the outdoors, showing that exploration isn't confined by physical boundaries.

During the pandemic, we also created virtual motivation programmes, such as 'Resilience: Lessons from Everest', where we shared our experience of overcoming extreme challenges. These sessions resonated deeply. Over 100 virtual programmes were conducted in 2020 and 2021, offering insights into resilience in an uncertain world.

As the pandemic's shadow receded and travel resumed, we noticed a paradigm shift in the people seeking out adventure. Having faced the fragility of life during the pandemic – whether through falling ill or losing loved ones – people yearned for something deeper: a true adventure, a challenge that would remind them of the thrill of living. 'Revenge travel' became the buzzword, and in 2023 and 2024, we saw a sharp rise in interest in trekking. Adventure Pulse was well positioned to welcome these first-time adventurers eager to explore the mountains and reconnect with nature.

Often, after many of our talks, the most common question we hear is: what's next? For us, our purpose has evolved beyond inspiring people through our adventures. It's now about enabling others to reach new heights and realise their mountain aspirations, regardless of personal limitations such as age, physical restrictions or even medical conditions. In this endeavour, we've guided people from all walks of life to the Himalayas – from a six-year-old to a seventy-four-year-old – all the way to Everest Base Camp. By prioritising safety and quality, we are honoured to have enabled breast cancer survivors, heart attack survivors and many others to experience the mountains. This ethos of care, safety and dedication to quality has now become the hallmark of Adventure Pulse, permeating through every member of our team.

As life resumed, we also pursued our personal climbing goals to strengthen our credentials as mountaineers. In October 2022, alongside Rahul Oak (our friend and Adventure Pulse climber) and Sauraj, I summited Ama Dablam (6,812 m), one of the world's most formidable and beautiful peaks. Reaching the summit of this mountain, often referred to as the Matterhorn of the Himalayas, was more than a climbing achievement – it was a testament to resilience and perseverance, a reflection of the inner strength we had cultivated over the years.

Today, as Adventure Pulse nears its fifteenth anniversary, we stand at the cusp of new adventures, with a growing community of trekkers and mountaineers. The lessons we've learnt, from Everest to the pandemic, are all part of this book's message: to inspire you to find your Everest, whether physical or metaphorical. The mountains may stand tall, but so does the human spirit, and we hope our journey has shown you that with the right mindset and support, no summit is too far.

As described right at the beginning, *What's Your Everest* isn't your conventional self-help guide offering a simple formula for success. It's a real-life account of our dreams and experiences. Everything in this book really did happen, and we hope our tale of struggle, determination, failure and success strikes a chord with you. As we finally conclude this chronicle, we would like to leave you with a parting thought. Be inspired by your dreams and aspirations. Look for your own mountains to climb, whether physical or proverbial. Only in our endeavour to reach new heights will we be able to overcome the mountains of our mind.

Acknowledgements

We are deeply humbled by the overwhelming support we have received over the many years it has taken to climb Everest and build Adventure Pulse. The success of reaching Everest's summit and the growth of our company are inseparable – each step on the mountain has mirrored the strides we have made as a team and a community. While it would be impossible to list every individual who has contributed to this dream – this book could never contain enough pages – we still want to express our heartfelt gratitude to everyone who has been a part of our epic journey.

First and foremost, we owe a tremendous debt of gratitude to our families. Their unwavering support, despite the inherent dangers of mountaineering, has been our foundation. With cautious optimism, they encouraged us, celebrating our triumphs and standing by us in our trials. From accompanying us on the trek to Everest Base Camp to supporting us through financially challenging times, they have been there every step of the way. We are profoundly grateful for their patience, understanding and belief in our vision, which has allowed us to pursue our dreams and ultimately build Adventure Pulse.

To our lifelong friends, who have stuck with us through all the mountain madness – though many haven't yet been able to trek with us to Nepal – their financial, emotional and psychological support has always been a steady source of strength.

A special mention goes to Smiti Kumar, without whom this book might have remained a dream. Her passion, enthusiasm and tireless energy in helping us put these stories into words were infectious, pushing us forward even when we doubted our writing abilities. Her invaluable contribution has helped bring this book to life.

We would also like to thank our friends and families in the Khumbu Valley of Nepal, who have adopted us as their own over the past fourteen years. Their warmth, support and respect have made it possible for two young adventurers to lead expeditions through the Everest region, and today we are proud to be one of the largest Indian operators in the area. Without their care, none of our treks or climbs would have been possible.

A huge shoutout to our batchmates from SIMS, Pune. This incredible alumni network played a critical role in helping us secure the financial backing we needed for not just one but three Everest expeditions. Whether through direct contributions or by creating opportunities for us to conduct speaking sessions and corporate workshops, their support has been instrumental.

Our heartfelt thanks also go to our former colleagues at Druva Software, Standard Chartered, Infosys and Sitel, who have supported us both emotionally and financially, and lived vicariously through our adventures.

A special thank you to Force Motors, whose sponsorship for our third Everest expedition gave us the financial boost we needed and, more importantly, restored our confidence and belief in the success of our mission.

To the Adventure Pulse community, your unwavering support over the past fifteen years has been invaluable. You trusted us to lead you on adventures around the world, and your constant encouragement also inspired us to put our experiences into words. Your belief in our vision, your financial support for our expeditions and your presence on our treks have been the foundation upon which Adventure Pulse was built.

Finally, we would like to extend our deepest appreciation to you, the reader, for choosing to pick up this book, for your curiosity and for the possibility that, in some small way, our story might inspire you to chase your own Everest.

Note

AVALANCHE

1 Shane Murphy, *The Sport Psych Handbook* (Champaign: Human Kinetics, 2005). Shane Murphy's work examines the psychological aftermath of achievement for athletes. His studies explore post-Olympic depression and emotional management after significant milestones. Research by Carsten Wrosch and Gregory E. Miller delves into goal disengagement and its effects on emotional well-being. Barbara L. Fredrickson has also written about how long-term goal pursuit shapes emotional experiences and the resulting emotional withdrawal when the goal is no longer present.

Index

Abel, 99–100
Adventure Pulse, 94–95, 150, 223, 235,
    242–245, 249–250
    birth of, 35–36
    business portfolio, 38
    corporate training in crisis
        management, 246
    Everest expedition, 38–39
    2018 expedition, 174–179
    financial challenges, 41–43, 46–47
    lean period, 167
    mountaineering costs, 39–40
    Nun expedition, 43–45
    planning and management at, 38
    preparation for Everest, 44, 47
    recruitment of Sherpas, 51
    sponsorships, 168–169, 172–173, 178
    Stok Kangri trek, 45–46
    training schedules, 47–48
    trekking expeditions, 35–36
    trek to Kilimanjaro, 177
adventure sports, 8–10
Alan, 105
altitude acclimatisation strategy, 51, 58, 99,
    107–109, 113, 117, 125, 169, 184,
    186, 189–191
Ama Dablam, 250
Asian Trekking, 121
avalanche disaster, 2015, 71–79
    descent back to Kathmandu, 91
    helicopter evacuations, 83–84
    impact of, 88
    impacts, 73, 75, 78
    rescue efforts, 77
Avalanche Simulation Workshop, 247

Babu, Malli Mastan, 14–15, 18, 52, 58, 99
Bahl, Sangeeta Sindhi, 190–191, 197
Bare Act, 11
Barpak village, 74
Beijing Olympics, 24
Bhandari, Rishi, 193
Bhonagiri, Shekhar, 10–11, 41
Bibek, 234
Boukreev, Anatoli, 118–119
British Everest expedition of 1953, 63
budget travellers, 25–26

Camp 3, 61
Camp 4, 61
Caroline, 183–184, 189, 191, 199
Caucasus Mountains of Russia, 99–100
Chadar trek, 35, 49
Chamonix village, 171
Chawale, Bhagwan, 107, 190–191
Chokdo, 171
Chukhung village, 106
The Climb, 118
climbers, 21–24, 38–39, 44–45, 50–52, 57,
    62–63, 66–67, 69, 77–78, 82–84,
    92, 97–98, 104–105, 107–109,
    111, 120–121, 123–124, 131–133,
    135, 137, 141, 143–144, 146, 152,
    156, 158–159, 170–174, 177–178,
    182–187, 189, 191–193, 199,
    202–204, 208–216, 220, 222,
    225–227, 230, 234, 250
climbing permit or royalty fee, 39
COVID-19 pandemic, 248
Crampon Point, 109
crowdfunding, 42

Dai, Bhim, 58, 63, 72, 76, 81, 104, 128
Dai, Mingma, 87
Dai, Tashi, 63–65, 67, 76, 81
Dalai Lama, 106
Dankude, Kishore, 83, 107, 148
Death Zone, 108, 130, 139, 184, 203, 210,
    223
Deboche, 184, 193
Dimri, Vikas, 96–97, 101–102, 105, 110,
    113–114, 119, 128, 131–132,
    135–137, 139–141, 146–147, 149,
    151–153, 159–160, 188, 194–195,
    198, 200–201, 205, 214, 220–221,
    223, 229–230, 235
Dorje, Pemb, 198
Dzo Jongo, 171–172

El Dorado, 32
Enduro3 race, 8, 10–12
Everest (film), 119
Everest Base Camp adventure, 19–27, 29–30,
    35, 37, 41, 44, 46, 48, 50, 56,

Index

62, 70, 74–75, 78, 81, 86, 91, 101–104, 119, 232–234
Camp 1, 65, 67, 69–71, 77, 83, 107–110, 112–113, 117, 127–128, 131, 188–191, 197, 232
Camp 2, 69–71, 77, 85, 107–110, 112–117, 121, 123–131, 136, 138, 152–155, 158, 188, 191, 194, 197–200, 202, 204, 218, 228–231
Camp 3, 61, 107–109, 113, 115, 124, 129–134, 137, 139, 154, 191, 198, 202–203, 227–228
Camp 4, 61, 108, 113, 125, 133–139, 143–144, 147–148, 150–157, 159, 173–174, 192, 206, 208, 222, 224–230
to Khumbu Glacier, 24
from Lukla, 20–21
mission, 2015, 50–59
mountaineering costs, 39–40
streets of Namche Bazaar, 21–22
to Tengboche Monastery, 22
walk to Gorakshep, 22
Everest Base Camp trek, 18–28
Everest Emergency Rescue (ER) team, 77
Everest 2015 expedition, 183
Everest expedition, 2017, 96, 103–125
acclimatisation strategy to climb, 107
challenges of storm and descent, 139–150
climbing teams, 105–107, 121
climb to Yellow Band, 136–137
climb up the Lhotse wall, 130–132
entering death zone, 140–150, 202–207, 210, 223
ETD (estimated time of departure), 140
experiences of smokers *vs* non-smokers, 105
as failed expedition, 151–163
final climb, 127–139, 207–224
high-altitude cough and upper respiratory tract infections, 119–120
members, 104–105
plan of rotation, 124
return and celebrations, 225–236
routine, 119
at South Summit of Everest, 190, 212, 215–217
three-stage rotation plan for climbing, 107–108
Everest 1996 tragedy, 119
Everest tragedy, 2014, 43

fear of failing, 244
Firodia, Prasan, 175–179, 239
Firodia, Sejal, 175–179
Fischer, Scott, 57
Force Motors, 175–177, 181, 223, 237–238
Force Motors Everest Expedition, 178
funding of trips, 41–43, 46–47, 52, 100–101, 168–169, 172–173

Ganesh, 160
Garhwal Himalayas of Uttarakhand, 46
Gawron, Wojtek, 186, 189–191
Geishi, Lama, 54, 105–106
gender diversity, 9
Geneva Spur, 137–138, 149, 154, 205
Giripremi Pune team, 107
Goel, Ritesh, 82
Gokyo Lakes, 181
'go/no-go decision,' 123
Gorakshep, 22, 87
Greg, 99–100, 169–171

Hawley, Elizabeth, 53
Headline Today, 94
high-altitude medicine doctors (icefall doctors), 62, 66–67, 78, 110, 121, 187, 191
Hillary, Peter, 183, 185
Hillary, Sir Edmund, 183
Hillary Step, 218–220
Himalayan Database, 53
Himalayan Hotel, 87
Himalayan Rescue Association (HRA), 62
Himalayan Trails campaign, 178
Himalayan Trust, 183
Himalayas, 20–21, 27, 55, 57, 80, 87, 93, 99, 133, 182, 249–250
Eastern, 247
Garhwal Himalayas of Uttarakhand, 46
Nepalese, 53
Western, 247
HIMEX (Himalayan Expeditions), 121
Hotel Everest View, 179

Ibrahimi, Uta, 122–123, 129, 133, 136
IMG (International Mountain Guides) and Adventure Consultants, 121
Indian Army dining camp, 62–63
Indian Army expedition camp, 75
International Federation of Mountain Guides Associations (IFMGA), 122
Into Thin Air (Jon Krakauer), 119
Island Peak (Imja Tse), 106

Jacob, Cyriac, 177
Jamwal, Major (Colonel), 62, 78, 82–83, 86, 97–98
Jhingan, Sauraj, 2, 5–16, 28, 30–31, 50, 86, 108–109, 114, 116, 140–142, 145–149, 195, 201–203, 205, 209, 214, 216–217, 243–244, 247, 250

Index

achievements in Enduro race, 16
at Druva Software, 34–35, 42–43
experience in Enduro, 10–12
first Everest Base Camp adventure, 19–27
HR career, 17–18
MBA programme, 5, 7–8, 15
at SIMS, Pune, 5–6
at Standard Chartered Bank, 17, 28
Joisher, Kuntal, 83, 97–98, 182–184, 189, 199–201
jumar, 68
Junior Mountaineering Course, 248

Kang Yatse 2, 171
Karishma, 29, 71, 103, 241
Karwal, Atul, 24
Think Everest, 24
Kathmandu, Nepal, 18–20, 26, 52–54, 74, 76, 78, 83, 86, 91–92, 117, 121, 159–162, 180, 184, 190–193, 199, 234–236
Khukri rum, 234
Khumbu cough, 157, 190
Khumbu Glacier, 74, 120
Khumbu Valley/Khumbu Glacier/Khumbu Icefall, 22–24, 55, 58, 60–63, 65–69, 71–72, 85–86, 97, 104–105, 108–111, 116, 121, 127–128, 173, 180, 184, 188–189, 191, 197, 199, 232–233
2014 avalanche disaster, 72
length and altitude, 65
Khunde village, 86
Kongmaru La pass, 171
Kumar, Ravi, 105, 116, 149, 155–156
Kuntal, 97–98

Lhotse peak, 108, 112, 114–115, 129–131, 135, 142, 150, 180, 190–191, 195, 200–205, 220
expedition, 181, 190–191, 195–198
Lobuche Peak, 27, 60–61, 89, 182–183, 186–187
expedition to, 186–192
Lobuche settlement, 184–185
Lukla, 20, 53, 83, 156

Malla, Vinayak Jaya, 117
marathoners, 234
Mazur, Dan, 104
MBA Institute, formation of, 33–35
Melanie (Mel), 56, 92, 97–98, 182–183, 185
Milaap crowdfunding, 42
money-making venture, 32
Mont Blanc expedition, 169–171
Mother Earth, 87
motivation programmes, virtual, 249

mountaineering, 7, 13–15, 28, 47
books, 39
logistics, 40, 50–49
Mt Elbrus, Russia, 98–100, 247
Mt Kilimanjaro, 35, 177
Mt Makalu, 222
Mulepati, Moni, 53
Murphy, Dr Shane, 242

Nakayama, Takeshi, 185–186, 194, 196–198, 205–206, 214, 220–221, 223, 229–230, 235
Namche Bakery, 182
Namche Bazaar, 21–22, 55–56, 85–86, 97, 181, 234
Nehru, Pandit Jawaharlal, 7
Nehru Institute of Mountaineering, 7, 15
Advanced Mountaineering Course, 43, 46
Nepal earthquake, 2015, 72, 74, 76–77, 103
death toll, 91
Nepal Mountaineering Association (NMA), 84
Nun Base Camp, 43–45
Nuptse, 112, 117

Oil and Natural Gas Corporation (ONGC), 107
outdoor training routines, 17–18, 32, 101
Oxygen Lodge, 185

Pangboche village, 54, 87, 105, 186
Pasang, 124, 139–140, 171–172
Peak XV Lodge, 87
People over Profit (Dale Partridge), 244
Pheriche, 87, 193
Piolets d'Or awards, 111
pooja ceremony, 64–65, 103, 182–183
Pumori High Camp, 70–71, 76

Queen Mary's Technical Institute for Differently Abled Soldiers (QMTI), 98

Rahul Oak, 250
Ravlekar, Mangesh, 47–48, 52, 101
'Resilience: Lessons from Everest,' 249
'Revenge travel,' 249
Rivendell Lodge, 55
river-rafting, 7
Rumdoodle restaurant, 26

Sagarmatha, 63
Sagarmatha Pollution Control Centre (SPCC), 61, 86
Sainik School, Satara, 15
Sam (Samir Patham), 6–8, 14, 16, 19, 28–30, 37–38, 44–45, 49–50, 68, 70, 77,

Index

93, 95–97, 100–101, 123–125, 127–130, 133, 138, 151–154, 160, 167–168, 220, 231, 235
Enduro race, 9–11
as HR recruiter, 17
at Infosys, Pune, 28
knee injury, 47–48
Samden, 104, 124, 133, 140
Satori Adventures, 155, 174, 181
Satyen, 13–14
Seven Summits, 99, 202
  Mt Aconcagua, 14
  Mt Denali, 14
  Mt Elbrus, 14
  Mt Everest, 14
  Mt Kilimanjaro, 14
  Mt Kosciuszko, 14
  Mt Vinson Massif, 14
Sharma, Brijesh, 184, 189, 192, 199–200
Sharma, Ghanshyam, 1–2, 51, 54–55, 59, 63, 65, 69, 73, 76, 103–105, 122, 129, 144–145, 147, 152, 154, 156–159
Sharma, Karan, 13–14
Sharma, Preeti, 9
Sherchan, Min Bahadur, 119–120
Sherpa, 72
Sherpa, Ang Temba, 87
Sherpa, Babu Chiri, 57
Sherpa, Dawa, 104, 124, 135, 139–140, 150
Sherpa, Jangbu, 103–106, 109–110, 115, 121, 124–125, 128, 130, 132–136, 139, 144–145, 147–148, 151–156, 161–163
Sherpa, Kami, 74
Sherpa, Lakpa, 75, 196–197, 199
Sherpa, Lambu, 75
Sherpa, Mingma Tenzi, 107, 148, 182, 185–186, 191–192, 194, 198–202, 204, 207, 227–228, 231–232, 234–235
Sherpa, Pasang, 75, 87, 104
Sherpa, Phurba, 186, 191, 201
Sherpa, Tenji, 117
Sherpa (Dai), Tashi, 51, 59, 69–70, 78, 104
Sherpa (Dai), Tendi, 122–123, 129, 133, 136, 156, 224
Sherpa Highland, 87
Sherpas, 25, 37, 43, 50–51, 63, 66–67, 84, 105, 121, 124–125, 130, 133, 146, 157–159, 171–172, 187, 189, 193–194, 206
SIMS Adventure Club, 10
Singh, Ricky, 188–191
sleeping mattress, 62

Snowy Horizon expedition camp, 83
Soman, Milind, 105
South Summit of Everest, 190, 212, 215–217
Srikanth, Kris, 100
Steck, Ueli, 111, 117–118
  preparation and acclimatisation schedule, 117
Stok Kangri, 35, 101, 171–172
Swiss Everest, expedition of 1952, 137
Sylvine, 183–184, 189, 191, 199
Symbiosis Institute of Management Studies (SIMS), Pune, 5, 14, 29, 31–32, 95, 252, 256
  SIMS Adventure Club, 10–11

TAG Nepal, 122
Tashi, 1–2
Tashi, Pemba, 192, 202–204, 208–213, 215, 226
Tatsuo, Matsumoto, 199
teahouses, 21
Temba, Dawa, 192, 209, 212–214, 216–217, 219, 221, 223
Tengboche Monastery, 22, 64, 180
tents, 78, 80, 111
  dining, 60–61
  of Himalayan Rescue Association (HRA), 62
  sharing of, 61
  size of, 61
  sleeping, 61
  toilet, 61
Tenzi, Lakpa, 192, 204
Thamel, 19
Thamel coffee shop, 92
Thame village, 86
Thukla Pass, 56–57, 184
Tibetan teahouse of Rivendell, 119
Times of India, 94
Tomer, Chris, 121–122
Tomer Weather Solutions, 122
Tres Cruces Sur, 55
Triangular Face, 212–213

Vikas, 101
Viru, 104

Western Cwm, 111–113, 128, 195–201, 205
  trek through, 196
'what if' questions, 167

Yellow Band, 136–137
Yeti foots, 26

About the Authors

Sauraj Jhingan is an accomplished mountaineer, adventurer, entrepreneur and TEDx speaker who traded a successful corporate career for the pursuit of his passion for the mountains. After completing his MBA from the Symbiosis Institute of Management Studies (SIMS, Pune) in 2007, he worked for Standard Chartered Bank as regional head of recruitment, Mumbai, before moving on to become head of human resources at Druva Software Pvt. Ltd. However, the call of the mountains proved irresistible, and he co-founded Adventure Pulse, one of India's leading adventure travel companies.

A qualified mountaineer from the prestigious Nehru Institute of Mountaineering, Uttarkashi, Sauraj has undertaken high-altitude expeditions across the world. He has successfully summited Mt Elbrus in Russia, Mt Blanc in the French Alps, Mt Kilimanjaro in Africa and Mt Aconcagua in Argentina, in addition to multiple expeditions in the Indian and Nepalese Himalayas. In May 2018, he stood atop Mt Everest, completing a journey of resilience, determination and perseverance. A certified skydiver with the Indian Parachuting Federation and a trained lifeguard from the Royal Life Saving Society, Australia, Sauraj continues to push the limits of adventure while inspiring others to do the same.

Samir Patham is a seasoned mountaineer, explorer and motivational speaker with a deep-rooted passion for adventure and the outdoors. He completed his graduation

About the Authors

in microbiology from the University of Mumbai before earning his MBA in human resources from SIMS, Pune. His professional journey began in the corporate world, where he worked as an HR manager at Infosys BPO before joining forces with Sauraj to launch Adventure Pulse.

A qualified mountaineer from the Nehru Institute of Mountaineering, Uttarkashi, and a PADI (Professional Association of Diving Instructors) certified Advanced Open Water scuba diver, Samir has led over thirty-four expeditions to Everest Base Camp, guiding more than 400 trekkers through the challenging Himalayan terrain. His mountaineering achievements include summiting Ama Dablam, Nun, Stok Kangri, Mera Peak and the Annapurna Circuit. Having climbed four of the Seven Summits, Samir reached the pinnacle of the world, the summit of Mt Everest, in May 2018.

Through Adventure Pulse, both Sauraj and Samir continue to inspire and empower adventurers from all walks of life, proving that with the right mindset and determination, anyone can achieve the extraordinary.

Scan the QR code to view photographs and videos and learn more about the authors' Everest expeditions.